George Bruce Malleson

The Refounding of the German Empire, 1848-1871

George Bruce Malleson

The Refounding of the German Empire, 1848-1871

ISBN/EAN: 9783337169077

Printed in Europe, USA, Canada, Australia, Japan

Cover: Foto ©ninafisch / pixelio.de

More available books at **www.hansebooks.com**

THE REFOUNDING OF THE GERMAN EMPIRE

1848-1871

BY

COLONEL G. B. MALLESON, C.S.I.

AUTHOR OF 'THE INDIAN MUTINY,' 'HISTORY OF THE FRENCH IN INDIA,'
'THE BATTLEFIELDS OF GERMANY,' ETC., ETC.

With Portraits and Plans

LONDON
SEELEY AND CO. LIMITED
ESSEX STREET, STRAND
1893

CONTENTS

—o—

CHAP.		PAGE
I.	THE EMPIRE OF CHARLEMAGNE—THE RENUNCIATION OF FRANCIS II.—THE NAPOLEONIC PERIOD—FROM 1815 TO 1848—1848 TO 1852,	1
II.	PRUSSIA FROM 1852 TO 1857,	36
III.	THE REGENCY OF THE PRINCE OF PRUSSIA—THE PERIOD OF AWAKENING,	49
IV.	THE KINGSHIP OF WILLIAM I.—THE POLICY OF 'BLOOD AND IRON,'	66
V.	THE AUSTRO-PRUSSIAN INVASION OF SCHLESWIG-HOLSTEIN, AND ITS CONSEQUENCES,	86
VI.	THE FOREIGN POLICY OF AUSTRIA—PREPARATIONS FOR WAR—ACTION OF THE LESSER STATES OF GERMANY—MOLTKE—PRINCE FREDERIC CHARLES—THE CROWN PRINCE—HERWARTH VON BITTENFELD—BENEDEK—THE WAR BREAKS OUT,	103
VII.	THE WAR OF 1866—HANOVER AND ELECTORAL HESSE—LANGENSALZA AND WILHELMSHÖHE,	119
VIII.	THE CAMPAIGN IN BOHEMIA—COMBATS OF LIEBENAU—OF PODOL—OF MÜNCHENGRÄTZ—OF GITSCHIN—OF TRAUTENAU—OF SOOR—OF NACHOD—OF SKALITZ—OF SCHWEINSCHÄDEL,	132
IX.	THE BATTLE OF KÖNIGGRÄTZ,	154

CHAP.		PAGE
X.	THE BATTLE OF CUSTOZA — THE CAMPAIGN IN BAVARIA—THE MARCH OF THE PRUSSIANS ON VIENNA—THE ARMISTICE OF NIKOLSBURG AND TREATY OF PRAGUE,	175
XI.	NAPOLEON III. AND BISMARCK—FOUR YEARS OF SMOULDERING IN PARIS AND BERLIN—THE HOHENZOLLERN CANDIDATURE—KING WILLIAM AND BENEDETTI AT EMS — EXCITEMENT IN PARIS—THE BERLIN FICTIONS RENDER WAR INEVITABLE,	194
XII.	THE FRANCO-GERMAN WAR—THE NUMBERS AND RESOURCES OF THE COMBATANTS—THE LEADERS ON BOTH SIDES—AUSTRIA AND ITALY—SAARBRÜCKEN—WÖRTH—SPICHEREN,	222
XIII.	COLOMBEY — VIONVILLE AND MARS-LE-TOUR — GRAVELOTTE,	255
XIV.	SEDAN,	279
XV.	THE LAST PHASES OF THE WAR,	296
XVI.	THE CROWNING OF THE EDIFICE,	314

LIST OF ILLUSTRATIONS

	PAGE
THE EMPEROR WILLIAM I.,	*Frontispiece*
PRINCE BISMARCK,	74
FREDERICK, CROWN PRINCE OF PRUSSIA,	166
COUNT VON MOLTKE,	230
MAP TO ILLUSTRATE THE INVASION OF BOHEMIA,	*To face* 135
PLAN OF THE BATTLE OF KÖNIGGRÄTZ,	156
PLAN OF THE BATTLE OF CUSTOZA,	178
MAP OF PART OF FRANCE INVADED BY THE GERMANS,	*To face* 225
PLAN OF THE BATTLES OF VIONVILLE AND GRAVELOTTE,	260

** *The Portraits of the* EMPEROR WILLIAM, PRINCE BISMARCK *and* COUNT VON MOLTKE *are engraved by permission of* Messrs LOESCHER & PETSCH; *that of the* CROWN PRINCE FREDERICK *by permission of* Messrs REICHARD & LINDNER.

PREFACE

THIS book deals especially with a period of German history of twenty-three years' duration. Beginning with the French Revolution of 1848 it records the rousing in Germany of passions long pent-up, and, for the time, difficult to be controlled or directed; the manner in which these passions were eventually mastered; the great void and the fierce longing they left behind them; the use made by one of the chief Powers of Germany of the feelings and aspirations thus dormant, and, finally, the complete reversal, by the means employed by that Power, of the positions held in Europe till that period by Austria and Prussia on the one side, by France and Germany on the other.

During this period of twenty-three years there occurred in Europe five wars; and although, of those five wars, two, the Crimean war and the Franco-Austrian war require in this volume but a cursory notice, the other three, viz., the Danish war, the Austro-Prussian war, and the Franco-German war constitute the three steps which made possible the refounding of the German Empire. The second and third of these wars would have been impossible without their predecessor. For if the first of the three, the Danish war, may be regarded as a small thing—the whole of Germany being pitted against the smallest country in Europe—it was, nevertheless, the necessary prelude to the wars that followed. That war, and the two greater wars of 1866 and 1870, had been predetermined in the mind of the regenerator of Germany before a shot in the first had been fired. The initial war, in fact, was needed to cause the second; the second to produce the third. The Danish war, then, far from being a war of secondary importance, was the first act of a deliberately planned system; the first consequence of the introduction of that policy of 'Blood and Iron' which, in one of his earliest speeches to the Prussian parliament, Count Bismarck declared to be necessary for the solution of the great questions which were agitating Germany.

The writer of a book professing to deal with these subjects had, therefore, to record (1st) the effect in Germany of that outburst in Paris of February 1848, which acted as a match to the inflamed imaginations of the populations of the great centres of thought in the Fatherland; (2d) the manner in which that outbreak seized hold of the German mind; how it was viewed by princes and peoples; the action it induced; the several movements that followed; the precipitancy of the mob, and the patient waiting of sovereigns; until the fire of the movement had been spent, and the sovereigns were enabled to recover all that they had temporarily lost. It will then be shown how the popular feeling, though crushed for the time, never died out; how it remained, a reminiscence full of hope, to encourage those to whom the

Preface

prospect of German Unity had ever been a living ideal; how, again, the feelings and aspirations which had been aroused were, whilst still dormant, utilised by politicians to prepare a machine which, placing the necessary power in the hands of men who knew their own minds, who had a fixed policy, and who were to be deterred by no scruples, would, at the proper time, deal the blows which were to secure for Germany the union which had been her dream; how the policy of 'Blood and Iron' was invented for that end; how other Powers, not in Germany alone, played into the hands of the masters of the machine. Then will follow the story of the wars which had been planned. It will be told finally, how, in 1871, the adventurous but far-sighted policy was crowned with success.

In preparing a continuous account of this policy and of these events the main difficulty of the writer has been to compress in the allotted number of pages events so momentous and so diverging: the diverse actions of Austria, of Prussia, of the German Diet, of France, of Italy. The battles of the three wars above noted—the secret plans and hopes of the several Courts have all demanded the most careful study. How difficult it has been to give a sufficiently clear description of the several battles, many of them of the first importance, may be gathered from the fact that Major Henderson, the most eminent of the younger officers of the British army, has devoted to the consideration of only one battle, that of Spicheren, a number of words at least equal to the whole of those contained in this volume.[1]

---

[1] 'The Battle of Spicheren,' by Brevet-Major Henderson. This volume counts three hundred pages, but, in the type of this volume, the contents would require a few pages more.

I am bound to add that in Major Henderson's volume I do not find a single redundant page. It is throughout admirable; for the military student invaluable. I call attention to the fact simply to illustrate the difficulty of a writer who has to describe, within a given compass equal to that considered by Major Henderson necessary for one battle, not one only, but many battles, some of them of even greater importance than Spicheren, for they were more decisive of the war. The author has been forced then to endeavour to produce, by bold and correct outlines, results which may atone for want of detail. He would fain hope that he has succeeded in producing such sketches of the principal battles as will convey a clear meaning of the movements on both sides to the general reader. With respect to some of them, those of 1866 in particular, he has enjoyed the advantage of a personal acquaintance with many officers who served in the campaign of Bohemia, and he can confidently assert that, although his account of that campaign may differ in some details from the story told by some English writers, it will be accepted in Vienna as the true one. He may add that a distinguished foreign officer, whom he consulted this year, has endorsed every word of it.

Regarding the political events, also, the writer is not without personal experience. He was in Westphalia in the summer and autumn of 1858, and again during 1863-4, and witnessed the growing discontent of large classes of the people, and their distrust of Count Bismarck. There never was a policy so unpopular as that involved by the military system of Von Roon; never a minister so detested as was Bismarck. The war of

Preface

1866 was, in its inception, nowhere so unpopular as in Prussia. But success atoned for everything. All the previous high-handed measures of the ministry were forgotten, and the annexations and other advantages which followed it produced the most complete revulsion in the public mind with regard to the minister theretofore so detested.

With respect to events generally, the writer has consulted all the German, and many of the English and French works written on the subject. He has also been allowed to peruse journals of some of the actors, hitherto unpublished. To all he is greatly indebted. But he is bound to admit that he has met with no writer whose knowledge of the incidents which led to the war of 1866 is so ample, or whose conclusions are so just, as those of Sir Alexander Malet, at the time H.M.'s Envoy Extraordinary and Minister Plenipotentiary at Frankfort. In his book, 'The Overthrow of the Germanic Confederation by Prussia in 1866,' the keys of the Foreign Office at Berlin are placed in the readers' hands, and the mind of the statesman who, after excluding Austria from Germany, completed his policy of 'Thorough' by the humiliation of France, is laid, an open book, before the generation that witnessed 'the refounding of the German Empire.'

G. B. M.

THE REFOUNDING OF THE GERMAN EMPIRE

CHAPTER I.

THE EMPIRE OF CHARLEMAGNE — RENUNCIATION BY FRANCIS II.—THE NAPOLEONIC PERIOD—FROM 1815 TO 1848—FROM 1848 TO 1852.

THE Holy Roman Empire, founded by Charlemagne, and dating from Christmas day 800, died on the 6th of August 1806. It had lived just over a thousand years. The hopes of the great Charles that the sceptre would descend in perpetuity to members of his own family had not been realised. The family became extinct in 911. From that date the numerous dukes and counts who had been content to serve as officers of the imperial court asserted their independence, and with it the right to elect their supreme overlord. The method of election, under the arrangement originally settled, was gradually found to be in practice crude, unwieldy, and unworkable. In the thirteenth century, then, the electoral basis was narrowed by restricting the voting power to seven of the most influential magnates of the land. In 1648 the number was increased to eight, and in 1692 to nine. It was reduced to eight in 1777, but the peace of Lunéville (February 9, 1801) increased it to ten. From the year 1407 onwards the electing body had, with rare

A

exceptions, conferred the dignity on the representative of the House of Habsburg.

Alike in his capacity as Emperor of Germany and the hereditary ruler of the several States he had inherited from his ancestors, the Emperor Francis II. had taken a prominent part in the wars of the French Revolution. Up to the year 1796 the victories gained and the defeats sustained by his armies and those of his allies were not very unevenly balanced. In 1795 the tide had seemed to turn rather decisively in his and their favour, but in the following year the genius of Napoleon Bonaparte turned the scale very effectually against him. The same genius forced him the year immediately following to accept a peace[1] by which he yielded the Low Countries and the Ionian islands to France, and Milan, Mantua, and Modena to the newly formed Cisalpine republic, receiving, by a secret article, Venice as compensation. The war was renewed a year later. Bonaparte was absent in Egypt, and Austria, powerfully aided by Russia, carried at the outset all before her. The return of Bonaparte on the 9th of October, his successful blow at the existing constitution exactly one month later, his nomination as First Consul, and, finally and chiefly, the campaign of Marengo, changed into despair the bright hopes to which the earlier successes of the war had given birth at Vienna. The peace of Lunéville which followed confirmed the advantages to France obtained by the preceding treaty, and in addition secured for her a preponderating influence in western Germany. The conditions imposed by the conqueror were lenient. It was the only time, if we may except the conditions regarding Russia of the treaty of Tilsit, when the young

[1] Treaty of Campo Formio, October 17, 1797.

The Consequences of Austerlitz. 3

conqueror whose work it was showed consideration to a defeated enemy. His subsequent words and acts proved that he had come to believe that in displaying that consideration he had made a blunder.

The peace between France and Austria lasted four years. Meanwhile the conqueror of Marengo had become Emperor of the French (May 18, 1804), and the Emperor Francis of Germany had, nearly three months later, assumed, by letters patent, the position of hereditary Emperor of Austria, under the title of Francis I. (August 11, 1804). When he assumed the rank and position of Emperor of the French, Napoleon was, and for some time previously had been, engaged in making gigantic preparations for the invasion of England. He was still pushing forward these preparations when, on the 5th of August 1805, the Emperor Francis, yielding to the solicitations of Pitt, declared war against him. How Napoleon, with marvellous skill, suddenly transferred his army from the shores of the ocean to southern Germany, how he compelled one Austrian army to capitulate at Ulm, and completely defeated another allied with the Russians, on the anniversary of his coronation (December 2) at Austerlitz, need not be told here in detail. Napoleon had prefaced the war by telling his soldiers that he would not again spare the enemy to whom he had been too merciful at Campo Formio and at Lunéville, and he kept his word. The treaty of Pressburg, the consequence of Austerlitz, rent Venice from Austria, transferred to Bavaria Tirol, Voralberg, the principality of Eichstadt, and part of the Bishopric of Passau; to Baden the greater part of the Brisgau, with Constance; to Würtemberg Augsburg and a portion of Suabia. The Electors of Bavaria and Würtemberg became kings, and Baden was recognised as a sovereign State. In the words of the latest English historian [1] of the period: 'The constitution of the empire ceased to exist even in name.'

But another and a fiercer blow directed against that constitution was to follow. Napoleon employed the comparative leisure which followed the signature of the peace of Pressburg (December 26, 1805) to devise a still more potent method for crippling Germany. On the ruins of the empire he had broken up he designed to constitute in Germany a new power, independent alike of Austria and Prussia, pushed in as a wedge between the two, a province of France in all but in name, and deriving from France all its motive power. He worked at this project with his accustomed energy during the earlier months of 1806. In July of that year he had arranged every detail. Sixteen prominent princes of western and southern Germany declared their separation from the German Empire and Emperor, and formed under the protection of the French Emperor, a league to be styled 'The Confederation of the Rhine.' On the 6th of August, the Emperor Francis, under the pressure of Napoleon, dissolved by decree the Germanic confederation, and formally abdicated his title as chief of the Holy Roman Empire. Before the close of the year the adhesion of Saxony had brought within that league almost every German who was not either Austrian or Prussian.[2] The territories thus amalgamated for offence and defence became virtually a French province. They counted a population of more than fourteen millions, and had an extent of over 125,000 square miles. The military forces they disposed of, fixed after the union of Saxony at

[1] Fyffe's *History of Modern Europe*, Vol. I. page 300.
[2] In December 1806 the Confederation consisted of France, Bavaria, Würtemberg, Saxony, and Westphalia, seven grand duchies, six duchies, and twenty principalities.

Its Strength and its Weakness. 5

119,180 men, were drilled by French officers. The frontiers were regarded to all intents as the frontiers of France. The Confederation, thrust into the very heart of Germany, was a standing menace to Austria and Prussia. Its formation, from the standpoint of the actual moment, seemed to its author and to Europe generally to be the outcome of the highest political genius. With the consent of a great part of Germany Napoleon had, it seemed, rendered German union against France for ever impossible. Nor can it be doubted that the German people admitted within the Confederation derived great immediate advantages from the amalgamation. Justice was made easy to all; the taxes were spread in more even proportions over the several classes; whilst to the ambitious a career was opened such as, under the petty governments which had been swept away, had been impossible.

Yet it can scarcely be doubted now that the measure in the form it took was adverse to the interests of France; that it really contributed, and greatly, to the cause of German unity. The existence of the Confederation was only possible under the condition of continued success on the field of battle. The campaign of 1812 in Russia, still more the campaign of 1813 in Germany, proved the instability of the foundations on which it rested. Nor was the evil—to France—confined to the sudden disaffection which immediately preceded and immediately followed the battle of Leipsig. The Confederation had introduced into the very heart of Germany that power of combination for the cause of national union which we have seen fructify in our own day. There were, indeed, in 1806 some shrewd men, some of them Frenchmen, who deprecated the policy of Napoleon because, in their view, it was bound to lead to such results. One of these, the Baron de Marbot, at the time aide-de-camp to Marshal Augereau, has detailed, in one of the most charming autobiographies[1] ever given to the world, the opinions he formed at that period. In the presence of accomplished facts they are worthy of being transcribed. 'Although,' wrote the Baron, 'I was very young at this epoch I thought that Napoleon committed a great fault in reducing the number of the small principalities of Germany. In fact in the ancient wars against France the 800 princes of the Germanic corps could not act together. There was some of them who furnished only a company, some only a platoon, many but half a soldier; so that the reunion of these different contingents composed an army totally deprived of any principle of combination, and disbanded at the very first reverse. But when Napoleon had reduced to thirty-two the number of the principalities he introduced the spirit of union into the forces of Germany. The sovereigns preserved and aggrandised formed a small but well-constituted army. That indeed was the end which the Emperor proposed to himself in the hope of thus utilising to his profit all the military resources of the country. This was the case so long as we were successful. But at the very first reverse the thirty-two sovereigns, having a common understanding, combined against France, and their coalition with Russia overthrew the Emperor Napoleon.'

The Confederation of the Rhine, wounded to the death by the campaign of 1812, and killed by the battle of Leipsig, was succeeded, in 1815, by a new league called 'The Germanic Federation.' In the autumn of 1814 the work of forming a scheme for the reorganisation of Germany had been committed to Austria, Prussia,

[1] *Memoires du Gen. Baron de Marbot*, Vol. I. page 275. Paris, Plon Nourrit & Co., 1891.

and three of the minor powers. The scheme itself, promulgated June 8, 1815, fell short of the hopes that had been roused during the life and death struggles of 1813-14. The blighting influence of Metternich had successfully restricted the wider-reaching aspirations of the patriots of northern Germany. That many difficulties existed in the way of satisfying the latter must be admitted. The kings whom Napoleon had made, released from his yoke, were resolved to maintain, as far as was possible, the absolutism which had characterised their rule during the preceding eight years. Austria was bound hand and foot to the same principle. And though the general feeling of Prussia, as a nation, was strongly in favour of progress, the King and his ministers were in their hearts not one whit more inclined to it than was Metternich himself. The outcome, then, of the deliberations of the five powers was unsatisfactory. Germany became federated only in name. The act of June 1815 created a Federal Diet at which seventeen members, the representatives of States, or groups of States or free cities, were to meet. These representatives were nominated by the rulers of the respective States or groups. The place of meeting was the city of Frankfort on the Main. From its first meeting, in November 1816, to its last, in August 1866, the Diet was powerless to assure the real union of Germany. Throughout that period the influence of Austria was predominant; and during the arbitrary rule of Metternich, 1815 to 1848, and again during the reaction which followed the outbreaks of 1848, Austria used that influence to stifle every aspiration for freedom. Her principle was, 'to aggrandise Austria, to humiliate Prussia.' During its life of fifty-one years, inclusive of the suspension of its powers from July 1848 to May 1851, the Diet, with opportunities favourable for the development of sound patriotic principles, displayed only a genius for intrigue and a capacity for repression.

To the Diet, thus playing a part at once subordinate and humiliating, the mouthpiece in matters pertaining to Germany of Metternich, the revolution of February 1848 in Paris was a very rude awakener. To the people of every State in Germany the same event acted as a call to prompt and resolute action. It happened that at the moment (February 27) a meeting of patriotic men was being held at Mannheim to devise how to procure for the Fatherland a few moderate reforms. These were, the freedom of the press, trial by jury, liberty to carry arms, national representation. The terror inspired in ruling circles by the movements in Paris caused these proposals to be everywhere accepted. Baden led the way. The other States followed. In a few days not only had the modest requests I have mentioned been all but universally granted, but the governments, those of Austria and Prussia excepted, had promised to revoke the exceptional laws; to impose on the army an oath of fidelity to the constitution; to declare the political equality of all creeds; the responsibility of the ministers of the crown; the independence of the judges; the abolition of the remnants of feudalism. But little opposition was offered by the rulers. In Bavaria, indeed, there were tumults; but the abdication of King Louis (March 20) promptly put an end to these. Meanwhile, in Frankfort, the population of which, like the populations of all the great cities in Germany, was wild with enthusiasm and excitement, the Diet had passed a resolution (March 3) empowering every federal State to abolish the censorship, and, under certain guarantees, to sanction the freedom of the press. On the 10th, noting the continued swelling of the storm, it despatched to the rulers of

Its First Effect in Germany. 9

Germany an invitation to send to Frankfort commissaries to discuss the reorganisation of the country. This invitation was its own death-warrant. In the tumult of the national aspirations it passed from the minds of men, and apparently expired. For nearly three years, from July 1848 to May 1851, it ceased to meet. But for Austria, fresh from her triumph over the internal foes of her unpopular sway, the Diet would never have been heard of again. But we shall presently see how, in May 1851, the powerful representative of the ambitious policy of that power needing the semblance of a national sanction to the schemes he was planning, summoned it from its tomb, and used its phantom form to impress the will of Austria on the Fatherland. How it existed for fifteen years, and then, under the treatment of Count Bismarck, went the way of other shams, will be told in due course.

In considering the course of events which in Germany followed the explosion of 1848 it must be borne in mind that during the first eighteen months Austria was too much occupied with her own affairs to take a decisive part in the settlement of German questions, and that it was not to her but to Prussia that the patriots of the Fatherland looked for the action which should make Germany a nation. It will then be only necessary to state that no country in Europe was apparently so completely shattered by the storm of the revolution as was the composite empire ruled over by the Habsburgs. For some time it seemed absolutely impossible that she could escape shipwreck. What with risings in Lombardy, at Venice, in Bohemia, in Hungary, in her own capital, Austria had the appearance of a gallant ship cast upon a lee shore combating with the breakers. The time came indeed when she righted herself, and made for a few years a show as proud and as defiant as that which she had presented before February 1848. But for the moment she seemed a wreck, and all eyes and all hearts turned with hope and expectation to Prussia and her king.

It seems advisable, under these circumstances, before we enter upon a sketch of the troubles at Berlin and at Frankfort, with their gradual subsidence in favour of a policy which, if responded to, might have anticipated by twenty years the great event at Versailles of January 1871, to examine very briefly the character of the sovereign who then ruled in Prussia.

Frederic William IV., King of Prussia, was in his fifty-fourth year when Paris dismissed the King of the French and his family. Though he had served as a youth in the stirring campaigns of 1811-14-15,[1] he had none of the instincts of the soldier. The term 'dreamer' describes accurately what he was. He had unbounded confidence in, almost a worship for the Czar Nicholas, a dread of offending Austria, a reverence for royalty and for ruling princes, such as placed them on a pedestal not to be approached by the common people. A sentimentalist, irresolute, enthusiastic, and indolent, he wished the happiness of his subjects provided they would leave himself and his nobles in the enjoyment of the power and privileges he and they had inherited. He was ever ready with soft cajoling words, but he would not give them, if he could avoid it, any of the political food for which they clamoured. He was ready to promise without intending to perform. If he had ruled in France in the place of Louis XVI. he would have displayed no more

---

[1] Baron Marbot records how his father, in 1812, earnestly begged Napoleon to allow the young prince to accompany him to Russia, on his staff, and how Napoleon, to his surprise, refused.

Berlin in 1848.

firmness than did that ill-fated monarch. But there was this difference in the positions of the two men. In France, in 1789-90, the army sided with the people. In Prussia, in 1848, the soldiers were loyal to the sovereign.

Popular aspirations and popular enthusiasm had, early in March 1848, found a very strong expression in Berlin. With the cry for constitutional freedom in its broadest sense was joined the demand for the reorganisation of Germany on the principle of unity. The King was not disposed to grant any but the very slightest concession. On the 5th of March he attempted to disarm the leaders of the movement by telling them that their proposals would be considered by the Prussian Diet, the periodical meeting of which had been assured. Three days later the public were informed that the revision of the press laws was under consideration; but these paltry and half-hearted concessions rather irritated than satisfied the people. For the six days that followed Berlin was paraded by an angry mob, which seemed inclined even to court a contest with the soldiery. On the 14th the King, who had been apparently delaying action until he should ascertain the results of the movements in other large centres, especially in Vienna, driven by the attitude of the people to do something, made another feeble attempt to calm men's minds. He issued a proclamation summoning the parliament to meet on the 27th of April, and promising that the question of unity should be considered at Dresden by a congress of princes. This ill-judged announcement drove the Berliners to fever heat, and for three days the city was a prey to continual tumult. The mind of the King was not relieved when, on the evening of the 15th, he received news of the untoward result of the outbreak at Vienna. Still he resisted; nor did a deputation from Cologne, warning him in threatening tones of the attitude of the people of the Rhine provinces, nor another from Berlin itself, urging him to comply with the popular wishes, move him to action. After a sleepless night on the 17th-18th he gave way. At midday of the 18th he issued an edict granting freedom of the press, summoning the united Prussian parliament for the 2d of April, and promising to aid with all his influence the meeting of a parliament for all Germany, to work out in the most practical manner the regeneration of the Fatherland. This manifesto seemed for the moment to satisfy the people. They crowded in groups round the palace, desirous to express their complete satisfaction. Then ensued one of those catastrophes which in times of revolution are brought about no one knows how. The scene was one full of excitement; there were groups round the palace, the King vainly striving to address and to make himself heard by the masses in the front rank. The position bore some analogy to that of the 20th of June 1791 in Paris. Behind the front ranks the people continued to press on until the pressure became intolerable; then to relieve it there was issued an order to disperse. The untrained elements which compose a crowd never disperse easily; there can seldom be that unity of thought and action which is the only insurance against disorder. On this occasion the crowd did not readily disentangle itself. The soldiers who had heard the order noticed that it was not obeyed, and two of them discharged their muskets. In the panic which ensued the cavalry and infantry charged the people and dispersed them. But the anger of the people had been roused, blood had been shed, bands of men from all parts of the city collected to continue the combat, and during the night to erect barricades. There was every prospect

Reconciliation between King and People. 13

of a terrible battle on the 19th, when on the early morning of that day the King, who had been greatly distressed at the occurrences, yielded to the advice pressed upon him and issued an order to withdraw the troops into the palace. The order was understood by those by whom it was received to mean withdrawal from the city, and this was done, the palace being left unprotected. The people now stood in the position of victors; they used their victory far more generously than did the Paris mob on the occasion I have referred to. Desirous only that the King should witness the effect of the precipitate action of his soldiers, they had the bodies of the slain brought into the courtyard of the palace and their wounds laid bare. The King descended from the balcony and stood with uncovered head in the presence of the victims. His manner, sympathetic yet dignified, produced a deep effect. The same day he issued a political amnesty, to be extended to all classes, granted permission to carry arms, dismissed his reactionary ministry, and formed one from the ranks of the liberals. The people, on their side, attributed none of the mischance to their King. It was his brother, afterwards the Emperor William I., to whom they assigned the *rôle* of adviser against their interests, and that prince, conscious of his unpopularity, seized the opportunity to depart for London.

On the 21st took place the formal reconciliation between the King and the Berliners. The former, wearing the tricolour emblematic of German unity, rode, the head of a procession, through the streets, saluted by the crowd as Emperor of Germany, and talking platitudes regarding the duties imposed on all by a common danger. To him, an utter contemner of the authority of the people, the shouts which greeted him as Emperor were most distasteful. He endeavoured by signs to signify his disapproval, and declared repeatedly that he would not despoil the other princes of the Fatherland. However, on his return he published a manifesto in which, whilst declaring himself ready to assume the leadership in the hour of peril, and announcing that thenceforth Prussia was merged in Germany, he told the people that the country could only be saved by the most intimate union of German princes and peoples under a single headship. But at this time neither his words nor his acts gave a true indication of his inner convictions. Talking confidentially to a deputy at a later period of his conduct on this very day, March 21, he described his famous ride through the city and its accompaniments as 'a comedy he had been made to play.'

Though internal peace was restored, and the victory of the party of progress seemed assured, the King's position was still surrounded by difficulties. The principality of Neuchatel in Switzerland, which had come into the hands of the King of Prussia as heir to the House of Orange, seized the opportunity of the general convulsion to sever itself from its liege lord. The Prussian Poles, to whose demands for a national reorganisation the King had listened, were pressing their claims. At this moment of perplexity a request from the people of Schleswig-Holstein for assistance against the Danes came to him as a positive relief.

The subject may be treated very briefly. On the 21st of March a deputation of Schleswig-Holsteiners had proceeded to Copenhagen to make demands affecting their national life, to which, as Germans, they were entitled. These were, the admission of Schleswig into the German Bund, a common constitution for Schleswig-Holstein, the freedom of the press, and the dismissal of their obnoxious Statthalter. The King of Denmark

Important Movements in Germany. 15

refused these demands, whereupon the duchies consummated (March 24) a bloodless revolution, dismissed their Statthalter, nominated in his stead a governing commission of five persons, summoned a common parliament, and appealed to Berlin for support in the struggle which they knew to be inevitable.

Frederic William IV. responded gladly to the appeal, and ordered Prussian troops to enter the duchies. These arrived just in time to prevent the collapse of the revolutionary movement. They proceeded to occupy the duchies, the Danes retaliating by employing their ships of war against the mercantile marine of Germany. Thus matters continued till the 26th of August, when Prussia and Denmark,—the latter refusing to admit to the deliberations the representatives of the National Assembly of Frankfort—signed an armistice for seven months.

It is time that I should advert to the proceedings at Frankfort, the outcome of the combined thought and action of the intellect of Germany. To those thinkers it had long been clear that the victorious issue of the struggle with Napoleon had not produced the results which had been hoped for. Napoleon had enslaved a great part of Germany because the Germans were disunited. After their release they remained almost as disunited as before. The yoke of Napoleon had been exchanged for the yoke of Metternich. Never had the freedom of thought and the freedom of the pen been more repressed than in the period from 1815 to 1848. But now a chance had occurred: the chance of recovering all and more than all Germany had been hoping and secretly struggling for during the past thirty-three years. Instantly there was a movement. Communications passed from hand to hand, from centre to centre. Finally it was resolved that some 500 men, who had for the most part taken a share in the discussions of the day, should meet at Frankfort, the central point between north and south, the seat of the Diet, and make there preparations for the assembling of a national parliament representative of the entire Fatherland. The 500 met, sat five days, framed resolutions for the election of members of the new parliament, and then began to quarrel. In a time of revolution there is always a party of extremists, and they were not wanting in the ante-parliament, as the assembly of the 500 was called. But they formed the minority, and after having been worsted in argument, and having risen in insurrection in Baden, they were defeated, and deported to America.

Meanwhile the elections had taken place, and on the 18th of May the national constitutional assembly was opened. The main object of its members was to frame a constitution which should ensure the unity of Germany. Recalling the circumstances of the times, the state of chaos existing everywhere, the energies, often badly directed, which had been aroused, the terror of the princes, and the madness of the people, we can see that their task was almost impossible of accomplishment. Some hundreds of excellent gentlemen, all enthusiasts, many of them deep thinkers, all eager for the unity of the Fatherland, had met in solemn conclave to devise a scheme which, without the support of an army, they would enforce on States till then disunited and independent. Their best chance of success lay in the rapidity with which the scheme should be formulated and adopted. Failing that, they could hope for success only by enlisting in favour of their constitution one of the two great German powers, Austria or Prussia. But instead of acting with the celerity absolutely necessary to success, the philosophers and fanatics of the National

Its Dilatory Proceedings.

Assembly threw away valuable time in searching for first principles, in debating theoretical objections, and in debating the Schleswig-Holstein question. The result was that by the time their constitution was ready Austria had reasserted her influence, and the enthusiasm of the peoples had in great part evaporated.

It is not necessary here to examine minutely the several phases through which the National Assembly of Frankfort passed in 1848-9. Meeting on May 18th, it was not until the 28th of June that it had defined its powers for dealing with foreign affairs. On the day following it nominated the Archduke John of Austria to be regent of the empire, the holder, until a permanent chief should be appointed, of the executive power. An order assuring to itself indirectly supreme power, issued by the Assembly on this occasion, and directed to be read to the troops garrisoned all over Germany, gave rise on the part of the rulers of different parts of the country to expressions of opinion which should have warned the makers of the constitution to hurry on. Frederic William of Prussia was especially indignant, and although a meeting with the Archduke John at Cologne stilled his animosity, he could not refrain from telling a deputation of the Assembly which waited upon him that it was as well they should not forget that 'in Germany there were princes, and he was one of them.'

Still the Assembly did not expedite the framing of the constitution. Early in June the consideration of the Schleswig-Holstein question had diverted it from the one path it should have followed, and served only to demonstrate its impotence. To the severance of its various parties, to the insurrectionary risings in Baden and their repression (September 24), it is not necessary to refer except to note the time diverted thereby from the main and pressing object. Nor is it desirable to do more than indicate the embroilment with Austria caused by the proposition of that power that the entrance of the Austrian empire into any scheme of union would mean the entrance of the whole empire, with its nearly 40,000,000 of inhabitants, the majority non-German. It must suffice to state that it was not until March 27, 1849, that the Assembly resolved by 267 votes against 263 to make the dignity of the future German Emperor hereditary; not till the 28th, that the constitution was read a second time, and that Frederic William IV. of Prussia was elected Emperor, 290 members voting for him, 248 abstaining.

Before we consider the reply made by Frederic William to the offer it is advisable to take a glance alike at the turn affairs had been taking in Prussia and to the position of Austria. We left Frederic William momentarily relieved from his internal troubles by the outbreak of war with Denmark, a valve, he thought, for the superabundant energies of the liberals. Shortly afterwards, May 22d, the constituent assembly met. It was composed of very mediocre men, the best heads in northern Germany having preferred seats in the Frankfort Assembly. It effected very little. For a time it could with difficulty repress the street riots which continued at intervals to rage. It rejected the constitution scheme put before it by the government as not sufficiently democratic. Thereupon the cabinet resigned (June 15), and ten days later a new ministry was constituted which styled itself a 'ministry of action.' At first it seemed to justify its title, but soon new complications arose which defied its capacity to unravel. At length the unlicensed demagogy of the streets paved the way by its excesses to a reaction. Gradually the party of order recovered courage, the army

Position of Frederic William. 19

was staunch, and when, after many trials, the King had found the assembly impracticable, he suddenly appointed Count Brandenburg minister, prorogued the assembly (November 8), and ordered that it should meet at Brandenburg. Meanwhile troops were concentrated round the capital, and a state of siege was proclaimed On December 5th, finding the assembly still bent on obstruction, the King dissolved it, published a new constitution, and summoned a new parliament, composed of two chambers, to meet on February 26th.

Such was the situation of Prussia during the later months of 1848 and the earlier days of 1849. The King meanwhile was watching with mingled feelings the action tending to the unity of Germany under the presidency of Prussia at Frankfort. Whether he should accept or refuse the offer which he felt sure would be made him was a question he debated long and seriously with himself. It can scarcely be doubted that in the earlier period of the consideration he was inclined to acceptance. This is evident from the fact that even at the last moment, when the imperial crown was actually offered, those about him believed that he would take it. But not only were his prejudices very strong, not only did he abhor the idea of accepting from inferiors that which he would have hailed if offered by men of his own caste, but the long delays of the Frankfort assembly, the indications of its waning authority, and, above all, the rapid revival of Austria, and the dictatorial tone she was assuming, set before his eyes every day more clearly the great difficulties to himself an acceptance would involve. But he wavered long. The smaller States of Germany had given evidence that the Frankfort plan would be acceptable to them. The King himself (Frederic William), in a circular note he addressed to the powers, seemed to favour it.

But before the offer actually was made the action of Austria, under the guidance of Felix Schwarzenberg, came not only to increase the difficulties of the situation but to efface as far as was possible all the records of the revolution.

From that revolution Austria had suffered more than all the other German powers together. She had lost for the moment Italy and Hungary. Her capital, Vienna, was more than once in the hands of the revolutionary party. But she had recovered with a celerity which astonished Europe. The victory of Novara (March 23, 1849), followed by the peace of Milan (August 6), restored to her her Italian possessions. The energy of Prince Windischgrätz had put down revolution in Prague and Vienna. From September 1848 to August 1849 she was engaged in a severe struggle with Hungary, to emerge from it, with the aid of Russia, given without stint, absolutely victorious. On the 2d of December 1848 the feeble Emperor Ferdinand had abdicated in favour of a nephew in the prime of early youth—he was but just nineteen—at Olmütz in Moravia. With the new Emperor, Francis Joseph, or rather preceding him by a few days (November 22), came the famous minister who for a short time was to impose his will upon Germany, Prince Felix Schwarzenberg.

The recovery of Italy, and the suppression of the national rising in Hungary, by invoking the aid of Russia, were the work of Felix Schwarzenberg. He assumed at once the high tone which would have befitted the ruler of a recuperated empire. His one aim for the moment was to abolish all disunion within his own empire, to restore to Austria in Germany the preponderance she had exercised between 1815 and 1848, if possible to augment it. He set to work in a manner which quickly assured temporary union within, and certain preponderance without, the borders of his country. Had he lived and retained his position there is no saying how far he might have rendered permanent the advantages he had gained, but he died (April 5, 1852) too early for his purpose. It is necessary to examine here how far his action affected the cause of German unity as that cause was progressing in 1849.

When, in the early days of 1849, the majority of the National Assembly at Frankfort had made it abundantly clear that they contemplated the union of Germany as a federated State under the leadership of Prussia, to be followed by a union with Austria, Schwarzenberg protested in the most positive manner against the subordination of the Kaiser to a supreme power centred in any other German prince (February 1849). On the 5th of April following, for reasons presently to be mentioned, he recalled all the Austrian deputies from Frankfort. Meanwhile, in March, he had dissolved at Olmütz the parliament which, during the prevalence of the revolutionary fever, had been summoned to meet at Kremsier, a town in Moravia, and the seat during the troubles in Vienna of the government; had set aside the constitution it had drafted; and had published an edict, known as the edict of Olmütz, which professed to bestow upon the entire Austrian empire a uniform and centralised constitution. This constitution, under the pretence of securing equal rights for all the subjects of the Kaiser, really established absolute government throughout his dominions, some of them still in a state of rebellion. It contained, indeed, clauses granting provincial institutions to the German and Slav districts, but the powers of these were practically extremely limited.

The action of Austria towards the National Assembly

in protesting against the subordination of the Kaiser to a central power vested in any other German prince had been indirectly supported by the four lesser kingdoms— Saxony, Bavaria, Würtemberg, and Hanover; for these had with one voice protested against any federation in which Austria was not included. Now, the Austria of Schwarzenberg would be included only on her own terms. She could make or mar. She could either, that is to say, impose terms, which, if accepted, would assure her a predominance in Germany, or she would restore the old Diet in which, for thirty-three years, her preponderance had been unquestioned. In the same note then in which he protested against the subordination of Austria Schwarzenberg proposed the entry into the Germanic federation of the entire Austrian empire, including all its foreign elements. This announcement, followed a month later by the edict of Olmütz, which merged into one mass the different nationalities which recognised the Kaiser, excited the greatest commotion at Frankfort, and hastened the action of the supporters of German unity under a Prussian king. It led directly to that election of the King of Prussia to the headship of the Fatherland (March 28) of which I have written in a preceding page.[1]

It must always be borne in mind, when considering the action of the King of Prussia with respect to the offer of the headship of federated Germany, that he was thoroughly cognisant of the policy of Austria, and knew well that acceptance on his part would almost certainly mean war. Now he was not prepared for war. The army of Prussia was not in a condition to enter upon a campaign with a first-class power. Neither could the King count upon the support of the Czar. Indeed

[1] Page 18.

a little later, he had to learn that the sympathies of that powerful sovereign were entirely with Austria. He had besides, and had always had, a reverence for Austria. And although, in the early part of 1849, Austria had not retrieved her affairs in Italy, and her armies were still engaged in Hungary, yet no one doubted her speedy success in both quarters. That success achieved, she would have at her disposal troops seasoned by warfare, and probably rendered enthusiastic by victory. But what weighed most of all, probably, with Frederic William was the fact that if he were to accept the offer he would accept it from an assembly founded by a revolution, and he would have thus to assert his rights, as champion of the revolution, against the supporters of the divine right in which he implicitly believed.

Still the temptation to him was great; and when, on the evening of the 2d of April, the members deputed by the Frankfort assembly to offer the crown to the King arrived at Berlin, the minister, Count Brandenburg, received them with such cordiality that the impression was general that Frederic William had been won over. But the events of the following morning dispelled the impression. Whatever may have passed through his mind during the night, the dawn of day found Frederic William true to the traditions in which he had been nursed. He would not, he told the deputation, accept the proffered crown unless he were summoned to take it by the princes of Germany, and unless, also, the constitution should be approved by the same princes. The answer amounted to an absolute refusal: as such it was intended: as such it was sorrowfully accepted.

The answer was indeed much more than a refusal.

Despotic Action of Frederic William.

It was the deathblow to the Frankfort Assembly: to that assembly of German patriots who had made a genuine and strenuous effort to heal the many wounds of the Fatherland, to remove all causes of discord, to anticipate, in a word, the work of 1866-71. For the answer of the King of Prussia was not only a rejection of the crown, it was virtually a rejection of the constitution, the result of so many debates and so many compromises. That part of his reply referring to the constitution supplied a keynote for all Germany, for Austria in particular. It was that reference which brought from Prince Schwarzenberg the order of the 5th of April to the Austrian deputies of the National Assembly, to which I have alluded, to quit Frankfort. The ground he took was that the Assembly had been guilty of illegality in publishing the constitution. It became clear that Bavaria and Würtemberg would act with Austria, and that neither Saxony nor Hanover would side with the Assembly. Frederic William followed up his refusal by dismissing his recently summoned parliament for passing a resolution in favour of the Frankfort constitution.[1] This was a blow the significance of which could scarcely be overrated. When, in reply, the Frankfort Assembly addressed a note to all the disapproving Governments, demanding that they should abstain from dismissing or proroguing the representative bodies within their dominions, in order thus to stifle the free utterance of opinions in favour of the constitution they had drawn up, the official press of Prussia denounced that Assembly as a revolutionary body.

Thus denounced, the Assembly, the basis of moral

[1] The parliament also protested against the continuance of the state of siege in Berlin.

power on which it had depended cut from beneath it, abandoned on all sides, had no choice but to succumb. Some of the most violent of the democratic spirits arranged a popular rising at Dresden (May 4). But five days later Prussian troops restored order in the Saxon capital. In Baden, despite the fact that the Grand Duke had accepted the constitution, and had issued summonses of election for the federal legislative body by which the Assembly was to be succeeded, insurrection broke out, the republic was proclaimed, the troops joined the insurgents, and revolutionists from beyond the borders poured in to assist them. The situation was a test situation for the Frankfort Assembly. Could it or could it not repress disorders the consequence of its own failure to ensure unity? It at least made the attempt. It called upon the regent of the empire it had appointed, the Archduke John, to put down the revolution in Baden, and to protect the expression of free opinion regarding the constitution where that expression was threatened. The Archduke refused, and on the consequent resignation of his minister Von Gagern, he placed a set of nobodies in office. Prussia then, anxious to finish with the Assembly, declared that it regarded the resolution passed by it on the 10th of May, calling upon the Archduke to employ all the forces of Germany in defence of the constitution as a summons to civil war, and ordered all the Prussian deputies to quit Frankfort. Saxony and Hanover followed her example, and a few days later, May 20th, sixty-five of the most respected of the deputies declared their conviction that under the actual circumstances the relinquishment of its task by the Assembly was the least of evils, and that their work must be regarded as ended. Their example was gradually followed by all but the extreme radicals. These withdrew first to Stuttgart (June 6). But their vagaries at that quiet capital roused against them the popular opinion, and on the 18th they were driven out and dispersed. The Baden revolutionists, to whom I have previously referred, made a longer stand, and a campaign of six weeks was necessary before the Prince of Prussia was able, after some reverses, to crush them.

Such was the end of the great attempt made in 1848-9 to secure the federal union of Germany. It was a bold, a generous, a patriotic attempt. Resting solely on moral force, it could only succeed by enlisting on its behalf one of the two great powers which influenced respectively the country north of the Main and the territories south of that river. Had the King of Prussia been other than he was, had his nature partaken of the adventurous, and his will been strong and resolute, had, moreover, the Assembly been more intent on quickly forming its constitution than on fruitlessly debating the Schleswig-Holstein question; in a word, had it made to the King in the autumn of 1848 the offer it submitted to him in April 1849, it is just possible that the scheme might have been accepted. But the delay gave time to Austria, and the opposition of Austria was fatal. The King of Prussia could not have accepted the offer of April 1849 without having to meet Austria in the field. That was a contingency which—it will be seen later on—with an unprepared army, he dared not face.

The failure of the Frankfort Assembly left Austria and Prussia practically face to face. The views of Frederic William and Prince Felix Schwarzenberg were essentially opposed. The former still desired, in the perfunctory manner habitual to him, to bring about some kind of German union, with Prussia at the head. The latter was determined to restore the state of affairs which had existed prior to March 1848. He would resuscitate the Bund with its Diet ensuring the preponderance of Austria. It is advisable to devote a very short space to the discussion of the methods they severally pursued, and note the results which followed therefrom. The story is another illustration of the maxim that, in politics as in war, the boldest player almost invariably chains victory to his car.

The secret hopes of Frederic William IV. of Prussia to obtain, not from the Frankfort Assembly, now through his action dying or dead, but from the princes of northern and central Germany, a position which should more than counterbalance the influence of Austria, had been inducing him, in the earlier months of 1849, to set on foot secret negotiations to bring about that end. When, on the 3d of April, he had refused the proffered crown, he had announced his determination to place himself at the head of a federation of States voluntarily uniting themselves to Prussia, under terms to be arranged; and, very soon afterwards, he had addressed to the several governments of Germany a circular, inviting such of them as might be disposed to attend a conference to be held at Berlin on the 17th of May. In the interval his government, by its reply to the resolution of the Frankfort Assembly of the 10th of May, had dealt to that Assembly the blow from which it never rallied. To transfer to himself, then, any moral power which up to that date might have been wielded by the Assembly as the promoter of German unity, and to calm the minds of the liberals at Breslau, Elberfeld, Düsseldorf, and other centres, the King, on the 15th, issued a proclamation to the Prussian people, declaring that despite the failure at Frankfort a German union was still to be formed. From the conference that he summoned, the smaller States, which had given in their adhesion to the Frankfort constitution, at first held aloof, though subsequently twenty-eight of them sent in their adherence. To guage its real object, Austria sent a representative, but he retired at the close of the first sitting. The Bavarian agent followed his example. There remained, then, besides Prussia, the representatives of Hanover and Saxony. These three, proceeding to work, formed the confederation of the 26th of May, known as the 'League of the Three Kingdoms,' and which had for its object the formation of a federal union for all the States of Germany willingly adhering thereto. An undertaking was given that a federal parliament should be summoned for this purpose. Meanwhile Frederic William despatched troops to put down the disturbances which, as previously noted, had broken out in Saxony and Baden, a military operation which, in the case of the latter, occupied six weeks. The League of the Three Kingdoms gradually attracted to itself the smaller powers of Germany, but Austria, Bavaria, and Würtemberg would have nothing further to say to it. With Austria all that could be accomplished was to renew the agreement of the 30th of September previously, which provided that, until the permanent settlement of the affairs of Germany should be accomplished, a joint commission should carry on the administration of the Bund. But, as the internal affairs of the Austrian empire righted themselves, the opposition of Prince Schwarzenberg to the action taken by the King of Prussia became more strongly defined. The victory of Novara (March 23) had restored to Austria Northern Italy; the surrender of Vilagos (August 13) gave her back Hungary. Thenceforward Schwarzenberg could reckon upon an army proved in war to support his policy. Accordingly he began to work with a purpose which there was no mistaking. He first succeeded in detaching Saxony and Hanover from the Prussian league. Prussia, nevertheless, though followed only by the twenty-eight minor States of Germany, pursued her plan, and held at Erfurt (March 20, 1850) a federal parliament for the consideration of a new system of federal union. A draft of a constitution, drawn up in Berlin, was submitted to it. But hardly had it been read when the insincerity of the King of Prussia became manifest. In the interval between June 1849 and March 1850 a great reaction had taken place in Prussia. The King had reconquered the power he had lost in March 1848, and he was entirely disposed to retract all the concessions he had made at the period when, to use his own words, he had been 'acting a comedy.' The very federal constitution he had had drawn up at Berlin whilst his fears held the ascendency had now become too liberal; and, although the parliament he had summoned to Erfurt would have voted it *en bloc*, his supporters demanded that it should be revised. This proceeding excited the scorn and contempt of all the right-minded liberals of Germany. It was plain to them that Frederic William IV. of Prussia was a shuffler, whose word was not to be trusted, and from whom no scheme for the real union of Germany was to be expected.

Meanwhile Austria, her hands now completely free, had been slowly working for the attainment of her aim, the restoration of the Bund of 1815 to the position it had lost in 1848. The vacillations and want of faith of Frederic William greatly helped her. Already there sat in Frankfort thirteen representatives of States composing the Bund as an extraordinary Diet with full powers. This Diet was ready to act as Prince Schwarzenberg might desire. It possessed the fullest authority, for, legally, it was the Bund, the representative of all Germany. A circumstance very soon arose which gave Schwarzenburg the opportunity of exercising its powers with decisive effect against Prussia.

Frederic William I., Elector of Hesse-Cassel, born in 1802, had become, September 30, 1831, by the virtual abdication of his father, ruler of the electorate when still in his twenty-ninth year. A despot at heart, the young prince had begun by administering the electorate under constitutional forms which he was always endeavouring to evade. The death of his father, November 20, 1847, made him ruler in name as well as in fact. Not foreseeing the coming storm, he then made an attempt to suppress the constitution, which he detested, but when the crisis came his army failed him, and he was baffled. Close upon that rebuff broke out the revolution of February 1848, and the popular enthusiasm it caused made itself felt in every town and district of the electorate. The Elector bowed before the storm, and, deserted on the night of the 5th of March by his unpopular minister, Scheffer, promised the reforms immediately asked for (March 7). Pressed still further, he gave way on all points, formed a new ministry composed of liberals, and summoned the estates for the 13th of March. They met on that date, and passed laws which removed grievances long passively endured. A new era of happiness seemed to dawn for the people of Hesse-Cassel. They sent deputies to the Frankfort Assembly, and on its dissolution the electorate adhered to the league formed by Prussia and known as the League of the Three Kings. A fresh parliament, elected in July 1849, endorsed this policy.

But by this time it had become clear to the rulers, who had divested themselves of absolutism, that the enthusiasm of March 1848 had waned considerably, and that the zeal for reform was abating. We have already noticed how this consideration affected the action of Frederic William IV. of Prussia. It acted similarly on the mind of the Elector of Hesse-Cassel. This prince, who had been waiting his opportunity, resolved now to strike a blow for the recovery of his lost authority. To attain this end he entered into secret negotiations with Austria; dismissed, February 22, 1850, his liberal ministry, when he found the change he suggested unacceptable to his parliament; dissolved the latter without warning (June 12); and despatched his unpopular minister, Hassenpflug, to represent Hesse-Cassel at the Diet then sitting at Frankfort. He then proceeded to undo all that had been accomplished in the way of liberal reform in the period between March 1848 and the actual date, and he persisted in this course despite the refusal of his troops to coerce the people, and the opposition of the constituted authorities within the electorate.

Meanwhile the action of Hassenpflug at the Diet brought to boiling point the differences between Austria and Prussia. The Hesse minister, backed by Austria and her allies, had persuaded the Diet to pass a resolution (September 17) pledging itself to use all its efforts to maintain the threatened authority of the Elector within his dominions. But Prussia had morally pledged herself to the support of the constitutional rights of the people of the electorate, and she could not, without abandoning her claim to the leadership of German union, forsake her confederates in their extremity. She began by issuing a diplomatic circular to the effect that an irregular body which called itself the Diet had no right whatever to interfere in the affairs of the electorate. The King followed up this declaration by directing

Prussian troops to enter Hesse. They did enter the country, and occupied the important posts of Cassel and Fulda.

This was the opportunity for which Prince Schwarzenberg had been longing, to reobtain for Austria her preponderance in Germany. Acting with Bavaria and Würtemberg, he upheld the authority of the Diet against the strictures of Prussia, and gave orders to an Austro-Bavarian army corps to march into Hesse from the east. It appeared impossible, if both the contending parties should adhere to their published declarations, that a conflict between the north and south could be avoided.

But just at this critical moment the Czar Nicholas, whose delight it was to pose as the arbiter of continental Europe, and who had but recently crushed Hungary at the urgent prayer of Austria, came to Warsaw. There he was met (October 29) by the Emperor of Austria and the brother of the King of Prussia. There also were Schwarzenberg for Austria and Count Brandenburg representing Prussia. The differences between the two great German powers were considered in detail by the Czar, and on all points he decided in favour of Austria. Indeed the reception he gave to the Prussian minister, Count Brandenburg, was so galling that that true-hearted man returned to Berlin only to submit his report and to die.

To a mind constituted as was that of the King of Prussia the opinions expressed by a potentate whom he had been taught to revere, and whom the history of the past forty years had identified so closely with his family and his country, came as an order from heaven. He had still able and patriotic men by his side. Prominent among these was his minister, General Radowitz, who urged him at this crisis to be true to Prussia and to his principles. But, on the other side, was Manteuffe whispering in his ear that the Prussian army was in such a condition that it could not possibly resist the hardy and well-tried soldiers of Austria, and that the consequences of defeat might be far-reaching. This information was not reassuring, but it was the dictum of the Czar that settled the question. At a council held at Berlin on the 2d of November the King decided to submit. Radowitz resigned. Manteuffel succeeded him. Prussia abandoned the lead she had assumed, and accepted, to hold it for sixteen years, the second position in Germany.

Prince Schwarzenberg was thus triumphant. The army corps of which I have spoken entered Hesse (November 1), occupied Hanau, and marching westwards, had a slight brush with the Prussian troops at Bronzell near Fulda. On the 9th he categorically demanded the dissolution of the Prussian union, the recognition of the Diet, and the evacuation of Hesse. Manteuffel conceded the first point. Whilst he was hesitating regarding the other two Schwarzenberg sent the order to the Austro-Bavarian army corps to advance, and demanded that Prussian troops should evacuate the electorate within four-and-twenty hours. Upon this Manteuffel begged for an interview, and, not waiting for an answer, started for Olmütz. There he had to give way on all points. He agreed, in the name of Prussia, to withdraw all her troops, one battalion excepted, from Hesse, and practically to recognise the Bund. He resigned, in fact, all that Prussia and her king had intrigued for persistently ever since they had recovered from the terror caused by the outbreak of 1848.

The triumph of Prince Schwarzenberg was, it cannot be denied, the triumph of reaction. Not only was the

Bund reconstituted on the principles on which it had been founded in 1815, but Austria herself, by decrees of August 1851 and January 1852, still further restricted the liberties of her people. In Prussia the restrictions imposed by the constitution of January 31, 1850, existed indeed, but did not prevent a near approach to absolutism. In most of the other German States, more especially in Hesse, the reaction exhibited an impatient and unsparing activity. In Schleswig-Holstein the retrograde action of Germany was even more pronounced. Austria and Prussia virtually accepted terms dictated by Denmark, which secured to the latter power supreme authority in the two duchies. In a conference held in London the right of inheritance to the duchies was secured, after the death of the reigning king, to the line of Glücksburg. To this the two larger German powers also agreed. Finally, the German fleet, the object of so much enthusiasm, was offered up to the reactionary spirit. After long deliberations it was resolved to break it up. Prussia bought some of the larger vessels, the others were sold by auction to the highest bidder.

But if the dreams of unity which inspired all hearts on the morrow of the revolution of 1848 were thus cruelly dissipated; if the one power to which every thoughtful German had turned with hope and expectation in 1848 had renounced the aspirations which had fitfully inspired it in the early days of the revolution; if the years 1851 and 1852 witnessed the re-welding of that central authority which secured for Austria the first, and relegated Prussia to the second place in the German hierarchy; if the cause of union seemed dead, not to be resuscitated except by a general convulsion, there were yet some shrewd men who, remembering the story of the mouse and the lion, worked quietly and unostentatiously to prepare the ground for a new opportunity. These men were Prussians, working under the despotism of Frederic William IV., and under the timid and reactionary ministry of Manteuffel. It is to the consideration of their operations that we must now turn, for, in the presence of accomplished facts, it has to be admitted that the ZOLLVEREIN, the NEEDLE-GUN, and, a little later, THE REORGANISATION OF HER MILITARY SYSTEM, were the factors which enabled Prussia to become predominant in Germany in 1866, absolutely supreme in 1871.

CHAPTER II.

PRUSSIA FROM 1852 TO 1857.

UNDER the ministry of Manteuffel Prussia retrograded to a system more despotic than that which had obtained prior to the revolution of 1848. She had had her chance and had thrown it away. The period of alternate fears and hopes had culminated in the capitulation of Olmütz, a capitulation made by the very man whom the King, Frederic William IV., delighted to honour, and to whom he now entrusted the administration of the country. All the measures of Manteuffel were tainted by the moral disgrace engendered by that capitulation. They were, in external affairs, petty, irritating, poor in conception, showing that their author had not realised the nature of the policy which had made Prussia great, and which alone could keep her great. Manteuffel's one aim appeared to be to keep Prussia out of sight, to yield with a good grace, to avoid all responsibility, to submit to moral effacement. Had the powerful Austrian statesman who had brought about the capitulation of Olmütz lived but a few years longer it is probable that Prussia during the period of which I am writing would have reached even a lower point of degradation. Felix Schwarzenberg had made no secret of the aim of his German policy. He had resolved to undo the work of Frederic II. He would first humiliate Prussia, and then destroy her. How effectually he had humiliated her the records of the con-

The Zollverein. 37

vention of the 29th of November 1850 clearly prove. But in April 1852 a stroke of apoplexy removed Felix Schwarzenberg from the scene. His sucessors, fortunately for Prussia, were men of inferior mental calibre. For some time, however, the shadow of his presence seemed to hover round the council chamber of the King of Prussia and his ministers, and to impel them to the policy of self-effacement which I have endeavoured to describe.

But whilst the King of Prussia and his minister were thus degrading Prussia externally, an internal process was going on, the development of the work of preceding statesmen, which was destined to bear abundant fruit. I find the early stages of this process so admirably and concisely described by Mr Fyffe in his history of modern Europe[1] that I venture to quote the passage. Writing of the internal administration of Prussia between 1828 and 1836 Mr Fyffe says: 'Under a wise and enlightened financial policy the country was becoming visibly richer. Obstacles to commercial intercourse were removed; communications opened; and finally, by a series of treaties with the neighbouring German States, the foundations were laid for that customs union which, under the name of the Zollverein, ultimately embraced almost the whole of non-Austrian Germany. As one principality after another attached itself to the Prussian system, the products of the various regions of Germany, hitherto blocked by the frontier dues of each petty State, moved freely through the land, while the costs attending the taxation of foreign imports, now concentrated upon the external line of frontier, were enormously diminished. Patient, sagacious, and even liberal in its negotiations with its weaker neighbours, Prussia silently connected

[1] Fyffe's *Modern Europe*, Vol. II. page 406.

with itself, through the ties of financial union, States which had hitherto looked to Austria as their natural head. The semblance of political union was carefully avoided, but the germs of political union were nevertheless present in the growing community of material interests.'

The extension of the Zollverein was steadily pushed on after the period of which Mr Fyffe writes, and in 1837, 1841, 1843, 1844, and 1845 various petty States joined it. After the revolution of 1848, when matters had returned in the manner described into the old grooves, Austria made an attempt to creep into the system. The manner in which her action in this respect was baffled proves that there were men in Prussia fully cognisant of the immense advantages which would accrue to their country by the exclusion from the Zollverein of the purely Austrian element. It happened in this way.

In November 1851 Prussia had announced to the members of the Zollverein that, at a conference which had been summoned to meet at Berlin in the spring of 1852, she intended to bring forward proposals for strengthening and enlarging its basis and its scope of action. Meanwhile the minister for commerce and public works at Vienna, Charles Louis von Brück, a native of Elberfeld, and therefore by birth a Prussian, had convinced Prince Schwarzenberg of the necessity of altering the prohibitive system then existing in the dominions of the Kaiser, and of proposing to the other States of Germany a closer commercial connection. Flushed with this idea, Schwarzenberg summoned a Zoll-Congress to meet at Vienna in January 1852. In this congress the majority of the members of the Zollverein, Prussia, Hanover, and some smaller States excepted, took part. These unanimously agreed to advocate the acceptance of the Austrian proposals, securing to Austria a footing in the Zollverein, at the meeting of the members of the latter to be held at Berlin on the 19th of April following. At a preliminary meeting at Darmstadt, on the 6th of April, Bavaria, Saxony, Würtemberg, both the provinces of Hesse, Baden, and Nassau, known in the history of the period as 'The Darmstadt Coalition,' bound themselves to make a special point of this admission. But at the Berlin conference Prussia, without openly opposing it, managed to get the scheme virtually shelved. Her representatives met the proposal of the Darmstadt coalition by a motion that the consideration of that proposal should be deferred until the conference should have pronounced an opinion on the plans they had submitted for the reconstruction of the bases of the Zollverein itself. After many discussions, all of which proved fruitless, the Zoll conference was adjourned for a month (July 20). In the interval the Darmstadt coalition met again at Stuttgart, and, when the conference reassembled at Berlin on the 21st of August, announced that they were willing to accept, on certain conditions, the scheme which Prussia had proposed. They insisted, however, that coincidently with the ratification of the Prussian scheme a customs union and commercial treaty should be signed with Austria. Prussia, supported by Hanover, Brunswick, Oldenberg, and Thuringia, agreed to sign such a treaty, but only after the Zollverein should have been reconstituted. On this the conference was again adjourned, and the Darmstadt coalition held in September a meeting at Munich. Further negotiations made clear the secret purpose of Prussia not to allow Austria to enter the Zollverein. Possessing no longer the guiding hand and resolute will of Felix Schwarzenberg, Austria, after an interval, agreed to a compromise, by which she made a treaty with Prussia (February 19, 1853) securing for her products a more moderate scale of import, export, and transit duties, the terms, in fact, granted to the 'most favoured nation.' The duration of the treaty was to be twelve years. In 1860 committees were to meet to discuss the possibility of a customs union, or, in case this should be pronounced impracticable, of a further mutual lowering of the scale of duties. Thus by masterly adherence to her main idea—the exclusion of Austria from the Zollverein—Prussia maintained during those years of waiting the enormous advantage of union of interests with the German principalities outside of Austria. Her policy in this respect was one great factor in the cementing of the union of hearts which followed the events of 1866.

Another factor, which preceded and had a large influence in producing those events, was the introduction into the Prussian army of the needle-gun. During the thirty-five years which had followed the peace of 1815 the several nations of Europe had shown a great disinclination to effect improvements in their armies. This disinclination had been manifested especially in England. The first Duke of Wellington, whose influence on this point was all-commanding, had set his face against the attempting any large change in the weapons which had won for him his great battles. He would agree to the replacement of the flint lock by the percussion cap, but nothing beyond that. The same line had been taken by the historian of the Peninsular war, the late Sir William Napier. By both of these the old musket known as 'Brown Bess' was extolled as the 'Queen of weapons' for the infantry soldier. Led by these high authorities, the nation adopted the same idea. Unsparing ridicule was cast upon inventors. When in 1850-2 a gentleman named Warner produced a gun capable of covering a range far in excess of that attained by the artillery guns of the period the ministry of the day laughed at him as a crack-brained enthusiast, and refused point-blank to sanction the trial he asked for. Thus no change in the arming of the soldier was then possible in England. Stranger still was the fact that a similar dislike to examining existing methods had likewise taken hold of France, though she had but just recognised as her Emperor a man who had not only served in the artillery but had written a book on the subject, advocating certain reforms. In Austria, in Russia, and in all the other countries of Europe save one the same fatuous contentment with the actual arming of the soldier prevailed. In the opinions of all, the weapons which had freed continental Europe in 1815 were good enough for their day. But, as I have indicated, to this reasoning there was one exception.

That exception was Prussia. It happened in this wise. John Nicolas Dreyse, born at Sömmerda in Saxony in 1787, the son of a master locksmith, had been gifted by nature with a remarkable faculty for working in iron. At the age of nineteen he followed his father's profession at Altenburg and Dresden. There he showed so much capacity that in 1809 he migrated to Paris, then the place in Europe for the development of genius. There Dreyse succeeded in obtaining employment in the small-arms manufactory of Pauli, under the immediate patronage of Napoleon. In that manufactory he completely mastered the technicalities of the trade, and suggested many improvements in the process then adopted. After the collapse of 1814 he returned to his native place, Sömmerda, and established there an iron manufactory, under the name of Dreyse & Kronbiegel.

In course of time the firm was entrusted with the replacement in the muskets for the army of the flint lock by the percussion cap. Whilst Dreyse was engaged in this work the idea came to him that he could improve on the percussion cap, and in 1827 he produced a weapon the cartridge of which, though still inserted at the muzzle, was ignited by a small steel rod or needle pressed through it by the hammer. This weapon he called the 'needle-gun' (Zundnadelgewehr). He greatly interested the government in his invention, but recognising that it was not yet perfect, he insisted on continuing to labour for its improvement, until in 1836 he produced a weapon which loaded from the breach, the cartridge being still ignited by the action of the needle. The government tried the weapon very severely at Spandau and Lübben, and then accepted it. They resolved to keep the invention a secret, and served out the needle-guns only to the fusilier battalions. But the storming of the Berlin arsenal by the mob in 1848 disclosed the existence of a very large supply of muskets of the new pattern. The reason for secrecy existing no longer, the weapon was gradually served out to the entire army, first to the light infantry, and then, as the men could be instructed, to the other regiments. A trial on a small scale of its efficiency in action was made when the Prince of Prussia led an army corps to put down the Baden insurgents in 1851-2. The prince, afterwards King William I. of Prussia, and later the first German Emperor, saw enough of it during this campaign of six weeks to realise that Prussia possessed a weapon in all respects superior to the weapons of every other nation in Europe, and under his influence the distribution of it to the remainder of the army was pushed on with the greatest rapidity. In the Austrian war of 1866 it was this weapon which largely assisted in giving success

Reactionary Internal Policy of Prussia. 43

to the policy of the daring statesmen who risked all on the endeavour to place Prussia at the head of Germany. Rightly therefore may the needle-gun be regarded as a factor in the realisation of that cherished dream.

But during the years in which Prussia was engaged, unostentatiously and with what secrecy was possible, in preparing herself for a contest which was ever looming in the future, she was, by her reactionary policy within, turning against the government the hearts of her own people, and by her self-effacing external policy earning the contempt of Europe. The King, gloomy, mystical, unsympathetic towards the new ideas, was sinking daily into the hands of the absolutist party. His minister of public worship and public education, Raumer, and his minister of the interior, Westphalen, tormented the people by the restrictions they introduced into the administrations over which they severally presided. The system they adopted was one of continuous irritation. Spies were encouraged, denunciations were rewarded, public utterances were forbidden. The members of the party which had been dominant in 1848-9 were watched, tracked and on the most insignificant pretences thrown into prison. The writer recollects well how at the time he asked a professor in Westphalia who had taken a lead in the revolutionary events of 1848, and whose every movement was watched in the period between 1852 and 1866, how it would all end, and received the reply, given in a whisper, and in a tone as though the speaker really believed that walls had ears, '*in einer Revolution.*'[1] And it might have so ended but for the victories of 1866.

The foreign policy directed by Manteuffel, soured by the surrender of Olmütz, was as humiliating to its author as it was degrading to Prussia. Otto Theodor, Freiherr von

[1] 'In a revolution.'

Manteuffel's Foreign Policy.

Manteuffel, born in 1805, had been an absolutist throughout his career. In the united Prussian chambers, in 1847, and again, on the morrow of the revolution in April 1848, he had spoken strongly against the principle of constitutionalism. The manner in which, during the reaction which followed 1848, the advantages gained by the people were gradually filched from them had only strengthened his convictions. He had succeeded Count Brandenburg as minister for foreign affairs, and in December 1850 prepared to gain peace for Prussia at any price so that he might inaugurate a policy of repression within. As minister-president (December 19) and minister for foreign affairs he had, during eight years (from the 4th of December 1850 to the 9th of November 1858), all the means in his hand for oppressing his country within, and for humiliating her without, and he thoroughly succeeded in doing both.

To explain the details of his internal administration —to show how the popular rights gained in 1848 were swept away; how the abuses which had been then swept away were restored; how the education of the people was as far as possible restricted, and the press taught to subserve or be silent—would be beyond the scope of this work. It is mainly with the foreign policy of Manteuffel that we have to deal: to observe how his action during the crisis of the Crimean war affected the position of his country.

When in April 1853 the Czar Nicholas despatched Prince Menschikoff to Constantinople to make demands to which it was impossible for the Sultan to agree without yielding the independence of his country, and Turkey appealed from the dictates of the Czar to the public opinion of Europe, the King of Prussia proposed a plan the acceptance of which by the Powers and the Porte might possibly, although certainly not probably, have prevented hostilities. The demands of Russia had included the conceding to the Czar of the protectorship of the rights of the Christian subjects of the Sultan. It is obvious that such a concession would have established an '*imperium in imperio*' throughout Turkey; that the influence of the Sultan would have waned before that of the Czar; and that the way would have been paved for the gradual obliteration of all the rights of the former. Amid many suggestions for a middle way there came one from Frederic William IV. of Prussia. This was to the effect that the transfer of the rights over the Christian subjects of the Sultan should be conceeded, not to the Czar, but to the five great powers, that is, that the powers should guarantee and protect the rights of the Christian subjects of the Sultan. Logically there was no difference in principle between the proposal of the Czar and that of the Prussian king. Under both the rights of the subjects of the Sultan would be placed under foreign subjection. It was not a proposition which a sovereign with any self-respect or regard to his own dignity and the maintainance of his supreme authority dare accept. So it seemed to the English ambassador at the Porte, Lord Stratford de Redcliffe, and he advised the Sultan, who with his ministers fully shared Lord Stratford's views, to reject the proposal. It was rejected accordingly.

It will suffice if I simply record here the events which immediately followed. The Sultan, confiding in the support of the two great western powers, refused the conditions sought to be imposed upon him by the Czar. Upon this Prince Menschikoff quitted Constantinople (May 21). Thereupon the Sultan, to prove the sincerity of the concessions he had already made with respect to his Christian subjects, published a 'hatt-i-sharif' (imperial edict) in which he confirmed to the Christians all their rights and privileges, and appealed to his allies to support him against the unjust aggression of Russia. Then followed a conference at Vienna of the representatives of England, France, Austria, and Prussia. These agreed on the 11th of July to a collective note, which on the 10th of August following was accepted by the Czar. But as this note virtually conceded all that the Czar had asked for it was natural that the Sultan should object to it. He did object unless it should be partly modified, and the allies showed their appreciation of his reasons for so acting by supporting him in his demand for such modifications. On the 7th of September the Czar rejected the modifications proposed, and maintained his troops, who had crossed the Pruth on the 2d of July, in Moldavia. Thereupon the Sultan, with the consent of the national council, declared war against Russia (October 5). On the 2d of November the English and French fleets entered the Bosphorus and—after the destruction of the Turkish fleet at Sinope (November 30) —the Black sea (January 4, 1854). After many attempts at negotiation the Vienna conferences closed (January 16). England and France sent to the Czar an ultimatum, which he left unanswered (February 27); Turkey entered into an alliance with those powers to oppose, by force of arms, the demands of the Czar (March 12), and on the 27th and 28th following they declared war against Russia.

During the negotiations which had preceded that declaration Frederic William IV. had displayed a resolution, based upon the strangest grounds, not only to keep Prussia out of the war, but to avoid as far as possible taking any active part in the attempts made to stave off hostilities. He had made one proposal, that mentioned in a preceding page; and he had permitted his ambassador to take part in the conference at Vienna. He had, moreover, corresponded directly with the Queen of England and, through the ordinary channel, with the English Foreign Secretary, Lord Aberdeen. His objections to the war were manifold. It was 'a war for an idea'; it was a war 'which did not concern the industrious Rhinelanders and the husbandmen of Riesengebirg and Bernstein'; it was a war which had brought about an alliance which had filled him with disgust,' the alliance of England and Napoleon III.; he would take no part in it unless England would guarantee him against being attacked by 'that adventurer'; it was a war which, undertaken to support 'Islam against Christians,' would draw upon those who should take part in it 'God's avenging judgment,' and the baffling of all their hopes; it was a war undertaken against a sovereign whom he had found an acceptable neighbour; who, he knew, was 'ardently desirous of peace,' and who only desired an excuse to accept terms. 'I know,' he wrote to the Queen, 'that the Russian Emperor is ardently desirous of peace. Let your Majesty build a bridge for the principle of his life—the Imperial honour. He will walk over it, extolling God and praising Him. For this I pledge myself.'[1]

In the spirit in which the words above quoted were written Frederic William IV. conducted the foreign policy of Prussia throughout the Crimean war. The drift of that policy may be summed up in a single sentence. It was a policy of isolation. It was a policy which deprived Prussia of all influence in the councils

[1] See Martin's *Life of the Prince Consort*, Vol. III. pages 41 and onwards; and Fyffe's *Modern Europe*, Vol. III. page 202 and note.

of Europe. Whilst England and France were battling with the great eastern Colossus; whilst Austria occupied, in sympathetic alliance with the western powers, the Danubian principalities; whilst Italy, represented by the House of Savoy, aided those powers with an army; Prussia, guided by her sovereign, stood selfishly aloof. It is not surprising that when the war was approaching its termination, and a Conference of the Powers met at Paris (February 26, 1856) to negotiate for peace, Prussia, though nominally one of the great powers, was excluded from the initiatory stages of the discussion. She was not admitted until the first articles of the draft treaty had been settled, and then only because it had become necessary to revise the treaties of 1841, of which she had been one of the signatories. Never, since the days of Jena and the six years which followed Jena, had Prussia sunk so low in the estimation of the world. Who could have foreseen, who would have ventured to prophesy at that period of her humiliation that, only ten years later, she would not only regain, and more than regain, her influence in Europe as a great power, but would obtain a position in Germany assuring her a predominance more real, more certain, more decisive than that which might have been gained had Frederic William accepted the offer made to him by the National Assembly of Frankfort in April 1849?

CHAPTER III.

THE REGENCY OF THE PRINCE OF PRUSSIA—THE
PERIOD OF AWAKENING.

THE peace of Paris, concluding the Crimean war, was signed on the 30th of March 1856. On the 23d of October the following year, Frederic William IV. of Prussia ceased to rule. He had long suffered from a cerebral disorder, and the increase of this compelled him, on the date I have mentioned, to withdraw, temporarily it was thought, into seclusion. As he had no children, the executive power devolved for the moment on the Prince of Prussia, not immediately as Regent, but as Stellvertreter, or substitute. The name of this prince has been mentioned more than once in these pages. But, as he will occupy a very prominent position in those which are to follow, it seems desirable to give a short sketch of his career prior to his acceptance of the office which the illness of the King placed in his hands.

The second son of King Frederic William III., Prince William of Prussia was born at Berlin the 22d of March 1797. On the 1st of January 1807, the period when his country was in the deadly grasp of Napoleon, he received his first commission in the army. Nominated captain in October 1813, he accompanied his father throughout the campaign of 1814, won the Iron Cross at Bar-sur-Aube (February 26), and entered Paris with the Prussian army. After a short visit to England with the allied sovereigns he returned to be appointed major in a battalion of the Guards, and set out to join the army on the frontiers of Belgium. He was too late for Waterloo, but he again entered Paris with the army. On his return to Berlin he devoted himself very earnestly to his profession, mastered all its technicalities, and in 1825 was promoted to be lieutenant-general and commandant of the Guards. Four years later he married the Princess Augusta of Saxe-Weimar. The death of his father in 1840 made him heir-presumptive to the Prussian throne. As such he took the title of Prince of Prussia, and became Statthalter of Pomerania and general of infantry.

In the first throes of the outbreak of March 1848 in Berlin the Prince of Prussia strongly urged upon his brother the necessity of putting down the revolt with a strong hand before making concessions to the armed mob. Suppress the disturbances, he said in so many words, then redress real grievances, and loyally carry out the promises you may make. His advice was not followed, but the people associated his name with the advocacy of repressive measures, and he became so unpopular that the King and his ministers urged him to retire for a time. He proceeded, therefore, for the second time to London, and there associating with the first men of the day, with the Prince Consort, with Peel, Russell, Palmerston, and Bunsen, he rapidly made up his mind as to the course which Prussia ought to pursue in the crisis through which she was passing. He did not believe in the ultimate success of the endeavours then being made to constitute a united Germany; but he formed a very just idea as to the position which Prussia should prepare herself to take in the Fatherland. Returning to Berlin, he made a speech in the National

Assembly (June 8) in which he declared himself a supporter of constitutional government. The same day he was nominated to the command of the Prussian army corps which was to put down insurrection in Baden and the Palatinate. A campaign of six weeks, during which he enjoyed many opportunities of testing the needle-gun, saw the complete collapse of the rebellion. Returning to Berlin, and appointed Governor of the Rhenish provinces and Westphalia, he witnessed with a bitter pang the action of his brother in the Hesse question, culminating in the surrender of Olmütz. Thenceforth, and during the ministry of the author of that surrender, he took no part in politics. Being an outspoken man, however, he lost no opportunity of expressing his opinion regarding Manteuffel and his policy, and these utterances, everywhere repeated, gained for him a large amount of popularity, and caused the leaders of the liberal party to sigh for the time when power should fall into the hands of a man so honest, so capable, and disposed to act so fairly towards the people.

What this man was, thus suddenly called to the highest office in the State, can be but dimly imagined from the slight sketch I have given. But to that something has to be added. The Prince of Prussia was a real soldier. He had given himself to the study of army organisation. He knew the deficiencies of the Prussian army, and he had stored in his mind the plans which were to repair them. He was essentially a sober-minded man. Partaking to a certain extent of the caste prejudices of his elder brother, he would yet, in cases of emergency, allow himself, though with great difficulty, when pressed by men in whom he had absolute confidence, to forego them. He was a marvellous judge of a man. On this crucial point, for a ruler, his judgment was never once at fault. When, moreover, he had found the man, and had proved him, he gave him his entire confidence. Yet so honest was his nature that even his most trusted counsellors knew that there was a point beyond which he could not be persuaded. In such a case, when they considered the concession they required absolutely essential to the success of their policy, they did not hesitate deliberately to deceive him. And this indicates one weak point of his character. He was so true himself, and therefore so trusting, that a statement regarding which he would have made inquiries if uttered by an ordinary adviser was accepted by him unreservedly, and without the smallest doubt as to its accuracy, when tendered by one of his inner counsellors. A remarkable instance of this occurred immediately before the breaking out of the war of 1870. His bearing was ever manly and frank and his *bonhomie* and knowledge of the world endeared him to all about him.

Such was the man. His first acts, after attaining power, seemed to justify the hopes which hailed his succession. For Manteuffel he entertained a dislike strongly tempered with contempt. The petty tyrannies of the minister in matters internal, and his cringing, lifeless policy in matters external, had combined to produce this feeling. Whilst still only Stellvertreter, or Deputy for the King, whose recovery was not then despaired of, that is, from the 23d of October 1857 to the 7th of October 1858, he felt bound in conscience, as simply his brother's temporary representative, to maintain in office that minister and his colleagues. How bitter the necessity was may be judged from the fact that his first act on being nominated Regent (7th October 1858) was to remove them. It is difficult to describe the popularity of this measure. The writer, who happened then to be at

Good Effect of His Early Measures. 53

Düsseldorf, cannot forget the enthusiasm displayed alike by officers of the army and the people. Nor was that popularity diminished when the names of the new ministers were known. Chief of them was Prince Anton of Hohenzollern-Sigmaringen, the head of the Swabian branch of the Hohenzollerns, a Catholic, and possessed of a lofty nature. His colleagues belonged to the moderate liberal party: the foreign affairs being in the hands of Von Schleinitz, and those of the interior entrusted to Count Schwerin-Putzar. On the 8th of November the Regent addressed to the new ministry a few remarks which were accepted as his programme. He was, he said, in favour of a moderate constitutional government; declared that the highest duty of Prussia was to support and maintain the interests of Germany; and insisted that, for Prussia, the most absolute necessity was the organisation of a powerful army. The country responded to these words by returning a ministerial majority to the parliament (January 12, 1859).

But before that parliament had met the question of Italy had begun, on the initiative of Napoleon III., to engross the attention of Europe. That sovereign had entered into an agreement with Count Cavour, the prime minister of the King of Sardinia, whereby the latter should renew the quarrel with Austria, with the view to expel her from Italy and to absorb her possessions there—France assisting her with all her strength, and receiving, at the successful close of the war, the districts of Savoy and Nice as her share of the spoil. The engagement was a secret one, but as the action of the French Emperor developed itself very shrewd guesses were made as to its tendency. I have now to examine how the Italian question was regarded by the Regent of Prussia and his people.

The fact that the Austrian Empire included many provinces which were non-German deprived her, in German opinion, of all claim to the armed assistance of Germany in the event of one or more of those provinces, and those provinces only, being assailed. This also was the opinion of the Prince Regent. But as the victory of the allies over Austria in Italy might possibly draw after it an attack upon German territory — an attack which could not be permitted with impunity — the Regent declared that it was necessary for Prussia to prepare for any eventuality. On the 20th of April, therefore, he caused the mobilisation of three army corps. The same month he received in Berlin the Archduke Albert of Austria. This prince had come to beg that Prussia would guarantee to Austria her Italian possessions, and by placing a large army on the Rhine, in an attitude threatening to France, would prevent that power from rendering to Sardinia efficient assistance. This request the Regent was compelled to refuse; but, to ascertain clearly the political aims of Austria, he despatched General Willisen to Vienna. In his journey thither Willisen ascertained that entire southern Germany was prepared to stand by and support Austria, and that, as far as Austria was concerned, the war which had broken out on the 26th of April was a war of self-defence. Resolved to be ready for any event, the Regent then, the day after the battle of Solferino (June 24) mobilised the 7th and 8th Prussian army corps and on July 4 the 9th and 10th corps of the Bund army. He at the same time demanded from the Diet the command-in-chief of the entire German force and the sole direction of the same. Austria, by her representative at the Diet, was willing to comply with the first demand, but desired that the direction of the troops should be controlled

To baffle the French Designs against Austria. 55

by the Diet, that is, by herself as paramount in the Diet. When the Regent refused to agree to this proposal there ensued a curious but characteristic phase in Austria's policy. At the very time when the Emperor Napoleon, frightened by the losses he had sustained at Solferino, and still more by the conviction that not only was he no general himself but that he had no good general under his command, was fronting the formidable quadrilateral, and negotiating at Villafranca terms of a peace which he felt necessary to France and to himself, Prussia, by means of the Regent, was arranging a plan by which a formidable German army should force Napoleon to forego the advantages which Solferino had apparently secured to him. The preliminaries of peace between France and Austria had been negotiated at Villafranca, and Prince Windischgrätz had taken them to Berlin to obtain the opinion upon them of the Regent. The latter expressed to Windischgrätz, as representing Austria, an opinion strongly adverse to their acceptance. He pointed out to him the insecure position of Napoleon III., the preparations of Prussia and the rest of Germany, and how the French Emperor might be forced to quit his prey. Windischgrätz carried back these opinions to his master. The question which Austria had to decide was whether she would give up Lombardy to Sardinia or maintain her position in Italy at the cost of seeing the Prince Regent of Prussia at the head of a German army, and invested with its sole direction. Jealousy of Prussia prevailed. Rather than witness the great increase of her influence in Germany, which must have resulted from the position of the Prussian Regent she renounced Lombardy.

The marked step towards Italian unity evidenced by the cession of Lombardy to the House of Savoy contributed largely, with the liberal administration of the Regent, to revive the longing for unity in Germany itself. On the 16th of September there was founded at Frankfort an association called the National Society (Nationalverein), which set forth the idea of centralisation of the executive power of Germany in the hands of the King of Prussia; one leadership, also that of Prussia, for the German armies; and one diplomatic centre. This idea, circulating all over Germany, provoked in all the smaller States manifestations in favour of the Prussian headship. The Regent had, however, nothing of the adventurer in his nature. Essentially a Prussian, and looking forward to regain for Prussia, by legitimate means, the position in Germany to which she was entitled, and which she had lost, he directed his efforts rather to the reform of the military principles of the Bund than to the fostering of an agitation which might disturb the confidence of rulers. He wished by his measures to gain the trust of the party which had at heart the real welfare of Germany rather than that of German rulers individually. Prominent amongst those measures was the reorganisation on a sound basis, not only of the Prussian army, but of the German army under the control of the Diet. To ensure an efficient direction of the latter, his representative at Frankfort proposed, in January 1860, that in the event of a war in which all Germany should be interested the army of the Bund should be divided into two equal portions, the southern portion to be commanded by a nominee of Austria, the northern by a general named by Prussia. But Austria would not yield an inch, and by her influence the proposal was rejected the following April. Nor was the opposition to the Regent's schemes for the general welfare of Germany confined to the southern States.

Noting how, in the event of a war, the coasts of North Germany, and the flourishing cities which commercial enterprise had built upon them, would be exposed, defenceless or nearly so, to hostile cruisers, he proposed, at a conference of States whose territories were bordered by the sea, held for the purpose at Berlin the same year, that by their united efforts a fleet should be built, consisting of ten ships of the line and twenty frigates, to protect the sea-coast. By the votes of the smaller States the proposal was indeed carried; but when it was further suggested to build a line of railway to connect Minden with Jade Bay (Jadebusen), an inlet of the North Sea, to the point where now stands, thanks to the efforts of William when he became king, the flourishing naval station of Wilhelmshaven, Hanover absolutely refused to permit the line to traverse one single ell of her territory.

Convinced by this refusal, by the action of the Diet, and by other facts of more or less significance, that he could expect neither sympathy nor support from the larger States of Germany, all of which preferred to lean upon stationary Austria, the Regent turned his attention to the modelling of his army on a basis which should make it strong and efficient. Already in the time of his brother certain reforms had been initiated. Not only had the needle-gun become the armament of all the infantry, but the number of men under the colours had been largely increased by the putting in force of the law, which during the period between 1815 and 1848 had fallen into partial disuse, requiring from the conscript a service of three years. The system which provided for the mobilisation of the Landwehr had grown rusty with time. When, on the breaking out of the Franco-Austrian war in 1859, the Regent had mobilised the Prussian army, he discovered that for all practical purposes the Landwehr battalions were most inefficient. He found them filled with middle-aged, even old men, who had indeed been soldiers in their early youth, but who, in the long interval between their actual service and the time of their recall to duty, had forgotten all that they had ever known; and from the habits contracted in the interval the majority were utterly unfit for warfare. To restore efficiency to the army it was necessary, he felt, to introduce a radical change of principle, to alter the basis of the organisation. To effect this he required a man whom he could absolutely trust: a man imbibed with his views regarding organisation, convinced of the necessity to Prussia of an army which could fight, of the necessity likewise that Prussia should regain her proper place in Germany and in Europe.

Here it was that his thorough knowledge of men, of which I have spoken, came into play. He had been intimately connected with the army for fifty years, and it is scarcely too much to affirm that he had read the character of every man of note in its ranks. When the hour for reorganisation arrived his thoughts then turned instinctively to a soldier whom, in the period of inactivity of Manteuffel's premiership, he had noticed, and with whom, since his assumption of his high office, he had come much into contact. This man's name was Albert Theodore Emil, Count von Roon. On the 5th December 1859 the Regent appointed him minister of war.

Of the new war minister, whose action contributed so largely to the gaining for Prussia of the position she now occupies in Europe and the world, it is necessary here to say something. A Pomeranian by family and birth, he was born in 1803, and spent his early years at Alt-Damm, near Stettin. He was sent in 1816 to the school of

The War Minister, Von Roon. 59

cadets at Kulm in West Prussia; joined two years later the cadet corps at Berlin; entered (January 9, 1821) the 14th infantry regiment as second lieutenant; visited, 1825-7, the military public schools; was transferred in 1826 to the 15th infantry regiment; and in October 1828 was nominated to command the Berlin cadet corps as its instructor. At the instigation of Karl Ritter, the famous geographer, who at that time was director of studies of the cadet corps, Von Roon compiled a handbook of geography, which was published in 1832 under the title of *Outlines of Information regarding Peoples and Countries*.[1] At a later period, 1847-55, the work was greatly enlarged, and had an enormous circulation. In 1832 Von Roon returned to his regiment at Minden, but, the following November, General Müffling, who had been appointed to command the corps of observation which was to watch the siege of Antwerp by the French (November-December 1832), summoned him to his headquarters. In February 1833 Von Roon inspected the citadel of Antwerp, was transferred to the topographical bureau, and, recommended by the knowledge he displayed of surveying and the technicalities of military science, was nominated, March 30, 1836, to be captain on the general staff. Whilst engaged in the heavy duties devolving upon him in that capacity he wrote a book entitled *The Military Chorography of Europe*,[2] and, his attention having been directed to the civil war then raging in Spain, another entitled *The Iberian Peninsula; from a Military Standpoint*.[3] Of this, however, only the first part appeared. Whilst engaged in 1841 in making a reconnaissance on duty through Bohemia, Moravia, and

[1] *Grundzüge der Erd-Völker-and Staatenkunde.*
[2] *Militärische Länderbeschreibung von Europa.*
[3] *Die iberische Halbinsel. Vom Standpunkte des Militärs.*

Hungary, he was attacked by a very severe illness. On his recovery he was nominated major (1842) of the general staff of the second army corps, but the year following was ordered back to Berlin, to resume there his lectures. In 1844 he was selected to give to Prince Frederic Charles lessons in geography and tactics, and accompanied him in 1846 not only to the University of Bonn but also in his travels through Switzerland, Italy, France, and Belgium. This companionship was the means of cementing a bond of friendship, respect, and regard between the young prince and his mentor. On the 13th of March 1848 Von Roon returned to the practical exercise of his profession, was appointed in May to the general staff of the 8th army corps, and on the 22d of August following became chief of that staff. In the difficult crisis of that year and its immediate successor Von Roon displayed a judgment and a knowledge which drew upon him the commendation of his superiors. He took part in the short campaign in Baden in 1849, and, promoted in 1850 to be lieutenant-colonel, was nominated in December of that year (1850) commandant of the 33d regiment of infantry, stationed then at Thorn, afterwards at Cologne. On the 2d of December of that year he was advanced to the rank of colonel. On the 26th of June 1856 he received command of the 20th brigade of infantry in Posen; was promoted less than three months later (October 15, 1856) to be major-general; and, November 22, 1858, was nominated commander of the 14th division at Düsseldorf.

His varied experiences in many offices, especially in the mobilisations of 1832, 1849, and 1850, had convinced Von Roon of the glaring deficiencies of the Prussian army system, and he had thought out many plans for remedying these, especially those existing in the infantry.

Great Qualities of Von Roon.

These plans he caused, in June 1858, to be communicated to the Prince Regent. In May 1859 he became lieutenant-general. The mobilisation of that year served to confirm in the mind of the Regent the representations made to him by Von Roon. He sent for him, therefore (September 2), to Berlin to work out in the office of the minister of war his plans for the reorganisation of the army. Von Roon accompanied the Regent to Breslau, and a little later was appointed member of two commissions, which, under the presidency of the Prince Regent and General Wrangel respectively, sat in Berlin to perfect the plans for the reorganisation. In constant communication with the Regent, he made so deep an impression on the mind of the latter that, on the 5th of December 1859, he was nominated minister of war. He held that post for fourteen years (1859 to 1873), witnessing the perfect working of the machine which he had made, and the accomplishment by it of results greater by far than those which his master had contemplated in 1859. He was the third man in the illustrious triad presided over by the sovereign. Like the three brothers described in the *Arabian Nights*, one of whom had the gift of supernatural sight, the second of supernatural transport, the third of supernatural healing, each of the Prussian triad was essential to his companions. The daring policy of Bismarck, the perfect strategical knowledge of Moltke might alike have failed but for the thorough organisation of the machine which had been accomplished by the genius of Albert Theodore Emil, Count von Roon

The plan of reorganisation worked out by Von Roon in conjunction with the Prince Regent, in 1859-60, may be thus briefly summarised. It began by reciting the existing law imposing universal liability to military service. This law was in the future to be strictly enforced. Such service was limited in the line to three years, in the reserve to four, in the Landwehr to nine, making a total service for each man of sixteen years, instead of the nineteen till then authorised. By this means the peace establishment was raised from 150,000 men to somewhere about 213,000; the yearly conscription was increased from 40,000 to 63,000 recruits; the infantry battalions were increased from 135 to 253; and eighteen fresh cavalry regiments were to be raised. On the occasion of a mobilisation the Landwehr were not to be called out, whilst the line and the reserve were to be strengthened, so as to permit the rapid assembly of an army excellent alike in quality and in numbers. The yearly increase of expenditure for these changes was calculated at something in excess of 10,000,000 thalers, the cost of the first dispositions at about 5,000,000. Such were the heads of the plan submitted by the new war minister to the Lower House of Parliament on the 5th of February 1860.

Its reception was not favourable. The deputies looked rather to the amount of money required than to the necessity that Prussia, with her straggling territories, should be ready for war. Some deputies questioned the wisdom of making any sweeping change. The increase of service in the line from two to three years caused especially great murmuring. The minister therefore, dreading a defeat if he should persist with the measure in its actual form, withdrew it, and submitted on the 5th of May another proposal to the House. In this he simply demanded an extraordinary credit of 9,000,000 of thalers for the purpose of maintaining the army for the space of one year—till the 30th of June 1861—in a higher state of efficiency for war than then existed. At the same time he emphatically declared

Nominal Modifications of the Plan accepted. 63

that he brought forward this measure in order that subsequent resolutions regarding the army might not be prejudiced; and he pointed out that the condition it proposed for the army for the year ending the 30th of June 1861 was only provisional. Though he said this, both he and the Regent were fully determined, come what might come, with the consent of the House or without it, that the law should be absolutely permanent. The Lower House, after some discussion, granted the credit, and gave a provisional sanction to the proposed reorganisation; that is, it limited its provisions to the 30th of June following. Beyond that date there was to be no sanction for their existence. The Regent, however, paid no heed to this limitation, but proceeded to raise the additional infantry battalions and the additional cavalry regiments, and to bestow upon them their names and their colours.

The army bill had but just been passed when an event occurred which at the time attracted the attention of Europe. The Emperor of the French had cherished, especially since his triumph over Austria in 1859, the secret hope that it might be possible, by fanning the jealousy between Austria and Prussia, to regain for France on the Rhine the frontier she had possessed in the time of the first empire. So early as 1851 his minister to Berlin, the Count de Persigny, had sounded Frederic William IV. on the subject of an alliance which should benefit Prussia at the expense of Austria, the reward to France for her assistance being left purposely vague. But Frederic William was not only disinclined to a policy of adventure, he detested the adventurer who proposed it. During the active part of his reign, then, the subject was not again referred to. But in February 1859, after the accession of the Regent, and before the declaration of war with Austria, Napoleon caused certain proposals advantageous to Prussia to be made at Berlin. The Regent declined to entertain them, and, as we have seen, mobilised the Prussian army to defend the soil of Germany in case the turn of events should bring hostilities near to her door. After the war, the Emperor still clinging to his ideas, and believing that the same tactics which had gained for France the cession of Savoy and Nice might procure for her advantages on the Rhine, again opened negotiations with the Regent, proposing a personal interview, on the ostensible ground that he might convince him of his peaceable intentions, and prove to the Germans, who had attributed to him aggressive tendencies, that they had misjudged him. The Regent consented, and the interview took place at Baden-Baden on the 15th-17th June 1860. But the Regent had not gone alone. With commendable foresight he had taken care to be accompanied by German princes whom any proposal for the aggrandisement of Prussia at the expense of her neighbours would certainly affect. Beyond, then, making a passing allusion to the advantages which would accrue to Prussia from the possession of Schleswig-Holstein the baffled Emperor confined himself to generalities, and the meeting had no result. It deserves, however to be mentioned, as indicating alike the inner hopes of the French Emperor and the caution of the Prussian ruler. The latter, engaged in the formation of an army the real object of which was to secure for Prussia her proper place in Germany and in Europe, and nothing, as he then believed, beyond that, had had the opportunity of considering contingencies which an aggressive policy was to open out to him. He had no desire that his policy should be aggressive; he was content to live at peace with his German neighbours, but it should be a peace which would include respect for Prussia, which should give her the influence in German affairs which was her due. Above all, he desired no secret understandings with the French Emperor.

The year 1860 passed away, then, without further events deserving notice. The Regent and his war minister gave all their attention to the reorganisation of the army —the first step towards the recovery by Prussia of the position which the feeble policy of Frederic William IV. had temporarily lost.

CHAPTER IV.

THE KINGSHIP OF WILLIAM I.—THE POLICY OF 'BLOOD AND IRON.'

ON the 2d of January 1861 Frederic William IV. died. The Regent succeeded him, under the title of William I. His accession was very popular. He was almost universally regarded as an honest man, a man of his word, a man who had at heart the good of his country rather than that of a caste or a section of the community. His first act, the granting of an amnesty for all political offences (12th of January) confirmed the hopes of the people. His speeches at this time give the best possible indication of the subject which had possession of his mind. In his proclamation assuming the kingship, dated January 7th, whilst stating that he regarded his duties towards Prussia as bound up with those towards Germany, he declared that the task which Prussia had to fulfil in and for Germany was dictated by her glorious history, and rested for its accomplishment on the development of the plans of military reorganisation actually in progress. In the speech from the throne on the opening of the chambers the same spirit made itself clear. That the Lower Chamber did not fully partake his views was manifest in the answer to the address which they voted. In this they said, in so many words, that the reorganisation of the army was very well in its way, but it was not everything ; that the reform of the Bund, and certain popular

The Prussian Progress Party. 67

demands required attention. They confirmed, however, the grant of the 9,000,000 thalers for reorganisation as an extraordinary expenditure, with the exception of 750,000 thalers, which they struck off (May 31). The session closed on the 5th of June. Four days later saw the formation of a new liberal party, known as the 'German progress-party.' Its programme was (1) the reform of the Bund in a sense favourable to Prussia; (2) the placing the central power in the hands of Prussia; (3) the representation of the German people; (4) the real responsibility of ministers, the trial of political and press offences by a jury, the reform of the Upper House, and economy in the army administration by the advocacy of two years service in place of three. This party at once attracted to itself all the wavering elements of the House and the country. It became the great principle with which the King and his ministers had to struggle for the accomplishment of their plans. At the moment, and up to the year 1866, it represented, there can be no doubt, the majority of the people of Prussia. But, pure as were its principles, its leaders wanted in one particular point the foresight and the political acumen which characterised their opponents. That point was the absolute necessity for the thorough reorganisation of the army. How, when the crisis came, they were reminded of this in a manner which neither Prussia, nor Germany, nor Europe will ever forget will be told in its place.

A general impression prevailed at this time throughout Germany that the King had not risen to the height of the situation he occupied as ruler of the kingdom which every Prussian believed would eventually be compelled to assume the leading part in the formation of German unity. The aspirations which had been called into prominence by the events of 1848, though tempered and cooled by failure, still glowed in many a German heart. An expression used by the Archduke John at a public banquet held at Cologne in 1849—'No Austria, no Prussia, but one united Germanland, which shall stand as firmly as our mountains'—had penetrated the hearts of the people, and was repeated with peculiar fervour at the period of the accession of King William. But as time advanced, and the King, from whom so much had been hoped, appeared to the minds of the unreflecting multitude to care for little but the reorganisation of the Prussian army, a feeling of disappointment arose, and men began to ask one another whether, after all, he was more likely than had been his brother to initiate a bold policy of union. This feeling vented itself at Baden-Baden in an attempt made by a young man, Oscar Becker, to assassinate the King. Becker, though born at Odessa, was of German parentage, well instructed in jurisprudence and knowledge of finance, a good mathematician, and learned in the Turkish and Arabic languages. To effect his purpose he had travelled on the 12th of July from Leipsig, where he was studying, to Baden-Baden. There, on the 14th, he met the King, who was taking the waters, in the Lichtenthal Alley, and at a distance of only three paces discharged at his face, point-blank, both barrels of a pocket pistol. One of the balls struck the King on the neck, but inflicted only a slight contusion. When arrested Becker admitted that the act had been committed in cold blood, and was the consequence of his conviction 'that the King had not risen to the height of his position, the effecting of the union of Germany.' Becker was sentenced by the Baden Court of justice to twenty years' imprisonment, with intervals of solitary confinement; but, on the intercession in 1866 of the King, whose action then had proved the shallowness of the reason for the crime, he was released on condition that he should quit Germany for ever. He died, two years later, in Alexandria.

That the King, whilst bent on preparing the instrument which alone could assure to Prussia her proper position in Germany, had neither forgotten nor neglected the position of the States of Germany, bound hand and foot by the action of the Bund to the car of Austria, was proved by the answer he gave in December of the same year to a suggestion emanating from the Saxon government urging the reform of the Bund. He stated his conviction that the remodelling of the Bund's constitution could only be accomplished by means of single close alliance between the several States which constituted the Bund. How such alliances were to be contracted was not stated, and it would have been difficult to state plainly. The fact was that at this period the reform of the Bund was a question which, though it was burning under the surface, each German power shrank from approaching, though each of them knew that in a very short time it must be approached and solved. The policy of William consisted solely in the preparing of Prussia for the day of solution. At that moment neither he nor any prominent statesman in Germany had forecast the manner in which, by the action of one man, the question was to become within one year so pressing, so burning, as to compel the invocation of the God of battles.

Meanwhile the position in Prussia was being very sharply defined. When the Parliament met in the beginning of 1862 it was at once apparent that the ministry was not strong enough to meet the attacks of the new progress-party supported by the old liberals. The King then resolved to maintain at all costs his army reorganisation scheme, dismissed his ministry, appointed a new one, with Prince von Hohenlohe as its chief, dissolved the parliament, and made a special appeal to the country to support his policy. The appeal was fruitless. On the 19th of May the new parliament met, and though for a brief period it seemed inclined to support the measures submitted to it by the ministers, it struck when the army budget came under discussion. It ruthlessly refused the sum demanded for extraordinary expenses, that is, the sum required to carry out the reorganisations planned by the King and Von Roon.

The King had anticipated this result. He had been long searching for a man who would dominate the parliament: a man who, recognising as he had recognised the necessity of recovering for Prussia her place in Germany, should devote all his energies to the attainment of that end. But he must be a strong man, a man of convictions, of nerve; he must be 'a man of instincts and insights; a man, nevertheless, who will glare fiercely on any object, and see through it, and conquer it'; a man who had 'intellect, who had will, who had force beyond other men.'[1] Such a man King William believed he had found in Otto Edward Leopold, Count von Bismarck. On the 8th of October 1862 he nominated this man to be minister-president and minister of foreign affairs.

The new minister was comparatively young. He was born the 1st of April 1815 at the family estate of Schönhausen in the district of Magdeburg. At the age of seven years he was sent to school at Berlin, and, with the exception of a few months spent in 1832-3 at the university of Göttingen to study law and finance, he remained there for some years. In due course he passed the examination in the two subjects mentioned, received

[1] Carlyle's *French Revolution*.

the licence enabling him to practise in the courts of law, went through the military course required by the law, studied agriculture at Greifswald in Pomerania, and then in 1839 assumed the co-management of the family estates. On his father's death in 1845 he took up his residence at Schönhausen, which he then inherited. The same year he became a member of the provincial parliament of Pomerania, and in 1846 of that of Prussian Saxony. In this capacity he took a leading part in 1847 in the constitution of the first united parliament at Berlin, posing as a most decided champion of the conservative-monarchical principle, in opposition to the efforts made to introduce constitutionalism into Prussia. With the second united parliament which met in Berlin after the revolutionary events of March 1848 Bismarck did not much concern himself. He preferred to remain on his estates, devoting his time to the earnest consideration of the problems which were perplexing all the statesmen of the day. He attended, however, in the summer of 1848 the meeting at Berlin of the conference of conservatives known as the 'Junker parliament,' and contributed articles to the *Kreuz-Zeitung* newspaper which caused great sensation. In the parliament which met on the 7th of August 1849, and in which the conservative element predominated, Bismarck took his position as recognised leader of the right. His great principle was the building up in Prussia of a powerful kingdom, and the maintenance of such an understanding with Austria as would enable the two powers to have complete control of German affairs. In this sense he opposed the efforts in favour of union made by the King at the assembly he had convened at Erfurt (1850), and even approved of the convention of Olmütz, regarding it as unavoidable under the circumstances.

As the ablest and most energetic supporter of ab

solutism Bismarck drew upon himself at this period the attention of the leading men of all parties. The reactionary government of Manteuffel especially appreciated a man of his strongly pronounced absolutist views. In May 1851, therefore, he was nominated secretary to the Prussian legation at Frankfort; three months later, he was appointed Prussian representative to the Diet. Bismarck went to Frankfort with the fixed determination to bring about that cordial understanding between the two great German powers which had been the dream of his early manhood. He quitted Frankfort nearly three years later, January 1855, completely convinced that no such understanding was possible; that the Austrian policy was based on the principle of using the secondary States of Germany for her own aggrandisement, and for the humiliation of Prussia; that for the latter power there was but one course—to carve out her own destiny by the continuation of the policy employed by Frederic II. in 1740-2. From having been the friend with whom it was desirable to work with cordiality, Austria had become, in his eyes, the enemy whom it would be necessary to smite to the ground.

On leaving Frankfort Bismarck proceeded as Prussian ambassador to St Petersburg. The embassy was especially agreeable to him, for, with the scheme for smiting Austria dimly forming in his mind, he was anxious to secure the friendship of the ministers of the Czar, then deeply disappointed with the 'ingratitude' of the court of Vienna. The conduct of Austria during the Crimean war, then raging, the semi-hostility she had displayed, and her understanding with the western powers, had been regarded at St Petersburg as a shameful return for the aid afforded to her by Russia in the Hungarian war of 1849. The conduct of Prussia, on the contrary,

Bismarck's Plans of Policy. 73

in steadily refusing to listen to the advances of England and France, had conciliated the gratitude of the Czar and his ministers. Of this state of feeling Bismarck took full advantage, and it cannot be doubted but that the three years of his residence at St Petersburg laid the foundation of that alliance which was so useful to Prussia in her struggles in 1866 and 1870-1.

In the spring of 1862 Bismarck exchanged the embassy at St Petersburg for that of Paris. There he came in contact with the sovereign whose inscrutable policy was then exciting the attention of Europe. Napoleon III. did not impress Bismarck. He looked upon him as a dreamer, a trickster whose policy would best be met by plain blunt phrases and decisive action. For the policy which allowed France to embroil herself in an expedition to Mexico when Europe was in a state of tension he had the most profound contempt. Such a policy, however, he recognised, might favour his designs against Austria, for it might paralyse the action of France in Europe at the critical moment.

Bismarck had been but a few months at Paris when he was summoned by his sovereign to return to Berlin, September 23, to assume an *ad interim* position in the ministry. A fortnight later, October 8, he became minister-president and minister for foreign affairs.

We have looked at his training: it is time for us now to discuss the character of the man.

Strong in his convictions, unshakeable in his determinations, a Prussian to the backbone, Bismarck had shaped in his mind a policy which was to place Prussia at the head of Germany. With the carrying out of that policy, which he took an early opportunity of announcing as a policy of 'blood and iron,' nothing was to be allowed to interfere, neither scruples of conscience, regard for truth, considerations of honour. All these must give way. Not only that, but all the elements which combine to aid the course of an unscrupulous man were to be enlisted in his service. If the policy was a policy of 'blood and iron,' it was also a policy of 'fraud and falsehood.' The reader will find that it required a large exercise of the two last-named agencies to force Austria to that war which finally excluded her from the rest of Germany. Well had Bismarck studied the career of Frederic II. He could not, indeed, concentrate in his own person the qualities which gave Frederic the first position in Germany. But working under a master the one idea of whose life at that period was to make Prussia great, and in concert with colleagues one of whom would provide him with an army whilst the other would think out a strategy, he could repress internal opposition; then, throwing himself with avidity into the arena of foreign policy, and taking up the dropped threads of 1740-2 and of 1756-63, he could complete the plan which the ablest and most unscrupulous of the Hohenzollerns so ably began and so unwillingly left unfinished. Such was the man, such was his policy: let us now consider his actions.

On the 23d of September Bismarck had accepted the post of first minister *ad interim* on the resignation of the Prince von Hohenlohe. With characteristic energy he went straight to the task. On the 29th he informed the House that if the budget of the ministry were defeated, he would reintroduce it in the next session, and with it a new bill for the reorganisation of the army. The day following, addressing the budget commission, he made use of the phrase, alike historical and prophetic, that 'great questions were not to be solved by speeches and the resolutions of majorities, but by blood and iron.' This

Bismarck over-rides the Parliament. 75

expression produced little effect on the committee, for on the 7th of October the Lower House rejected the reorganisation scheme. Bismarck then caused the scheme to be passed by the Upper House, and prorogued the parliament. He had invented the theory that if the three great constitutional bodies could not agree the view taken by the majority of the three should prevail. He would in the meantime govern and levy taxes without a budget. In vain did the Lower House protest that the decisions of the Upper House were contrary to the constitution, and therefore illegal. The 'man of insight and instincts' was not to be moved by mere words. On the 13th, five days after he had assumed the office of foreign minister, he sent them back to their constituents.

From their constituents the deputies received thanks and congratulations for their patriotic conduct. The country evidently was with them. The people could not understand the daring conduct of this new minister, inexperienced in parliamentary affairs, who would thus trample upon the privileges of their representatives, and declare he would levy taxes, not only without their sanction but against their express decisions. The three months that followed were spent by both parties in preparing for a renewal of the struggle—a struggle regarded by the large majority of the people as affecting the very basis of constitutional government; by the Crown and the ministers as involving the very existence of Prussia as a great power.

The Lower House reassembled on the 10th of January 1863. Its members had returned in a very resolute mood. In reply to the speech from the throne they launched complaints against the statesman who had administered the affairs of the country without a budget, had disregarded the votes of the majority, and had spent money which had not been voted. A new cause of complaint soon arose from the action of the government in signing a convention with Russia (February 8) for the mobilisation of an army corps on Prussian Poland, in view of the disturbances in Warsaw and its neighbourhood, without communicating the same to the Lower House. The opposition fully believed that this mobilisation, coinciding as it did in date with the reintroduction of the army reorganisation scheme, would be used by the government to extort support for their measures. In effect, on the 8th of February, Von Roon did introduce his new army bill. It was found to be in principle a reproduction of the old one. It was then submitted to a committee. On the 24th of April this committee made a report, not only condemning the measure as it had been drafted, but taking it paragraph by paragraph and making its own amendments in each, entirely altering its scope, and representing it to the House as a bill which fixed the period of service with the line at two years. A fierce debate, in which the war minister, Von Roon, was repeatedly called to order by the vice-president of the Assembly, Herr von Bockum-Dolffs, followed the presentation of the report (May 11). But the action of the vice-president only stimulated the audacity of Bismarck. The following day he announced to the House that the members of the ministry would not again appear within its precincts until the president of the Assembly should have renounced all disciplinary authority over them. As the House declined to accept this condition the members of the ministry withdrew. A crisis followed. On the 21st the King announced that he fully supported his ministers in their contention. The following day the House voted an address to the King to the effect that the wide differences

Bismarck's Foreign Policy. 77

existing between his advisers and the deputies could only be healed by a change of men and a change of system. The reply of the Government was to prorogue the parliament (May 27). Three days later (June 1) a royal ordinance placed the press under police inspection and governmental superintendence.

Whilst the King and his ministers were thus engaged in forcing upon an unwilling, because uninstructed, parliament a scheme for army reorganisation which alone would enable Prussia to assume that position in Germany which was not only her due, but which the very liberals who opposed the scheme wished her to assume, Bismarck was introducing that aggressive system of foreign policy which could not fail to lead sooner or later to a rupture. It happened that the affairs of electoral Hesse, temporarily settled by the convention of Olmütz, again demanded the interference of the Bund. The hand of the Elector had been so heavy that his subjects loudly called for interference. In 1850, it will be recollected, Prussia had championed the cause of the people, Austria that of the Elector, and Austria had prevailed. This time Bismarck resolved that the influence and the hand of Prussia should be felt. Whilst, then, the Diet was nodding over the appeal which had been made to it, Bismarck addressed directly to the Elector a pressing demand to concede and to maintain the just rights of the estates of his realm. Then, again, Austria had expressed her dissatisfaction with the effect on her trade of a commercial treaty which Bismarck when at Paris had negotiated with France, and with the proposals regarding it which Prussia had made to the Diet. Bismarck seized the opportunity to address a very sharp despatch to Vienna, in which he charged the Austrian government with deliberate hostility to Prussia, and shadowed forth in plain terms the disruption of the

Bund in case Austria and the central States of Germany should persist in their hostile action. In the course of the correspondence which ensued Bismarck indicated very clearly the thoughts which directed his policy and the end he proposed. He told Austria that she would act in her best interests if she were to remove her centre of gravity to Buda-Pest instead of seeking to root the same, by her repeated attacks on Prussian influence, in Germany. Although such utterances tended to the isolation of Prussia in Germany, by inducing the central and southern States to cling more closely to Austria, they were nevertheless deliberate. Bismarck felt that to effect his end it was necessary that Prussia should break with past traditions, should show herself ready to look the rest of Germany in the face, should be ready to make good her pretensions, not by means of despatches and protocols, but by 'blood and iron.' The utterances were then simply preparatory to an action which in the inner circles of the Prussian capital was avowed.

As a step in the same direction we have again to consider the dealings of the same minister with Russia. We have seen how careful he had been to conciliate the friendship of the statesmen of the Czar during his residence at St Petersburg. An event happened shortly after his accession to the foreign office which gave him the opportunity of cementing the friendships and union of interests he then had formed. On the 22d of January 1863 an insurrection, which gradually extended to all Russian Poland, broke out at Warsaw. The sympathies of Paris and London went deeply with the Poles. Not so those of Bismarck. There were Poles in Prussia. Insurrection might breed insurrection. Bismarck had no sympathy with Polish aspirations. More than that, the opportunity was an excellent one for coming to a thorough understanding with St Petersburg. The time, he felt, was not very distant when Prussia would require the friendly neutrality of her northern neighbour. Bismarck then concluded a convention with Russia for a combined operation against the insurgents in the event of their crossing the Prussian frontier, closed that frontier against all fugitives, and, through Von Roon, directed the mobilisation of a strong army corps, which he placed in observation to watch events. Austria, who had likewise Polish subjects, displayed no such readiness to meet the wishes of the Czar. It can readily be seen, then, how this action on the part of Prussia contrasted with the hostility of the western powers and the callous indifference of Austria; how it impressed the minds of the statesmen of St Petersburg, and predisposed them to return in kind the service thus rendered.

There were two other questions which came to the front during this and the following year which tended to sharpen the differences, and eventually to cause an open breach, between Prussia and the rest of Germany. These were the reform of the Bund and the Schleswig-Holstein question.

There was no desire now on the part of Austria to avoid the solution of the first of those questions. Under the guidance of her Emperor, Francis Joseph, a single-minded and honourable man, Austria had been led into the path of constitutional government, and in her orderly methods, and in the frank and sincere co-operation of her statesmen, she presented a very favourable contrast to her northern rival. The high tone assumed, and the pressure exercised by Bismarck, had, however, frightened the Austrian statesmen, and they were as willing now to conciliate as they had been formerly unbending. In the autumn of the year the two Emperors had met at Gastein, and

Francis-Joseph had endeavoured to win the consent of his nephew to a scheme which he had formed, in conjunction with the princes of middle and southern Germany, for the assembling at Frankfort of a congress of German rulers to deliberate on the reform of the Bund. But Bismarck was not at Gastein, and although King William expressed tentatively his approval of the scheme, he decline to commit himself until he should have seen Bismarck. Before the matter had been finally settled King William quitted Gastein. The invitations addressed to all the countries represented at the Diet were a little later duly despatched. By sixteen of the States represented at the Diet they were accepted; by the seventeenth, Prussia, the invitation was declined. The King had at Berlin come under the influence of his minister, and although the princes assembled at Frankfort despatched one of their number, the most acceptable of all, King John of Saxony, to William, to induce him to change his mind, the King persisted in holding aloof, and the projected congress fell through.

It is easy to understand why Bismarck persuaded his master to decline. The only conditions, he declared, upon which a resettlement of the Bund was possible were—absolute equality of Prussia and Austria in the Diet; the right of veto to each with respect to the declaration of war; and a representation of the German people proceeding from direct voting on a franchise common to all. These were his three points, not one of which, he argued, would be conceded by a congress of princes. It is probable he was right.

On the failure of the congress there quickly followed the reopening of the Schleswig-Holstein question. The treaty of London[1] had laid down, in terms accepted by

[1] *Vide* page 34.

Strained Relations with Denmark.

Austria and Prussia alike, the recognition of the integrity of the Danish monarchy, and of Prince Christian of Glücksburg as heir-presumptive of the whole dominions of the reigning king. It had been arranged, however, that the rights in Holstein of the German Bund should remain unprejudiced, and the King, Frederic VII., had promised to conform to certain rules in his treatment of both principalities. This agreement the King had, in his zeal for union in the territories under his sway, persistently and continuously broken. The German population of the duchies had more than once appealed to the Diet to interfere on their behalf. There had been correspondence, even threats, but still their wrongs remained unredressed. But in March 1863 the Diet refused any longer to hold its hand. It plainly informed King Frederic that if he did not recall an edict he had then recently issued, imposing unauthorised burdens on the duchies, it would proceed to federal execution. Frederic replied by incorporating Schleswig with the rest of the monarchy. In consequence of this act the Diet, on the 1st of October, decreed federal execution, that is, armed intervention against the King of Denmark as Duke of Holstein.

Before the execution could be enforced the King of Denmark died (November 15). If his successor, Prince Christian of Glücksburg, would but withdraw the obnoxious edicts it appeared possible that the German intervention might be avoided. But the feelings of the Danes had been roused to a height too great to permit of a peaceable solution. The new king was forced to bow to the popular will, to give his assent to a constitution which included Schleswig as a part and parcel of Danish territory, and which levied taxes for the national expenditure from Holstein. But the popular feeling in Germany had been roused to a level higher than it had reached since 1848. From the moment King Christian had given his assent to the new constitution intervention was not to be avoided. From all parts of the Fatherland the cry came to Frankfort to abolish the conditions of the treaty of London, and to bring Schleswig-Holstein under the Duke of Augustenburg into a close federal union with Germany. The cry prevailed, and the Diet committed the execution of its orders to Saxony and Hanover.

Never in the history of Europe has the truth of the wise saying of King Solomon been more thoroughly manifested than it was upon this occasion.[1] Although the execution of the decree of the Diet had been openly entrusted to Saxony and Hanover, and the contingents from these two kingdoms had entered Holstein to accomplish one accepted purpose, the federal union with Germany of the two duchies under a prince of their own, Bismarck had resolved not only to thwart this accepted and partly executed scheme of the Diet but so to manœuvre as to win the duchies for Prussia alone, with the aid mainly of Prussian troops, and to incorporate them into the Prussian monarchy.

He carried out this scheme with all the audacity, all the deception, all the masterfulness of his bold and unscrupulous nature. His first care was to hoodwink Austria. Since the death of Felix Schwarzenberg Austria had not possessed a statesman capable of taking a comprehensive view of her requirements as a nation which, largely German, was still more largely composed of foreign elements. The minister who, at the period at which we have arrived, possessed the confidence of his master in the direction of the foreign

[1] 'The beginning of strife is as when one letteth out water.'—Proverbs xvii. 14.

Bismarck seizes the Direction of It. 83

policy of the empire was Count Rechberg, a statesman of the school of Metternich, regarding all other dangers as small compared with the spread of democratic influences. Bismarck had been associated with this man at Frankfort. He knew him well, his weak points as well as his good qualities, and he played with him as a cat plays with a mouse. By persuading him that the gratification of the popular demand for the admission into federal Germany of the two duchies would intensify and rouse to fever heat democratic influences throughout the Fatherland, and by guaranteeing the possessions of Austria in the case of a war arising from her union with Prussia, he persuaded Rechberg to unite with him in treating as null and void the resolution of the Diet; to join the troops of Austria to those of Prussia in order that they, the conservators of order, might enter the duchies, not as mandatories of the Bund but as the instruments of two independent and allied powers.

It seems incredible that Austria, the Austria whom Bismarck had told that she must remove her centre of gravity to Buda-Pest, the Austria whose measures he had constantly and openly thwarted, should walk quietly into the transparent trap he had laid for her, should run the risk of forfeiting all her influence with the minor states of Germany for the sole purpose of playing into the hands of her hereditary enemy. The only possible explanation is the reality of the dread felt by Rechberg, painted in exaggerated colours by Bismarck, that the action of the Bund, obeying the popular impulse, would open the floodgates of revolution, and restore the dreaded days of 1848. Austrian statesmanship with regard to foreign affairs has rarely been conspicuous for its excellence, but we shall see as we progress that, during the period between 1863 and 1866 inclusive, it was at its very lowest ebb. But, bad as it was in 1866, no mistake which she made equalled in its terrible consequences the initial mistake made by Count Rechberg when he not only agreed that Austria should draw the Schleswig-Holstein chestnuts from the fire in order that Prussia might eat them, but ran the risk of forfeiting the support of the rest of Germany, and laid his country open to the after consequences—the sudden turning upon her of the long-pent hatred of the unscrupulous man who had duped him. How high Austria would have stood had Rechberg refused to betray the Bund, how unassailable she would then have been, how complete would have been the exposure of the designs of Bismarck, it is easy to see now. Unfortunately for Austria it was a sealed book to Count Rechberg.

Having secretly arranged for the co-operation of Austria, Bismarck took the next step. That step was to pose as an upholder of the sacredness of treaties. The treaty of London had agreed to recognise King Christian as King of Denmark and as sovereign of the duchies. Bismarck declared to the Diet that by that treaty Prussia would abide. This declaration turned all Germany, the hoodwinked Austria excepted, against Prussia. Never had she, or rather never had her minister, been so unpopular. For the voice of Prussia coincided with the voice of Germany. The Lower House of Parliament at Berlin refused, we shall see, the supplies asked for a Prussian attack on the duchies. Nor in the Diet did the Prussian policy find a single supporter, except, of course, that of her deluded victim. The proposal Bismarck made to the Diet to despatch a summons to King Christian to annul the constitution of the previous November, and, in the event of his refusal, to occupy only Schleswig, was all but unanimously rejected. Then Bismarck laid his cards on the table. He would have his way despite the Diet. In concert with Austria he despatched an ultimatum to Copenhagen demanding the repeal of the November constitution. King Christian refused. Whereupon, on the 1st of February 1864, Prussian and Austrian troops entered Schleswig. The Danish war had begun. Bismarck had let out the waters which were not to subside until his ally, Austria, should be excluded from the rest of Germany.

CHAPTER V.

THE AUSTRO-PRUSSIAN INVASION OF SCHLESWIG-HOLSTEIN AND ITS CONSEQUENCES.

WHILST Bismarck had, in the manner described, directed the foreign policy of Prussia, the King and Von Roon had, despite the opposition of the liberals, been pushing on the reorganisation of the army with giant's strides. By the legal fiction which Bismarck had invented, and to which the King had given his public sanction, the taxes refused by the Lower House, but approved by the Crown and the Upper House, were still levied. But the discontent of the people was great. In the quiet corners of the cities the word 'revolution' was muttered in no dulcet tones. The more advanced liberals had persuaded themselves that the private soldiers, mostly men sprung from the people, would fire[1] in the air. These feelings found expression in the parliament newly elected, which met on the 9th of November 1863. The government had taken extraordinary pains to secure a majority in this parliament, but the feeling of the country had proved too strong for them. The first act of its members was to vote an address to the Crown requesting that the Schleswig-Holstein question might be settled by the recognition of the rights of the Duke of Augustenburg.

[1] I write this from personal knowledge. I was much in Prussia in 1863-4, and was assured, over and over again, that in the cause of constitutionalism the troops would not fire on the people.

Opposition of the Prussian Parliament. 87

Any other course, the address added, would threaten the solidarity of the two duchies, and would produce strife and civil war in Germany. Bismarck spoke against the address, but in vain. In his reply to it the King, whilst evading compliance with its prayer, demanded a loan of 12,000,000 thalers to enable him to carry out the policy of the government. The House, roused to indignation, not only refused the loan but rejected also the budget, the army reorganisation bill, and the law muzzling the press. The government, careless of its opposition, passed the budget through the Upper House, and then on the 25th of January dissolved the Lower House. The King's speech on the dissolution, written and read by Bismarck, abounded in reproaches against the Lower House. They had sinned grievously against patriotism. In the main he was right. The Prussian people had not comprehended that, for Prussia to resume her place in Germany, it was essential she should have an army on the model devised by the King and his war minister. Seven days later Austrian and Prussian troops entered Schleswig and occupied Eckenforde. The day following they attacked the Danewerke, an ancient fortification, consisting of a very thick wall from thirty to forty feet high, extending for about ten miles along the southern frontier of the duchy, from the North Sea to the Baltic. In the attack upon this work there happened something which gave great confidence to the Austrians, and produced an impression regarding the Prussian soldiers which continued till 1866.

The extreme left of the Danewerke rested on Missunde, a town situated on the river Schlei, a narrow inlet of the Baltic. It was arranged that whilst the Austrians, under the Freiherr von Gablenz, a very capable officer, who had served under Radetzky, should attack the centre, the Prussians, led by Prince Frederic Charles, better known as the 'Red Prince,' a cousin of the King, should assail the left at Missunde. The arrangement was carried out, but notwithstanding the needle-gun, now distributed to every soldier in the Prussian army, the Red Prince was repulsed; nor was it until Gablenz, victorious in his attack in the centre, brought his men against the flank of the defenders that Frederic Charles was able to force his way in. The Danes, yielding to numbers, fell back on Düppel, a fortified village covering the narrow channel which separates the isle of Alsen from the mainland. Whilst the Prussians took a position at Flensburg, at the west end of the fiord of the same name, thence to watch Düppel, Gablenz, marching northwards, occupied the town of Schleswig on the 6th of February, caught and defeated the Danish rearguard, after a very bloody battle at Oeversee, and entered Jutland on the 8th of March. There he remained until a month later he was joined by Frederic Charles.

That prince had experienced more difficulties than had Gablenz. Düppel was strong by nature, and had been made stronger by art. Its front works, ranging over an extent of 3000 metres, had been fortified according to the newest methods. Raised on an elevated plateau, they commanded the country in front, whilst the flanks resting on the sea were protected on one side by the Danish fleet, on the other by the batteries of Alsen. Before this place Frederic Charles had appeared on the 11th of February. After very many skirmishes he opened his batteries on the 16th of March, bombarded the place that day and the day following, but, making but little impression, sat down on the 29th to a regular siege. On the 17th of April his engineers reported the breaches practicable

The following morning he led his troops to the assault, and in a very brief space of time carried the place. The garrison retreated into Alsen, whither the Prince could not, by reason of the extreme narrowness of the channel, in the face of the protecting batteries, pursue them. He pushed on rather to join the Austrians in Jutland. The Danes, not strong enough to contend against the united forces, evacuated the province (April 29). The allies then proceeded to occupy the mainland as far as the series of inland water basins known as the Lümfiord, extending from the North Sea to the Kattegat.

So far as actual fighting was concerned the war was over. Europe had looked on with folded arms whilst a treaty signed by all the great powers only eleven years before was being deliberately broken. It is true that two of the parties to the treaty which guaranteed the succession of the Danish possessions, inclusive of Schleswig and Holstein, to the Glücksburg family,—the Duke of Augustenburg renouncing his claims for a compensation in money,—were the infringers of the treaty. Of the other three, Russia was bound by promises to support the policy of Prussia. The conduct of England and France would, however, seem to demand explanation.

It has been customary to attribute the inaction of the western powers in this grave European question to the increasing coldness between the courts of St James and the Tuileries, and to the fact that, because the former had not responded favourably to the invitation of the French Emperor to a congress to be held at Paris in 1863, therefore the latter rejected the proposals regarding Denmark which might, if acted upon, have saved her. But the refusal of Napoleon III. to co-operate with England was prompted by considerations of a character altogether different. No one more than he had fanned the frowning mistrust between Austria and Prussia. Ever since he had compelled Italy to cede Savoy and Nice he had nursed the hope of being able to play a similar game with the two great German powers. To set them against one another, to witness their gradual exhaustion, then to step in as arbitrator, receiving as payment either the frontier of the Rhine or the liberty to annex Belgium, had become to him a fixed resolve. It is remarkable that whilst cherishing such dreams he should have directed his foreign policy on lines which would most certainly prevent the fulfilment of them. That, at a period when Bismarck was beginning that series of intrigues which had for their object the compelling Austria to fight at a disadvantage, Napoleon should have entered upon the Mexican adventure was a madness paralleled only in history by the tenacity with which his uncle had clung in 1812 to the possession of Spain. When the hour arrived for which he had been hoping and scheming he was then powerless to utilise to his advantage the chance which it offered.

He declined then, in 1864, to respond favourably to the advances of England, because he sympathised with Bismarck's avowed intention to thrust Austria from her seat of predominance. For Denmark he really cared very little: for a civil war in Germany a great deal. It was not, then, pique, but a well-thought-out policy which dictated his reply to England: a policy excellent for France if he had carefully husbanded his resources to support it, but which, in the absence of any such statesmanlike action, would blunt his sickle on the barren sand.

As for England, it is only necessary to state that, under the guidance of the aged Lord Palmerston and the aged Lord Russell, her policy was a policy of words only. Those words, however bold, were not intended to be the precursors of action. 'I look upon Lord Russell's despatches as so much waste paper,'[1] said the Bavarian representative at Frankfort, the Baron von der Pfordten to the English minister, Sir Alexander Malet.

But, though they did not interfere, the neutral powers made an effort to settle the differences by diplomacy. A conference met in London on the 20th of April, two days after the storming of Düppel, and after three weeks of negotiation induced the belligerents to accept an armistice. At the time Schleswig, Holstein, and Jutland were in the occupation of the allies. Denmark was powerless. At the conference, however, she was misled by the expressions of sympathy emanating from the English and French representatives, and she refused an offer which, taking from her Holstein, would leave her the northern part of Schleswig. The war, consequently, recommenced (June 26). The result was such as everyone foresaw. Alsen was bombarded and taken, the Danes were driven to the northern extremity of the mainland, and they were finally compelled to accept terms far harder than those they had rejected in May. An armistice was agreed to on the 18th of July. On the 26th a conference of the powers was held at Vienna. On the 30th of October a treaty was signed by which Holstein, Schleswig, and Lauenburg were ceded to the allies. Denmark also agreed to pay a large sum to defray the expenses of the war.

After successful war follows the distribution of the spoil. Before they entered Denmark the invading powers had made no precise stipulation as to the manner in which the territories to be conquered should be appropriated. It had simply been settled by agreement that the two

[1] *Overthrow of the Germanic Confederation by Prussia in* 1866, by Sir Alexander Malet.

powers 'engage to establish the future condition of the duchies only by way of mutual understanding.' The time for the settling of the nature of this mutual understanding had now arrived. It was a question abounding with difficulties for Austria, for, as we now know, it was the full intention of Bismarck to arrange, not 'a mutual understanding,' but, rather, such a 'mutual misunderstanding' as would enable him, at any chosen moment, to fix a quarrel upon that Power.

It was Bismarck's firm determination to procure the cession of the duchies to Prussia. They supplied all that of which Prussia was in need: in Kiel, a magnificent harbour; in the narrownesss of the peninsula the possibility of uniting the North Sea and the Baltic by means of a canal—a frontier which might easily be made defensible. The acquisition of such a territory was so valuable that the utterance of falsehood and the practice of fraud might well seem, to an utterly unscrupulous man, not only justifiable but patriotic. That he had been able to delude Austria to go so far with him as to be a partner in the expulsion of the Danes was a marvellous feat of diplomacy. But it was a part only of the great scheme. The awakening for Austria would come when the time for the division of the spoil should arrive. Then, with an army increased and reorganised, supplied with an irresistible weapon, he could easily find means to pick the quarrel, the solution of which would either place Prussia at the head of Germany or roll her into an abyss more terrible than that formed by the whirlwind of 1801-7.

Such was the policy of Bismarck: a policy truly of adventure, a policy which could succeed only by deliberately deceiving Austria until the pear should be ripe—a policy rightly called 'of fraud and falsehood,' to be supported at the proper time by force. It had two dis-

Plans of Bismarck. 93

tinct bases: the deceiving of Austria and the preparation of an army which should be irresistible.

Yet it cannot be concealed that in this policy of adventure Bismarck was encouraged by four or five potent factors. He could count upon the sympathy of Russia; upon the blindness, and, above all, on the pride of the Habsburgs, always displaying itself at the wrong moment, always damaging to their country; upon successfully deceiving phlegmatic England; upon the secret sympathy and neutrality of the Emperor of the French, who, believing that the struggle would be long and exhaustive, and in the end disastrous to Prussia, hoped to step in towards its conclusion, as the armed arbitrator, and claim as his spoil the frontier of the Rhine. But he too was hoodwinked, and, unlike his fellow-adventurer who armed whilst he plotted, he plotted but did not arm.

To carry out his plans Bismarck proceeded with his accustomed dissimulation and his accustomed audacity. The first question to arise was as to the division of the spoil. On this point, as I have said, the two powers had had, before the outbreak of hostilities, but the vaguest understanding. It was necessary for Bismarck to break to his ally only gradually his intentions. Accordingly, in the first instance, the occupation of the conquered country was thus arranged. One Austrian brigade, consisting of five battalions of infantry, two squadrons of cavalry, and a battery of artillery, occupied Holstein, whilst two Prussian brigades of infantry, amounting to eighteen battalions, eighteen squadrons of cavalry, and three batteries of artillery, held Schleswig. It was understood by Austria that the occupation should only continue until the Duke of Augustenburg should have subscribed to certain necessary conditions, the claims of this prince having been recognised by all the powers, inclusive of the

Prussian representative, at the later conference of London.

But it was no part of Bismarck's policy to hand over the duchies to the Duke of Augustenburg. Accordingly, he obtained an opinion from the crown jurists of Berlin to the effect that the claims of King Christian (whom he had just dispossessed) to Schleswig-Holstein were legal, and that the Duke had no rights whatever in the duchies. To give to Austria some idea of this tendency of his policy he communicated to Vienna, February 22, 1865, the terms[1] upon which Prussia was ready to admit the claim of the Duke of Augustenburg. These conditions scarcely veiled the determination of Bismarck to seize the duchies for Prussia. They provided a system under which the Duke would be a mere puppet, and the duchies would be Prussian all but in name. Needless to say that they raised a storm on all sides. Austria would not have them; the Duke himself declined to listen to them; almost the entire population of Schleswig-Holstein protested against them. Austria, partially awakened now to the aspirations of Bismarck, formally demanded the re-establishment of the independence of both duchies, and that their future relations to Prussia should be regulated in consonance with the federal compact. The Diet, too, on the motion of Bavaria, Saxony, and Hesse, passed a resolution expressive of a hope that pending the final solution of the question the duchy of Holstein should be handed over to the Duke of Augustenburg. It was clear to Bismarck that, whilst his preparations

---

[1] They were: that the finance, postal, and railway systems should be assimilated to and combined with those of Prussia; that Prussian law, including the obligation to serve, should be introduced; that the regiments should take the oath of fidelity to the Prussian king; that the principal military positions should be held by Prussian troops.

He hoodwinks Austria. 95

for war had not been completed, the feeling of all Germany was opposed to the pretensions he had raised for Prussia. It was necessary, therefore, to temporise. After some correspondence he arranged to meet the Austrian minister, Count Blome, at Gastein; and there, on the 14th of August 1865, he signed with him a treaty —known as the Convention of Gastein—in virtue of which Holstein was transferred to Austria, and Schleswig to Prussia, 'without prejudice to the continuation of the rights of both powers to the whole of both duchies.' The second article provided for the establishment of a German fleet and the fixing of the port of Kiel as the federal harbour, under conditions which gave Prussia complete control; the third, for the establishment of Rendsburg as a federal fortress, to be garrisoned alternately by the troops of the two powers; the fourth stipulated that, until the carrying out of the partition agreed to in the first article, Prussia should have possession of two military roads through Holstein, the one from Lübeck to Kiel, the other from Hamburg to Rendsburg; the fifth gave to Prussia the privilege of erecting and using a telegraphic wire between Kiel and Rendsburg, and the right for its post-office carriages, with its own employés, to circulate on both railway lines throughout the duchy of Holstein, her railway line from Lübeck to Kiel being also assured a passage across the Holstein territory; the sixth provided for the entry of both duchies into the Zollverein; the seventh assured to Prussia the right of directing through the Holstein territory the intended North Sea canal, under her absolute control throughout its course; the seventh freed the duchy of Lauenburg from all contribution to the costs of the war; the eighth conferred that duchy upon Prussia, that power binding herself to pay to Austria, in exchange for the cession, 2,500,000 Danish rix-thalers within four weeks of the ratification of the treaty; the tenth provided that 'the execution of the hereinbefore agreed upon partition of the joint sovereignty shall follow as speedily as possible upon the ratification of this Convention'—by the two sovereigns—'and at latest be carried out by the 15th of September.'

The plain English of this convention was to secure absolutely to Prussia Schleswig and Lauenburg, and the right of constant interference, under any number of pretexts, in the affairs of Holstein. The Emperor of Austria met his uncle the King of Prussia to ratify it at Salzburg on the 20th of August, and there it was signed and sealed. Both sovereigns signed in good faith, the King regarding it as a most favourable agreement for Prussia, the Emperor as the best bargain he could make to escape the consequences of the entanglement Count Rechberg had unwittingly made for him. At this period, and from this period onwards, the King of Prussia was not in the complete confidence of his chief minister. An honest man, he would have started back from Bismarck, as Hazael did from the prophet Elisha, with a similar exclamation on his lips, had Bismarck opened to him his whole heart, told him of the necessity of hoodwinking his nephew, of striking him down in due season, of keeping him in good humour until the war preparations, then fast approaching completion, should be completed. The convention was bad enough for Austria. Had it rested there there would have been indeed constant misunderstandings and bickerings. But the matter was not to rest there. The convention was to be made the instrument for casting down the supremacy, for annihilating the influence, of Austria in Germany.

So confident was Bismarck that he had now laid the train which he could explode at any moment that immediately after the ratification of the convention he hastened to Biarritz, there to engage the Emperor of the French to permit him to secure the active alliance of Italy, and to observe himself absolute neutrality during the war he was projecting.

The Italian government had greatly at heart two objects: the cession of Rome and the cession of Venetia. The first was in the hands of Napoleon III., whose troops occupied the eternal city, the second depended solely upon Austria. Bismarck had argued that the desire to possess the Venetian territories was so intense in the Italian heart that it would move Italy to form an aggressive alliance with Prussia to gain them by force of arms. He was conscious, however, that Italy would not move without the sanction of Napoleon. Were that sanction to be given, and were that alliance to be concluded, he would succeed in dividing the Austrian forces, and compel her to maintain half her troops in Italy. He had already made guarded overtures to Italy, but these had not been very favourably received, and on the conclusion of the Convention of Gastein the Italian minister, La Marmora, believing that the distribution of the spoil of the Danish war had been amicably arranged, had actually despatched a confidential envoy to Vienna to ask if the Emperor would cede Venetia on the payment by Italy of a very large sum of money and on the assumption by her of a fair share of the Austrian public debt.

Such was the situation when Bismarck arrived at Biarritz. No authentic record of the proceedings at that famous meeting has been published, and there is but one man living who could supply one. But we can imagine the scene. On the one hand, the tempter from Berlin, who had read the character of his august host, who understood every movement of his mind, who could divine his every thought on the subject of the impending war; and this tempter, with one distinct settled purpose before him, a purpose which he could attain only by the silent cooperation of his host; a tempter ready to humour, to promise, to agree by word of mouth, but determined to sign nothing—as determined not to perform what he might be compelled verbally to promise. He had gone there absolutely convinced that, for his influence with Italy, for his own neutrality, Napoleon would demand his price. His price he knew to be the cession of the Rhine frontier or of Belgium, possibly of both. For the services to be rendered he was prepared, I have said, to promise largely, to humour the French Emperor to the full extent of his hopes, little caring for the fact that he was leading him into a fool's paradise. As little cared he for the rude awakening of his ally when his point should have been gained, his victory achieved. The Prussian army would fight the more confidently for the victory it had won. The French army was in Mexico.

On the other side was Napoleon III. A plotter by nature, accustomed to intrigue, he had encouraged Bismarck in all his schemes against Austria. Bismarck had a very frank nature, especially with those he desired to gain. With Napoleon III. he had been especially frank. None of his aspirations had been withheld from him. This frankness had thoroughly misled Napoleon. He never before 1866 credited Bismarck with the great talent he undoubtedly possessed. He looked upon him rather as a boaster, a sort of Bobadil, who, with abundance of ambition, overrated his own capacity. Such a blunt man, speaking so openly of his aims, could easily be overreached. He did not think for a moment that as a military power Prussia was a match for Austria. He was the more ready, therefore, at Biarritz, to listen to the suggestion that he should signify to Italy his approval of her making common cause with Prussia. He was content to accept from his frank, outspoken guest—in return for his whisper to Italy and his engagement that France should be neutral—vague, possibly, indeed, definite promises of cessions on the Rhine frontier or of a free hand with regard to Belgium. But these promises were merely verbal promises. Confident that the war would be a long one, Napoleon required no more, fully resolved that before the chance should arrive France should be ready.

He had in his mind the recollection of his transaction with Cavour. He did not, possibly, reflect that the circumstances differed from one another in almost every particular. In 1859 he had helped Cavour with his army, and he was in a position to insist on the carrying out of the contract. In 1865-6 he was almost in the position of a general without an army.

Bismarck quitted Biarritz, taking with him the consent of the French Emperor to all his plans. On his arrival at Berlin he set to work to accomplish the three purposes he had immediately in view: the goading of Austria to the point of quarrel, the cementing of an offensive and defensive alliance with Italy, the presentation to the honest mind of the King of the conduct and motives of Austria in a light the absolute reverse of the true light. He accomplished these three necessary schemes. When he had in March 1866 goaded Austria, in the manner to be indicated, to arm in self-defence, he arranged, and on the 8th of April signed, an offensive and defensive treaty with Italy. This treaty provided that if within three months Prussia should take up arms for the reform of the German federal system Italy would immediately declare war against Austria. Both parties were to put into the field their whole strength, and peace was not to be made until Austria should have agreed to cede Venetia to Italy.

Bismarck's representation that Austria, by her conduct in Holstein, was pandering to the democratic principle for the purpose of fostering internal discontent in Prussia gained the King. Bismarck had drawn up the Convention of Gastein in such a manner that he could use it to create and to foment difficulties with Vienna. His policy was based on the principle which, according to Æsop, animated the wolf in his conduct towards the lamb. He had instructed the statesman whom he had sent to govern the duchy of Schleswig, General Manteuffel, a son of the minister of that name, to maintain the strictest discipline in his duchy, to allow no meetings, to repress every expression of opinion. The Austrian governor of Holstein, on the other hand, had been directed to introduce into that duchy the tolerant principles which guided constitutional Austria in her dealings with her German subjects. It followed that public meetings, conducted in an orderly manner, were permitted in Holstein. It is quite possible that at some of these meetings observations were made regarding the different systems prevailing in the two duchies, and that regrets were expressed that a union of the two under the Duke of Augustenburg had not been effected. Bismarck used these expressions of the Holsteiners—not, be it remarked, of the Austrians—to fix the blame on Austria, and to press home, in his intercourse with the King, his charges against Austria, indicated in this paragraph.

Then, the King having been gained, he openly charged Austria with disturbing the peace of Germany. Vainly did Vienna protest that her intentions were of the purest. Fruitlessly did the Diet propose an alternative arrangement for the administration of the duchies. The only alternative scheme acceptable to Bismarck was their bodily transfer to Prussia. He would even have rejected that, for it would have deprived him of the goad he held in his hand for the tormenting and exciting of Austria. To such a length at last did his complaints proceed that, on the 16th of March, Count Karolyi, the Austrian ambassador at Berlin, received orders to demand point-blank from Bismarck whether 'Prussia meant to break the treaty of Gastein.' Bismarck was not quite ready for war, the alliance with Italy not having been signed. He therefore replied with a decided 'No,' but he is said to have added: 'If I had the intention, do you think I should tell you?'[1] Count Karolyi, however, a shrewd diplomatist, read between the lines, and in his despatch reporting the conversation informed his government that he considered war inevitable. From that moment Austria began, slowly indeed and hesitatingly, to arm.

Prussia had been arming for five years. By the efforts of the King and his ministers, in direct opposition to the votes of the national parliament, she had organised an army which could be made in three weeks superior to any force that Austria could put into the field at the end of two months. Yet, when Bismarck heard of the slow and hesitating movements of Austria in the way of arming, he did not hesitate to accuse her of endeavouring to force on war. In this sense he addressed a circular to all the States of the Germanic Confederation, in which he informed them that 'he had seen with surprise that Austria was preparing for a great war'; asked them: 'what is the object of Austria

[1] *Overthrow of the Germanic Confederation by Prussia in* 1866, by Sir Alexander Mallet, Bart, K.C.B., late H.M. Envoy Extraordinary and Minister Plenipotentiary at Frankfort. Sir Alexander adds: 'Determined to provoke Austria to act in some way that should put her in the wrong, M. de Bismarck did not find it an easy task to irritate the Imperial Government beyond endurance.'

in this armament?'; told them that Prussia 'had not made the slightest counter-armament'; intimated that, 'in the face of the Austrian dispositions, we on our side,' *i.e.* Prussia, 'can no longer delay.' He concluded by asking the federated States separately whether, in the face of the threatening 'armaments of Austria, and to what extent, Prussia could count upon their good dispositions.'

These expressions, paraphrased by Sir Alexander Malet, may thus be rendered: 'Prussia has irrevocably broken with Austria. The imperial government takes a menacing attitude. Prussia rather courts the issue, and is ready to fight. Prussia expects that all Germany will side with her against Austria. The confederation is antiquated, and must be remodelled. Prussia must have the control of the armed force of Germany.'

This circular bears date March 24th. A fortnight later the treaty with Italy, the terms of which had then been almost arranged, was signed. The Prussian army could be made ready in a fortnight. The circular was a bid for the support of those parts of Germany not subject to the Austrian Emperor. Whether their replies should be favourable or the reverse, Prussia would make her spring. Before I describe how she made it I must ask the reader to accompany me to Vienna, to examine briefly the action of the Austrian statesmen; then, reviewing the combatants on both sides, and glancing at their leaders, he will be ready to consider dispassionately the conduct of the war.

CHAPTER VI.

THE FOREIGN POLICY OF AUSTRIA—PREPARATIONS FOR WAR—ACTION OF THE LESSER STATES OF GERMANY—THE COMBATANTS—THE GENERALS—MOLTKE—PRINCE FREDERIC CHARLES—THE CROWN PRINCE—HERWARTH VON BITTENFELD—BENEDEK—THE WAR BREAKS OUT.

IN the preceding chapter I have told how, just before the meeting of the French Emperor and Bismarck at Biarritz, the Italian prime minister, General La Marmora, had sent an envoy to Vienna to ascertain whether the Emperor was inclined to cede Venetia to Italy on terms very advantageous to Austria. These were a large money payment to Austria and the assumption by Italy of a proportionate part of the Austrian national debt. When we consider the terms on which Austria had first obtained Venetia in 1797, that the cession has been branded by historians as one of the most disgraceful transactions entered into by a great power, there would have been nothing humiliating to Austria if she had taken advantage of the crisis with which she was threatened to restore the abducted child to the Italian fatherland, receiving due compensation in money. During the period she had possessed Venetia she had failed to conciliate affection. The people of the lagoons hated their foreign master with a hatred which displayed itself in abstention from all social intercourse. It is at least questionable whether, putting on the one side the hatred of the people and the expense of occupation ; the fact that her retention of the city was a festering sore in the heart of every Italian ; the advantages to be derived from holding Venetia were not quite balanced by the drawbacks. Had Austria complied at that time with the suggestion of La Marmora she would have rid herself of an incumbrance, have won the applause of the neutral powers, and have baffled two intriguing plotters, Bismarck and Napoleon III.

Austria has always boasted of her politicians, but from the time of Kaunitz onwards those politicians have succeeded either in subjecting her to a considerable loss of territory or in laying up for her, as did Metternich, heavy burdens for the future. When the offer of La Marmora reached Vienna the chief minister of the Emperor was Count Mensdorf-Pouilly, successor of the Count Rechberg, who had brought about the Schleswig-Holstein imbroglio. Mensdorf was the son of a soldier, and himself a soldier. He had fought at Magenta and Solferino, and after the Italian campaign had entered the diplomatic service. He was a favourite at court, but he had had but little experience, and in the events about to be recorded he figured rather as the mouthpiece of the inner court circles than as a minister with a policy of his own. The responsibility of the Austrian policy of 1866 rests therefore with the Emperor.

The Emperor was a very honest man, but he had no chance in the game of politics with either Bismarck or the French Emperor. He rejected, then, the one plan which would have defeated those unscrupulous schemers, and haughtily replied to the suggestions of La Marmora that he would not bargain away any part of his dominions.[1]

---

[1] Sir A. Malet describes this reply as 'a fatal political error.' Mr Fyffe writes : 'Had this transaction been effected it would probably have changed the course of European history.'

Austria, Italy, and France. 105

But the sentimental feeling which had prompted this reply died away when a despatch from Paris informed Francis Joseph of the treaty signed between Prussia and Italy on the 8th of April. The Emperor resolved then at once to offer Venetia to Italy as the price of her neutrality in the war which he saw was inevitable. The offer was made by the French Emperor on behalf of Francis Joseph to Count Nigra, the Italian ambassador in Paris, and transmitted by the latter to Florence. The Italian prime minister would have gladly accepted it, for it procured for him all the results of a war without its expense, had he received it earlier. But he felt he could not with honour recede from the engagements he had entered into with Prussia, and he therefore declined it. For Austria it was another example of the fatal 'too late.'

The refusal of La Marmora was followed by a proposal made by the French Emperor. The time had arrived, in the opinion of that prince, when the treaties of 1815 might be absolutely set aside. He suggested therefore to Bismarck, towards the latter days of May, that France should join Prussia with an army of 300,000 men, if the latter power would transfer to her the Rhenish provinces. He repeated offers of this nature in various forms during the weeks which immediately followed. The proposal savoured strongly of pure brigandage, for France had no quarrel with Austria. It indicated, also, poor statesmanship, for there were many other ways—the breaking of the Italian treaty, for instance—in which Napoleon could have made his co-operation necessary and rendered his reward secure. Bismarck, recognising the need to humour his neighbour, to maintain him in an expectant mood, did not absolutely reject any of his proposals. But he gave him no decisive answer.[1] Meanwhile the English government had made overtures to France and Russia, and on the 28th of May these powers proposed a congress of all the powers, at which to settle every point in dispute, and to reform the federal constitution of Germany. Of the three powers to whom invitations were sent, two, Italy and Prussia, accepted unconditionally, the third, Austria, conditionally. She stipulated that no arrangement should be discussed which should give increase of territory or power to any one of the States invited. This condition was naturally interpreted as a refusal. Probably the Austrian government saw that, with Russia, Italy, France, and Prussia arrayed against her in the congress, she would have no choice but to lay down her arms before she had fought. The course she actually pursued strengthens this view. Simultaneously with her answer to the neutral powers she called upon the Diet to take the affairs of Schleswig-Holstein into its own hands, and convoked the Holstein estates. Bismarck, recognising in this act a movement which he could use to render war certain, declared the treaty of Gastein to be at an end, and ordered Prussian troops to enter Holstein. The Austrian general, Von Gablentz, protesting that he yielded only to superior force, immediately marched the brigade he commanded to Altona, thence by a masterly manœuvre, in the face of superior forces, into Hanover. Furious at the breach of treaty committed by Prussia, Austria demanded and obtained from the Diet, by nine votes against six, the

[1] 'Bismarck procrastinated; he spoke of the obstinacy of the King his master; he inquired whether parts of Belgium or Switzerland would not better assimilate with France than a German province; he put off the Emperor's representatives by the assurance that he could more conveniently arrange these matters with the Emperor when he should himself visit Paris.' Fyffe, Vol. III. pages 368-9.

order for the mobilisation of the federal armies. The Prussian representative at Frankfort, declaring that this act dissolved the federal union, handed in the Prussian plan for the reorganisation of Germany,[1] and quitted Frankfort (June 14). The day following Bismarck demanded of the sovereigns of Hanover, Saxony, and Hesse-Cassel that they should put a stop to their military preparations and accept the Prussian scheme. On their refusal he directed Prussian troops to invade their territories. The war then began. Nearly the whole of Germany, disgusted with the high-handed action of Bismarck, sided with Austria. With the solitary exception of having weakly yielded to Prussia on the question of the duchies, she had respected the federal rights of her neighbours, whilst Prussia, led by Bismarck, had displayed a constantly increasing desire to trample upon all rights which might set a bar to his ambition.[2]

The battle to be fought for supremacy was then to be waged by Prussia, in Germany, against the undivided force and opinion of the Fatherland, for in all Germany Prussia could count only on the support of Mecklenburg, Weimar, and some pretty States in the north. Had she entered into the war without an external ally it is just possible that, despite the needle-gun, the result might have been adverse to her. She was about to fight, she well knew,

---

[1] This plan contained ten articles, the most salient of which were the convocation of a national representative body to sit periodically, and the exclusion of Austria from the Confederation. Malet, page 188.

[2] Amongst the propositions made by Prussia to Austria on the eve of the war was one transmitted by the King himself, proposing the cession to Prussia of Holstein for a pecuniary indemnity, and a division of Germany into North and South, separated by the river Main, under the respective presidial direction of the two great powers. Austria summarily rejected it on the ground that 'she declined to violate the federal law of Germany.' *Vide* Malet, page 185.

for supremacy in Germany or for degradation. The former, indeed, would be the consequence of her victory. But in war nothing is certain; and defeat, in her case, would have meant the cession of Silesia to Austria; of the parts of Saxony she had filched in 1815 to that power; and probably of the Elbe duchies to Hanover. She had done her best to prevent the possibility of so great a misfortune by obtaining the alliance of Italy. This alliance diminished by at least a third the military resources of her rival, for it forced Austria to maintain in Italy a large army capable of making head against the undivided force which that power could bring against her.

One word as to the sentiments of the several populations respecting the coming war. In Prussia it was unpopular with all classes, except with the upper classes and the immediate surroundings of the King. William himself had been persuaded by subtle reasoning on perverted facts to believe in its necessity. The result of his own efforts for peace had confirmed this reasoning. Had he not offered to Austria control of Germany beyond the Main, and had she not refused it? Why should she refuse the south unless she desired the north as well? But the parliament, the people, the very soldiers sprung from the people, hated the thought of fighting with their brethren to uphold the policy of Bismarck. No one in Prussia at this period, except the King and the court, believed in Bismarck. The people not only mistrusted him: they hated him He was regarded as a flighty politician, full of vain ambition, with neither foresight nor prudence. Before a hostile shot had been fired the bulk of the army shared these sentiments, though when in the presence of the enemy they behaved magnificently. They went unwillingly to the war. Something more than persuasion was often required to make them march beyond the borders.[1]

In the other parts of Germany the war was popular. The federal States had been so bullied, trodden upon, and insulted by Prussia that even war was preferable to the continuance of subjection to her insults. Few in Germany had a doubt but that the war would result in Prussia's overthrow. Their wishes dictated their opinions. They had not watched the five years' reorganising of the Prussian army, they knew but little of the needle-gun, they had been told that the Austrian troops had made a better impression on the Danes than had those of Prussia, they had never heard of Von Moltke, Benedek was a household word. As to the co-operation of Italy, they gave it but scant consideration.

Nor had they paid sufficient attention to the fact that there was one great drawback in the composition of the Austrian army. Austria had not effected that reconciliation with Hungary which was subsequently found to be essential to the well-being of the two countries. The Hungarian leaders, tired of struggling against the principle of autonomy, saw no chance of salvation from the victory of Austria. Hence the Hungarian soldiers were less well affected to the cause than were the other troops of her empire. If Austria had had more time to prepare, or if her military administration had been conducted on the lines of common sense

[1] A relative of my own who happened to be at Cologne at the time related to me an incident he had witnessed at that city. The men of a Landwehr regiment ordered to the front had declined to move unless their wives should go with them. When threats and persuasions were found useless the authorities gave way, on the condition that the wives should be stowed in separate carriages. This was done. The soldiers took their places in the front part of the train, the wives in the rear compartments. Just one second before the whistle sounded the couplings of the rear compartments were unloosed and the soldiers went on alone.

Sympathy of Germany with Austria.

this evil might have been greatly lessened by the transferring of more Hungarian regiments to the army of Italy. But it would seem that no effort was made in this direction.[1]

The feeling of Germany regarding the combatants was well illustrated when the troops of the two nations which formed the garrison of Frankfort quitted that city.

When the Austrian regiment marched out, the entire population poured into the streets, and accompanied the men to the railway station. 'Flowers were showered on them by fair hands from the windows, cigars and refreshments of all kinds thrust into the railway carriages, the notabilities of society and of commerce joined wishes of speedy and happy return with their farewell benisons.'[2] When the Prussians quitted the town there was not a voice to cry, 'God bless them'; no sympathising crowd accompanied them. 'Egypt was glad at their departure.'

[1] On the contrary, I am personally cognisant of an instance in which the Vienna war office lost the services of a very valuable officer because it persisted in taking a step prompted by a very opposite spirit. A Prussian friend of mine had entered the Austrian cavalry, had served with distinction during the many disturbances which took place in Hungary in the years 1860-64, and had become a captain. His regiment had received orders for Italy, when, on the eve of the war, he was transferred from it to a cavalry regiment told off to take part in the war against Prussia. He hurried to the war office, explained that he was a Prussian born, and could not fight against his own countrymen, although ready and willing to fight against the Italians, and begged to be re-transferred to a regiment serving in Italy. But the war minister was inexorable; he seemed to take a petty delight in wounding this officer's feelings because he was a Prussian, and rudely refused his request. The officer, who, I believe, is still living, resigned his commission rather than fight against his own countrymen.

[2] Malet, page 204. The author adds that the sympathy for the Austrians was the more significant inasmuch as the regiment was a Bohemian regiment, scarcely a man in which spoke German. The sympathy was emphatically for Austria.

The Prussian Army.

One word regarding the Prussian army. The reorganisation designed by Von Roon and approved by the King had been persistently carried on despite the equally persistent opposition of the parliament. In vain had the King, when the parliament of 1865 opened in January, expressed the hope that in the presence of the threatening aspect of affairs the differences between the two great powers would be smoothed. The Lower House rejected the reorganisation bill and the war budget, refused to pass the bill for the expenses of the war with Denmark, and declared the spending of money not voted by parliament to be unconstitutional. It persisted in the same spirit when it was reopened in January 1866. The King dismissed it after a sitting of only eight days, and continued to levy taxes as he had levied them in the preceding years. He had in the treasury the savings of preceding years, amounting to 20,000,000 thalers. The sale of the State railway from Cologne to Minden brought him a considerable sum, whilst he enforced the budget sanctioned by the Upper House and himself notwithstanding that the Lower House had rejected it. Independent thus of his parliament, independent likewise of the wishes of his people, who poured in petitions[1] begging for the continuance of peace, he pursued the policy dictated by Bismarck, determined to solve, by blood and iron, the question of Prussia's position in Germany. Meanwhile Von Roon had succeeded in bringing the army to a very high state of efficiency. It numbered 326,600 men, well drilled, well fed, the infantry armed with the new weapon of precision, the cavalry well mounted, the artillery admir-

---

[1] It is significant that whilst the petitions from every other part of the King's dominions pleaded strongly for peace, the city of Breslau, capital of the province which Frederic II. had filched from Austria, adhered resolutely to the policy of Bismarck.

ably appointed. The order to mobilise was given at intervals between the 3d and 12th of May. In fourteen days from the latter date the entire army awaited only the order to advance.

It remains now to introduce to the reader the distinguished man, the last mentioned of the triad to whom Prussia owes the position she now occupies in the world. If Von Roon organised victory, if Bismarck by his aggressive policy brought the question of Prussia's future to the point when blood and iron alone could solve it, it was Hellmuth Karl Bernhard von Moltke who when the moment of action arrived laid down with an accuracy not to be surpassed the decisive points which were to be struck. Von Moltke was a strategist of the highest order. Born on the 26th of October 1800 at Parchim, in Mecklenburg-Schwerin, he was educated for the most part at Copenhagen, and entered the infantry of the Prussian army as second lieutenant on the 12th of March 1822. From October 1823 to the same month in 1826 he attended the classes at the public military school (Allgemeine Kriegsschule) in Berlin, and gained there more than ordinary distinction. From 1828 to 1831 he was engaged in land surveying. On the 30th of March 1832 he was appointed to the general staff; was promoted to first lieutenant in it in 1833, and to captain in 1835. The same year he undertook a journey to Constantinople, and was requested by the Seraskier, Muhammad Chosref Pacha, to remain there some time in the interests of Turkey. Maintaining a perfectly independent position, he took a very leading part in the reorganisation of the Turkish army, accompanied Sultan Mahmud II. in a journey through Bulgaria, and carried out the mandates he received for the fortifying of Rustchuk, Silistria, Varna, Schumla, and a little later of the Dardanelles. About

His Earlier Career. 113

this time the Turkish government obtained from Berlin the prolongation of Moltke's leave for three years, and the sending to him thence of three officers to aid in the task he had undertaken. In 1838 Moltke proceeded to the army in Asia Minor, and utilised the assistance sent to him in making military roads. He took part also in the campaign against the Kurds, and against the Egyptians in Syria. On the death of Sultan Mahmud (1st of July 1839) Moltke returned to Prussia, was nominated to the general staff of the 4th army corps (April 1840), was promoted to be major in 1842, became permanently a member of the general staff in October 1845, and accompanied Prince Henry of Prussia to Rome in the quality of adjutant the same year. During his stay in Rome Moltke made a topographical survey of the country surrounding the city. On the death of Prince Henry he returned home, and was sent to the general staff of the 8th army corps (December 1846). In May 1848 he was nominated divisional chief in the principal general staff; on the 22d of August of the same year chief of the general staff of the 4th army corps. Whilst holding this position he was promoted, September 26, 1850, to be lieutenant-colonel, in December 1851 to be colonel. On the 1st of September 1855 he was appointed first adjutant to the Crown Prince (afterwards the Emperor Frederic) with the rank of major-general. He accompanied this prince in his journeys to London, Petersburg, Moscow, and Paris. Returning, he was nominated to act, October 29, 1857, as chief of the general staff of the army, and in September of the year following was confirmed in that post. In May 1859 he became lieutenant-general.

In the Danish war of 1864 Moltke took part as chief of the general staff under the command-in-chief of Prince

Frederic Charles. On the conclusion of the war he reassumed his post as chief of the general staff of the army. Early in the spring of 1866 he took part in the consultations held at Berlin as to the possibilities of success in a war against Austria. To the council of superior officers presided over by the King he submitted plans of operations which he contended must lead to success if carried out with energy and vigour. On the 8th of June he was nominated general of infantry, and attached to the headquarters of the King as the real director of the movements of the army.

Such, told baldly, was the previous career of the man who was to astonish Europe by his strategic insight—to inspire a confidence such as soldiers can feel only in men of combined genius and action—such as inspired the soldiers of Hannibal, of Alexander, of Cæsar, of Cromwell, of Turenne, of Clive, of Eugene, of Marlborough, of Villars, of Frederic, of Loudon, above all, of Napoleon. I do not assert that history will place Moltke on the level of the greatest of these, for it was his fortune never to meet an opponent who soared above mediocrity. But as a strategist, as a master of the art of war, as a general whose combinations were bold yet prudent, who could detect the weak point of his enemy, who could inspire officers and men with the most absolute confidence in his leading, he may claim admittance to the Walhalla in which rest the shades of the world's most famous warriors. He was a very modest man, kept himself always in the background, was jealous for the acknowledgment of the merits of others rather than of his own. His superiority therefore excited no feeling of envy or of hostility. He was singularly devoid of ambition. In common with the first Duke of Wellington, he claimed duty as his polar star.

A few words, and only a few, must be said of the

Prince Frederic Charles.

generals commanding the Prussian army corps when the war broke out. They were three: Prince Frederic Charles, the Crown Prince of Prussia, General Herwarth von Bittenfeld.

Prince Frederic Charles, only son of Prince Charles, younger brother of the actual King of Prussia, was born at Berlin on the 20th of March 1828, and from his days of boyhood was trained for the army. Whilst yet in his teens he was placed under the care of Major von Roon, later minister of war, who accompanied him to the University of Bonn (1846-8). The Prince took part in the Danish war of 1848, having the rank of captain, and thus early displayed the qualities of an excellent cavalry officer. He served on the staff of his uncle in 1849, when the latter was engaged in suppressing the insurrectionists of Baden, distinguished himself at the combat of Wiesenthal (June 20), in which he was twice severely wounded. On his recovery he devoted himself to military studies. A soldier from the bottom of his heart, he read and re-read the histories of the campaigns of Frederic II. and of Napoleon. He became a perfect soldier in theory, and wrote in 1860, for private circulation, a pamphlet in which he severely criticised the tactics displayed by the French Emperor in the Italian war of 1859, and compared, advantageously to the former, the German and French armies. Made general of cavalry in 1861, he commanded the right wing of the Prussian army corps which invaded the duchies in 1864. In this war he displayed many of the qualities of a commander, being quick in his decisions, rapid in his movements, and thorough in his plans. On the conclusion of peace he returned to his studies. He had gained a considerable reputation in Prussia, and was regarded by many officers as the coming man. His popularity with his men was great.

The Crown Prince.

The second commander mentioned, Frederic, Crown Prince of Prussia, the only son of the reigning king, was three years younger than his cousin, having been born the 18th of October 1831. This prince had received a military education, but, as heir to the throne, greater care had been taken to fit him for the duties which would devolve upon him as chief of the State. He possessed a noble character, being frank, open, resolute, just in his views, and courteous in his manners. No one knew better than he how to disarm opposition or to conciliate public opinion. He had had but little experience in the field, having served only, and not prominently, in the Danish war of 1864. To place him at the head of an important army, with a distinct mission of its own, was therefore an experiment. It will be seen, however, that at the most important crisis of the campaign, the results of which depended upon his action, he displayed a capacity and judgment which more than justified his selection.

The third officer, Herwarth von Bittenfeld, who was an older man than his comrades, having been born in 1796, had entered the army in 1811, and taken part in the campaigns of 1813-14. After the peace of 1815 he remained for twenty years with his regiment, serving five years as adjutant, and becoming captain in 1821. He became major in 1839, colonel in 1848, and in that rank was placed in command of an infantry brigade. Soon after the 'surrender of Olmütz' he commanded the Prussian troops at Frankfort, became a major-general in March 1852, commander of the 7th division in August 1856, and was promoted to lieutenant-general two months later. He held various important commands till the Danish war broke out in 1864. He then received command of the 1st mobilised army corps, and at the head of this gained a great reputation by the manner in which he captured the island of Alsen. But it was his reputation as an unsurpassed handler of masses, his character as a daring, cool, capable leader which procured for him in the seventieth year of his age the position of leader of one of the three aggressive armies of Prussia.

Of the army put into the field by Austria and her allies I shall write more at length when the time shall arrive to recount their exploits. But it is necessary to say a few words here of the commander of that army in Germany—Ludwig von Benedek.

Benedek was a Hungarian, having been born at Oedenburg in July 1804. He was, however, educated in the military academy at Wiener-Neustadt, issuing from it in 1822 with a lieutenant's commission. He became major in 1840, lieutenant-colonel in 1843, colonel in 1846. In that rank he served in the suppression of the insurrection in Galicia, and gave numerous proofs of courage and conduct. He fought in the Italian war of 1848-9, and was promoted to major-general in the Hungarian war of 1849, receiving therein many wounds. After the submission of Hungary Benedek was appointed chief of the general staff to Marshal Radetzky, became field-marshal-lieutenant in 1853, and during the Crimean war was placed in command of the army of observation located in Galicia. In the Franco-Italian war of 1859 he took an active part. At Solferino he commanded the right wing of the Austrian army, the only part of that army which was not beaten, for he completely repulsed the Italian attack. Promoted in November 1859 to be Feldzeugmeister (Inspector-General of Ordnance), he became, two months later, quartermaster-general of the whole army, and in the April following was nominated to be civil and military governor of Hungary. From this post he was moved in October to take the command-in-chief of the Austrian army in Italy, and of its reserves in the Alpine country north of Verona. Beloved by the troops, and regarded as the most capable general in the army, he was moved thence when, in May 1866, war with Prussia was seen to be imminent, to take command of the Austrian forces in Germany, the Archduke Albert relieving him in Italy. Regarding his talents as a commander, no opinion could be formed by those qualified to form one. He had certainly gained the confidence of his men, but he had never commanded in chief. Victory in war is to the general who makes the fewest mistakes. The reader will see that in the operations of the hostile armies neither general-in-chief was free from the commission of error; but the error of Benedek was far greater than the error of Moltke, and, committed at a critical period, was fatal.

Having presented to the reader the leading generals on both sides, I propose to take them to the battlefields on which were to be decided the claims for supremacy in Germany of Austria and Prussia.

CHAPTER VII.

THE WAR OF 1866—HANOVER AND ELECTORAL HESSE
—LANGENSALZA AND WILHELMSHÖHE.

ON the 13th and 15th of June the Prussian government notified to the several generals commanding corps and divisions to be ready to push forward at the first intimation sent by wire. On the 15th the same government declared war against Hanover, electoral Hesse, and Saxony; on the 18th[1] against the other members of the alliance. At the first of these dates the Prussian army was thus disposed. The first army, commanded by Prince Frederic Charles, consisting of the 2d, 3d, and 4th army corps, and numbering 93,000 men, occupied the Saxon frontier as far as Görlitz. The second, led by the Crown Prince, composed of the 1st, 5th, and 6th corps, and the Guards, numbering in all 115,000 men, was concentrated at Neisse in Silesia. The third army, called the army of the Elbe, commanded by Herwarth von Bittenfeld, composed of one division of the 7th corps and of the 8th corps, numbering 46,000 men, and having a Landwehr reserve of 24,300, which, however, was not engaged, stood on the left bank of the Elbe facing Saxony. The three armies, counting the reserve, numbered 278,000 men. But they constituted only a

[1] Austria was comprehended in this declaration; but the actual date on which the document declaring war was handed in at the Austrian advanced posts was the 21st.

part of the Prussian forces available for immediate action. At Minden was the 13th division, 14,300 strong, under General von Falkenstein; at Hamburg the corps of Manteuffel, 14,100 strong; at Wetzlar, ready to dash into electoral Hesse, Beyer's division, 19,600 strong.[1] Altogether the Prussian troops, ready for immediate action, counted 326,600 men.

If the forces of the enemy somewhat exceeded these in number they were neither so ready for immediate action, so united, so well armed, nor so dominated by one imperious will. It was the misfortune of Austria that she was compelled to divide her forces; that whilst maintaining one army, called the army of the north, under Benedek, in Germany, she was compelled, by the hostile action of Italy, to keep a second army, called the army of the south, in or about the Italian quadrilateral. To that army, under Archduke Albert, I shall refer later on. The northern army was composed of seven corps, the 1st, 2d, 3d, 4th, 6th, 8th, and 10th, each consisting of four brigades; of an artillery reserve of six batteries, of two light and three heavy reserve cavalry divisions. Its total strength was 247,000 men; but that strength was raised to 271,000 by the co-operation with it of a corps of Saxon troops, 24,000 strong. Besides these, the garrisons of Cracow, of Olmütz, of Theresienstadt, of Josephstadt, and of Königgrätz,[2] absorbed 54,000 men. Austria, moreover, had contributed 7000 men to the Bund army.

The Bund army was formed of 52,000 troops contributed by Bavaria; of 16,250 by Würtemberg; of 10,850 by Baden; of 9400 by Hesse (Hesse-Darmstadt); of

---

[1] These three corps were afterwards united to form the army of the Main.

[2] It is scarcely necessary to state that Olmütz is in Moravia; the three places last named in Bohemia.

The Position of Hanover.

5400 by Nassau; of 18,400 by Hanover; of 7000 by electoral Hesse (Hesse-Cassel). But these corps were neither ready nor united when Prussia declared war.

Although Prussia despatched her cartel to Austria only on the 21st of June she had, as I have said, notified to her generals on the 15th, the very moment she had understood that neither Saxony,[1] Hanover, nor electoral Hesse would make common cause with her, to move on those States at a moment's notice. It was a repetition of the policy of Frederic II. in 1756, viz., to dash upon an assured enemy before his resources should be complete.

Hanover, long coveted by Prussia, was one of the first to feel the blow. It would have been impossible for Hanover to arm at any time previously without provoking an attack from her more powerful neighbour. Her troops, therefore, were utterly unprepared for war. They were about to assemble for their peaceful summer manœuvres. But learning on the 15th the hostile dispositions of Prussia, and that orders to the Prussian army to march had been given, the King of Hanover summoned his whole army to assemble at Göttingen with the utmost haste. His soldiers obeyed his instructions with alacrity, and on the 18th the whole army, with the exception of three companies of artillery left at Stade, and some small detachments, joined the King and the Crown Prince at the given rendezvous.

Nothing was ready for them. The force was deficient in camp equipage, in means of transport, and in ammunition. It counted 15,000 infantry, 2000 of whom were recruits of only two months; 2200 cavalry, and forty-two [2]

[1] Hanover was not given a chance of neutrality. She was told she must join forces against Austria or accept war. Malet, page 211 and note.
[2] *Vide* Malet's *Overthrow of the Germanic Confederation in* 1866, pages 210-12.

field-pieces. The ammunition train consisted of forty waggons, and there was a reserve of ten guns. The King, his generals, and his subjects generally, worked incessantly to make good the deficiencies, but time was short, the means of the country were inadequate, and when the enemy approached, the Hanoverians were but ill-supplied with the means of moving. The feeling, however, of the troops was excellent. Recognising that they were about to be sacrificed to the long pent-up greed of their neighbour, they threw all their energies into the cause which was at once their King's and their own.

Whilst they were thus working the enemy were carrying all before them. On the 13th the Prussian general to whom had been committed the task of occupying Hanover, General Vogel von Falkenstein, a veteran in his sixty-ninth year, commanding the 13th division, received orders to hold himself in readiness to move at a moment's notice by wire. Crossing the Elbe on the 15th, he sent Manteuffel to seize Harburg that night; thence pushing forward detachments, he occupied on the 16th, Lüneburg and Brunshausen. On the 17th Manteuffel forced the fortress of Stade to surrender. Whilst Emden and the strand batteries on the Ems and the west were attacked by and surrendered to the Prussian maritime force during the four days, from the 19th to the 22d, another division of the Minden army, led by Von Goeben, himself a Hanoverian, marched straight on the town of Hanover, and entered it the evening of the 17th. A portion of Manteuffel's division joined him there the night of the 19th, whilst the other brigade entered Celle on the 20th.

It was on that day that the Hanoverian army at Göttingen had been brought into a condition in which it might attempt to move. Many were the consultations held as to the direction it should take. As always

Retreat of the Hanoverians. 123

happens under such circumstances, the diversity of opinion was great. The most obvious course seemed to march in the direction by which an early junction could be effected with the Bavarian corps then gathering in the Main. But it was not until the evening of the 20th that the decision was arrived at to march on Eisenach in Saxe-Weimar, thence to traverse Thuringia to a point where a union with the Bavarian force under Prince Charles would be easy.

The King had entrusted the command of his little force to General von Arentschildt. It consisted of four brigades: those of Knesebeck, De Vaux, Bülow, and Bothmer, besides reserves, altogether about 18,000 men. It set out on the morning of the 21st. On the evening of that day the advanced guard (Bülow's brigade) was at Helmsdorf, the rearguard at Geismar. It seemed possible that by pushing earnestly forward the little force might carry out the intentions of its leaders, for between it and its destination there was but one Prussian brigade, that of Fliess, about 9000 strong, posted at Gotha. The next day, the 22d, the advanced guard reached Heroldshausen; but reports coming in that the Prussians were in force in the vicinity, Arentschlidt decided to change slightly the plan of advance, and to move the next day on Langensalza instead of on Eisenach. Accordingly on the 23d the headquarters of the army were established at Langensalza, the advanced posts being pushed on to Heningsleben and Merxleben, the rear posts at Mulhäusen. No Prussians had been seen, and had the force made a serious effort the following day to push across Thuringia it is almost certain it would have succeeded, for its numbers were to the enemy fronting it at Gotha in the proportion of two to one. It was their one chance, but Prussian cunning induced them to neglect it.

For whilst the Hanoverians were marching to Langensalza the Prussians were gathering on the path and round them. General Goeben had reached Göttingen on the 22d; Manteuffel's division was but one march behind him; Von Falkenstein entered the same town on the 23d. Here, however, the Prussian commanders were all at fault. Whilst Wrangel's brigade made a vain reconnaissance in the direction of Heiligenstadt, General Beyer had been detached with his force to guard the passage of the Werra, where no enemy attempted to pass. Two battalions of the Guards had been hurriedly sent from Berlin to occupy Eisenach, from which place the Prussian Landwehr, alarmed by the reports of the Hanoverian advance, had fallen back on Gotha—but they arrived there only on the night of the 23d. I have already stated that there were 9000 Prussians at Gotha. In war nothing is absolutely certain; but, mathematically, it is more than probable that if the 18,000 men at Langensalza on the 23d had pushed on, either by Eisenach or by Gotha, on the 24th they would have escaped the Prussian toils.

But they did not push on. The Prussians had ascertained the position of their enemies, and dreading lest they should escape, they employed the stale but telling device of propositions for terms to detain them. Deceived by the false statement that the passes in front of them were strongly guarded, and by the idea, stated with an air of conviction, that by negotiations they could obtain terms which would preserve to Hanover its army, the King and his general counter-ordered the directions to advance on Eisenach. Then followed the result which those who knew Prussia and her chief minister might have expected. Conditions were offered from Berlin which could not be accepted. The march on Eisenach was delayed till the afternoon. By that time the garrison there had been effectually reinforced; and when the Hanoverian army appeared before the place in the evening they found it strongly occupied. They therefore halted where they were, between Langensalza and Eisenach, the headquarters at Gross-Behringen. For reasons not to be satisfactorily explained they halted there the next day, the King being still deceived by negotiations intended only to make his surrender certain.

The Prussians employed their time far more practically To make the doom of their foes certain they marched to positions encircling them with all their immediately available forces. On the evening of the 25th the position of the Prussian army was as follows: Fliess was at Gotha with his 9000 men; Von Goeben at Eisenach with the same number; Von Glumer was at Kreuzburg and Treffurt with 6000; Wrangel was at Cassel with 12,000. Manteuffel's division occupied the country about Göttingen and Minden. The headquarters were at Eisenach, at which place Von Falkenstein arrived on the 25th to take supreme command.

It was on the evening of the same day only that the King of Hanover and his general came to the conviction that they had been entrapped. Nothing remained then but to fight. Accordingly Arentschildt concentrated his force between Gross and Oster-Behringen, with Knesebeck's brigade at Henningsleben to protect a retrograde movement on Langensalza in case of a repulse. It is necessary to call particular attention to the disposition of Knesebeck's brigade, for it shows that the Hanoverian leaders had not yet arrived at the true bearings of the situation. No retreat would save them. The one course open to them was to mass their forces and endeavour to cut their way through the foe in front of them. Defensive operations could only mean ultimate ruin.

This should have been made clear to them by the fact that the Prussians, after much vapouring, made no attack that day. They were waiting for the further reinforcements which were approaching. During this the King prepared for the battle of the morrow, hoping that the messengers he had despatched to Prince Charles of Bavaria and Prince Alexander of Hesse on the 19th and 21st, to explain his situation and to ask assistance, might bring him aid.[1]

The rumour of a Bavarian advance had reached the Prussian camp, and it disposed the general commanding to make his attack at once. The Hanoverians, meanwhile, had taken a position on the left bank of the river Unstrutt, their forces being disposed in the following manner: Bülow's brigade, with the reserve artillery, on the right; De Vaux's brigade in the centre at Merxleben, connected with Bülow by the village of Thamsbrück, occupied by a detachment, and with the left by Henningsleben, occupied by the Cambridge dragoons. Bothmer's brigade held the left towards Nagelstädt, with one battalion at the bridge over the Unstrutt, and one squadron and a half guarding the flank towards Tennstedt and Bruckstedt. Knesebeck's brigade formed the reserve. The headquarters were at Merxleben, the King was at Thamsbrück. The Unstrutt covered the whole front of the position. It had steep banks, was not easily fordable, and was impassable for cavalry save by bridges. The difficulty of approach was greatly increased by the fact that the road to the south-west, beyond the

---

[1] In point of fact they brought none. Neither prince was ready for offensive operations. The Bavarian prince, however, tendered his advice that the Hanoverians should cut their way through.

Battle of Langensalza. 127

river, ran for about eighty yards between a bank from ten to fourteen feet high and the Salza brook. The key of the position was Merxleben and the eminence of Kirchberg, immediately to the south of it.[1]

In obedience to orders he had received, General Fliess marched, at half-past seven on the morning of the 27th, with his force of nearly 9000 men, from Warza upon Langensalza. His advanced guard reached the entrance of that town at eleven, and drove before it the small Hanoverian party which had occupied it. The latter, however, encountered in its retreat the brigade of Knesebeck which had been despatched to its support. Knesebeck at once occupied a strongly defensive position, and held the Prussians at bay until, at half-past eleven, all the Hanoverians who had been posted on the right bank of the Unstrutt had traversed the defile leading to Merxleben. The Prussians then seized a position on a hill known as the Judenhügel, but the Hanoverian guns on the more commanding position of the Kirchberg opened on them, and inflicted so much loss that they maintained themselves only by being reinforced.

By this time the entire force of Fliess had come up. That general then made a resolute attack on the Hanoverian centre at Merxleben. The attack was repulsed, whereupon Bothmer on the left and Bülow on the right crossed the Unstrutt to attack the Prussian flanks, De Vaux's brigade supporting the attack, whilst the reserves were brought up nearer to the centre. Owing mainly to the great difficulties of the ground, Bothmer's attack failed, but Bülow, who crossed the

---

[1] For the graphic description of the position, and for many interesting details connected with story of the Langensalza episode, so advantageous to Prussia and so damaging to her enemies, I am indebted to Sir Alexander Malet's book, already repeatedly quoted.

river about one o'clock, drove back the Prussians and took a position between Unstrutt and the Salza. There he was joined half an hour later by the first and second battalions of the Guard. He then advanced, stormed a strong position known as Kallenberg's mill, and pushing on, drove the Prussians from the Judenhügel. Other positions were stormed, and about two o'clock the Prussians were driven out of Langensalza.

But though Fliess's attack had failed he had accomplished one main purpose of his mission. He had secured the detention of the Hanoverians for another day. Strong reinforcements, he knew, were marching up, and could the enemy be induced to stay where they were till the following morning it would be impossible for them to escape the 40,000 men who would then surround them. Not desirous, however, to expose his own troops to further loss, Fliess began a retreat about half-past three, leaving to the Hanoverians all the honours of the day. The latter pursued the Prussians for about an hour. Their own loss in killed and wounded was greater than that of the Prussians, but they took 907 prisoners, of whom ten were officers. The course of events not only released these the next day, but restored also the two guns and 2000 stand of small-arms which the Hanoverians had captured.

It was about half-past four when the pursuit ceased. The question then arose as to what course should be pursued; whether to remain on the ground or to endeavour to march all night into Thuringia. A Prussian writer, generally very accurate,[1] has thus summed up the situation: 'Although the Hanoverians had undoubtedly won a victory which had at last made it possible for them to escape to the south and effect a junction with the

[1] Brockhaus's *Conversations-Lexikon*, 12th edition, Vol. IX. page 525.

Bavarians, they did not profit by it.' Whether they could have escaped may be doubtful. According to the testimony of the superior officers the men were exhausted, the dead remained unburied, they possessed ammunition only for one more serious combat, the supply of food in sufficient quantities was impossible, the Prussians were closing in from several directions, the further expenditure of blood could lead, in their opinion, to no good result. For these reasons the King and his officers resolved to remain where they were, and to treat the day following for a capitulation. The terms were drawn up on the 28th by the Prussian chief commander at Eisenach, General von Falkenstein, and after having been submitted to and revised by the King of Prussia, were agreed to by the Hanoverian commander-in-chief. They were to the following purport: (1) that the King of Hanover, the Crown Prince, and such entourage as they might select, should fix their residence wherever they pleased except in Hanover; (2) that the officers and civilians of the Hanoverian army should engage not to serve against Prussia; that they should keep their arms and receive their pay, and stand in the same relations towards the Prussian administration of Hanover as they had done towards the independent government of that kingdom; (3) that the rank and file should give up their arms and return to their homes, engaging not to serve against Prussia; (4) that arms, horses, and war materials should be handed over to Prussia.

There was no mistaking these conditions. The order had gone forth that the House of Guelph should cease to reign in Germany. Surely it would have been better had the representative of that ancient House and his army attempted a retreat across Thuringia, even at the risk of encountering superior numbers and being slaughtered to a man. Better that than to await in camp the tender mercies of a Bismarck-inspired King. It was a case of Might against Right. The King of Hanover had been told that he must either espouse a cause against which his conscience and the conscience of his people revolted, or be attacked. He was in the position of a private man who is told that he must either join in a robbery or be himself despoiled. The King of Hanover chose the right, and suffered accordingly.

I have dwelt at some length on the actions which led to the surrender of Hanover because it was one of the most important events of the war. It was the first great blow in that war, and it tended enormously to the advantage of Prussia. War with Austria had only been formally declared on the 21st of June, and a week later Prussia had succeeded not only in neutralising one of her enemies but in securing for herself the advantages accruing from the command of the resources of a territory containing about 2300 square miles and nearly 4,000,000 inhabitants. It was a blow which struck terror into the minds of her weaker foes. And although the conquest could not be attributed to the superior valour of the Prussian soldiers— for they had been beaten in fair fight—it gave evidence that the director-in-chief of the Prussian armies thoroughly understood the time-honoured principle that the way to win a battle is to concentrate the greatest number of men on the decisive point.

Not less expeditiously did Prussia act towards electoral Hesse. General Beyer, stationed with 19,000 men at Weitzlar, broke up from that place on the 16th, and before the troops of the electorate could be organised for action occupied Cassel (June 19). The Elector, surprised, had but time to direct his troops to march on Hainau and Fulda. This they attempted to do, and most of them succeeded eventually in joining their several corps at Frankfort and Mayence. But the unfortunate Elector, who persisted in remaining at his palace at Wilmelmshöhe, was taken prisoner by the Prussians, underwent many annoyances at their hands, and was eventually transferred under arrest to Bremen by the express order of the Prussian King. The electorate, left defenceless, was annexed by Prussia.

We have thus seen how two limbs of the German Confederation were lopped off before the war was a fortnight old. It remains now to examine the action of the other members, and of Prussia towards them.

CHAPTER VIII.

THE WAR OF 1866—THE CAMPAIGN IN BOHEMIA—
COMBATS OF LIEBENAU, OF PODOL, OF MÜNCHEN-
GRÄTZ, OF GITSCHIN, OF TRAUTENAU, OF SOOR, OF
NACHOD, OF SKALITZ, OF SCHWEINSCHÄDEL.

THE Prussian leaders thoroughly understood the advantage of promptitude in war. Ready themselves, and opposed to an enemy whose preparations were not yet completed, but who occupied a large extent of territory, some of which overlapped that of Prussia, it was a matter of life and death to strike a blow which should paralyse before the several opponents could combine to utilise the natural advantages open to them. It was, for instance, quite possible—and I mention it here because the points had been considered by the Prussian generals—that had Prussia delayed her forward movements, a capable Austrian commander—and Benedek had that character—might, by uniting with a portion of the Bund army, have dashed in between East and West Prussia, thus preventing combined action between the two parts, whilst a Bavarian army, dashing into Hanover and Hesse, and picking up the troops of those allies, might make possible a march upon Berlin.

How Prussia prevented the possibility of such action by paralysing both Hanover and Hesse has been already shown.

In point of fact there was no such thing as 'dash' on the part of the allies. They had not an irresponsible general, nor were their preparations for war nearly com-

Action of the Allies.

pleted. The prompt success of the divisions of Manteuffel, Von Falkenstein, and Beyer, in Hanover and Hesse, had proved this to the hilt. There remained, then, to Prussia the obligation to pursue a similar course towards Austria, Bavaria, Saxony, and their lesser allies, with the conviction that boldness was prudence, and that to succeed as they had succeeded in Hanover they must give no respite to the enemy. How rigorously they acted on this principle I shall now show.

Before war had been declared, but when it was still imminent, the representatives of Bavaria, Saxony, Würtemberg, Baden, Hesse-Darmstadt, and Nassau had met at Munich, and had fixed the contingents which should be furnished severally by those powers. It was not, however, till the 14th of June that the Diet called those troops into activity. It was then further arranged that whilst the contingents from the four last named of the allies, and the contingents to be furnished by Austria and Saxony, should be sent to Frankfort, to be placed there under the command of Prince Alexander of Hesse, an officer who had served with distinction in the Austrian army, the command of the Bavarian forces, which were to assemble on the Upper Main, should be given to Prince Charles of Bavaria, a veteran in his seventy-first year, who had seen no service since 1815, when he was a mere boy. It was decided further that the troops assembling at Frankfort under Alexander of Hesse should be subject to the command-in-chief of Prince Charles.

By the 18th and 19th the two armies were ready for movement. It had been quite possible for its commander to detach a sufficient body of troops to save the Hanoverian army. But, in reply to the earnest request of the blind sovereign of that State, Prince Charles had sent only advice. Now that Hanover had fallen, the turn for action of the Bavarian prince had arrived, for the Prussian army of the Main, formed of the three divisions which had acted in Hanover and in Hesse-Cassel, and led by Generals von Goeben, Beyer, and Fliess, were on his track, eager to bring him to battle.

Before I notice the action of these generals and their opponents it is necessary to follow the movements of the main armies—the armies destined to operate against Austria in Bohemia—commanded respectively by Prince Frederic Charles, the Crown Prince, and General von Bittenfeld, under the supreme direction of the chief of the general staff of the army, General von Moltke

On the 19th of June the second army, commanded by the Crown Prince, and cantoned, as previously stated, about Neisse, in Silesia, received orders to leave one corps, the sixth, at Neisse, and with the remainder to press forward into Bohemia, and there effect a junction with the first army. That army, commanded by Prince Frederic Charles, was similarly directed to march by way of the upper Lausitz to Reichenberg, seven miles beyond the Bohemian frontier, and to unite with the second army at Gitschin, fifty miles to the north-east of Prague. The Elbe army (Von Bittenfeld's) was to push on from Dresden, and, barred by the Saxon occupation of Königstein from attempting the Elbe valley, to make for Gabel, fifty miles to the north-east of Prague. To secure the upper Silesian frontier two detachments, commanded respectively by General von Knobelsdorff and General Count Stolberg, were left behind.

Meanwhile the Austrian commander-in-chief, General Benedek, had been indefatigable in bringing into line the considerable forces of which the Austrian empire could dispose. Benedek was not at all inclined to play a waiting game. He had noticed the positions of the

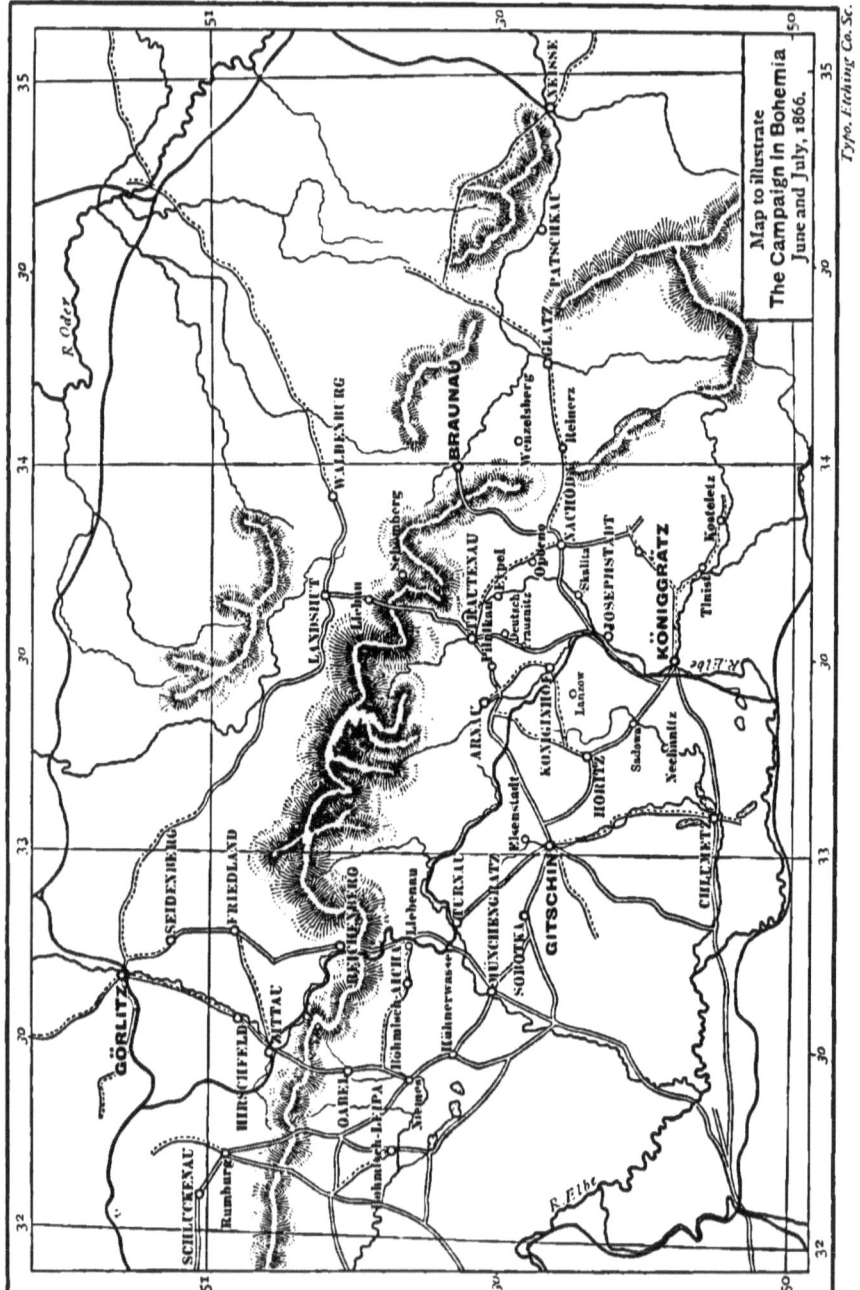

three Prussian armies, and it had occurred to him that by a speedy movement in advance he might strike a disabling blow at the second Prussian army whilst it was debouching in separate columns from the passes leading into Bohemia. With this plan in view he set out from Olmütz on the 17th June, but he had not proceeded far when information reached him that the first and third Prussian armies had entered Bohemia. He still, however, hoped. The army of the Crown Prince was separated, he ascertained, from that of Prince Frederic Charles by a distance of about 139 miles (225 kilometres), and it was yet possible, he thought, to carry out his plan. But he had been forestalled. The possibility that Benedek might attempt to overwhelm the second army whilst it was threading its way through the passes, had not escaped the penetrating eye of Moltke. To render such an attack impossible, he had arranged that the first and third armies should make three marches before the army of the Crown Prince should have started. The two former would thus be able seriously to engage the attention of the Austrians whilst the latter was making its way through the difficult passes of Bohemia, and if they could only gain an initial advantage they would compel Benedek to concentrate all his efforts against the foe immediately in front of him.

The event fully justified this wise prevision. Benedek had entrusted to the corps of Count Clam-Gallas, backed by 24,000 men of the Saxon army, led by the Crown Prince Albert of Saxony, the defence of the Silesian frontier. Clam-Gallas had his headquarters at Münchengrätz on the Iser, fifty-five miles nearly due north of Prague. He had posted one brigade at Reichenberg, the second largest provincial town in Bohemia, about thirty-two miles to the north of his own position, seventeen to the south-east from Zittau in Saxony. Between München-grätz and Reichenberg he had one detachment at Podol, a village three or four miles from Münchengrätz, where the Iser was spanned by the railway bridge; a second at Liebenau, some eleven miles to the south of Reichenberg. At Hühnerwasser, a village in the mountainous district north of the road leading to Böhmisch-Leipa, he had placed likewise a brigade to command the approaches from the direction of Dresden.

Meanwhile Prince Frederic Charles had broken up from Görlitz on the 22d, had reached Seidenberg the same evening, crossed the frontier by the passes of Schönwald and Neustädtl the morning of the 23d, and directed his march on Friedland,[1] sixteen miles due north of Reichenberg. Simultaneously General von Bittenfeld led the Elbe army along the highroad from Dresden leading from Schlückenau to Rumburg. The next morning Frederic Charles marched on Reichenberg: Bittenfeld on Gabel, twelve miles to the right of the first-named place. They both expected they might have to fight for the possession of Reichenberg, covering as it did the junction of the roads leading across the mountains by Gabel, Grottau, Friedland, and Hirschfeld. But Clam-Gallas was too prudent to encounter two armies with the much smaller force at his disposal, and he had directed the troops at Reichenberg to fall back on the approach of the enemy on Liebenau. This they did in a perfectly orderly manner. The Prussians occupied Reichenberg the same night and the following morning.

The village of Liebenau stands about midway between

---

[1] Close to the village of Friedland stands out in bold relief the castle of that name, formerly the castle of the famous Wallenstein, but now the property of the Clam-Gallas family.

Combat of Liebenau.

Reichenberg and Turnau, the latter being nine and a half miles from Münchengrätz. It was on the road leading to Turnau, immediately south of the village, that the Austrian commander had taken his position, more to test the prowess of the enemy than with the hope that with his vastly inferior force he could defeat him. For he had but four regiments of cavalry, two batteries of horse artillery, and a mere handful of infantry. With these he made an imposing show. He placed his guns on the summit of the hill which looks down from the south upon Liebenau, and kept his cavalry in hand ready to cover his movements. As the Prussians reached the ground which rises gradually to the summit of the hill the Austrian guns opened fire: those of the Prussians immediately responded, and in a few seconds a dense smoke hid the combatants from one another. It soon became clear to the Austrian commander that the two batteries at his disposal were far inferior to the enormous firing capacity of the enemy; he therefore limbered up and retired, halting occasionally to fire two or three rounds in the direction of Kositz. Vainly did the Prussian cavalry dash in pursuit. The ground was against them, and before they could come within striking distance the Austrians had reformed on the Kositz hill. Thence they opened a smart fire on the Prussian horse, and only ceased when the arrival of the enemy's guns gave the Prussians the superiority. Then they retired in excellent order on Podol. The affair had been but a skirmish, but it had satisfied both parties: the Austrians, because in the presence of vastly superior numbers they had displayed coolness and discipline; the Prussians, because they discovered that the Austrian artillery fire was not so dangerous as it should have been, many of their shells penetrating the earth without bursting, and that their practice was indifferent. The same evening the Prussians occupied Turnau, at which place the retreating Austrians had broken the bridge across the Iser. An advanced division of the army of the Elbe likewise occupied Böhmisch-Aicha on this day.

Podol, which the Austrians now held in some force, is the point below Turnau where a wooden bridge and the railway bridge cross the Iser, here about a hundred yards wide. At this place Count Clam-Gallas had placed six battalions of infantry, intending to hold the place until his entire force should have time to concentrate at München-grätz, thence eventually to fall back on Gitschin. It was his object not to fight a general action, but to delay the Prussian advance as long as possible, so as to give Benedek time to complete his preparations. In this object he only partially succeeded.

It was eight o'clock on the evening of the 26th when the advanced division of Prince Frederic Charles's army pushed on to within 1400 yards of the wooden bridge of Podol and came in contact with the Austrian outposts. The six battalions of the latter occupied the village in such a manner as to make their dislodgment a work of time and difficulty. A large farmhouse before the entrance into the village, strongly occupied, presented the first obstacle to the Prussians. From it, and from the skirmishers covering it, and who had formed across the road, a heavy fire poured upon the advancing enemy did considerable damage. Nor were the defenders unscathed. The needle-gun had enabled the Prussians to open fire from a distance beyond the range of the Austrian smooth-bores, and though the increasing twilight prevented them from taking a certain aim, their fire was nevertheless too well concentrated to fail in effect. Gradually their superiority in number made itself felt, and the Austrians, slowly falling back, took a second position behind some abattis hastily thrown up across the road leading into the village. The Prussians pressed on till within a few feet of this abattis and halted. There was scarcely three paces between the combatants, and the men on both sides fired point-blank at the breasts of their foes. Again, however, the power of firing much more rapidly, possessed by the breachloading weapons of the Prussians, made itself felt, and the Austrians again slowly retired. Yet for them there was still some consolation. The advancing Prussians were exposed to a murderous fire from the upper storeys of the loopholed houses and from the balconies. This fire, poured into the serried masses pressing through a narrow street, had a deadly effect. Every shot told. The Prussians nevertheless pushed steadily onwards. They knew that the river was behind their enemy, and that the occupants of the houses must become their prisoners as soon as they should have forced the front enemy across the bridge. But on this occasion the Austrian soldiers fought in a manner worthy of their ancient renown. Pressed back by superior numbers, armed with a superior weapon, they fell back in the darkness (for the moon had not yet risen) coolly and without panic, disputing every inch of ground. At last they were forced on to the bridge. There they turned, and, confronting their enemies, began again a resistance as stubborn as it was murderous in its effects. Before their fire the Prussian officers and men fell rapidly. When the enemy advanced too close the Austrians charged them with the bayonet. But again the weight of numbers and the superiority of the weapon told their tale. After a combat, terrible in its slaughter, the defenders were driven back, reaching the other bank of the Iser in time to join their comrades, who, after similar deeds of heroism, had been forced from the railway bridge. The two parties, uniting slowly, retreated for about a quarter of a mile, to a large house which commanded the highway. Here they made another stand, gathering in many of their men who had been cut off in the darkness. But the Prussians were not to be denied. They pressed on with increased numbers, until at last the Austrians, having fulfilled the purpose of their general, fell back at four o'clock in the morning in unbroken order on Münchengrätz. The Prussians made only a show of following them. The losses on both sides were heavy. But the Austrians left about 500 prisoners, the men who had occupied the houses and balconies of Podol, in the hands of the enemy.

The same day the 8th corps, commanded by Von Bittenfeld, marching from Gabiel by Niemes, on the Münchengrätz side of Böhmisch-Leipa, pushed on thence towards Hühnerwasser, and drove before it the skirmishers, all hussars, who had been thrown beyond that place to reconnoitre. The Austrian brigade which had occupied Hühnerwasser fell back then on Münchengrätz, carrying to Count Clam-Gallas the information of the arrival on the field of the Prussian army of the Elbe.

The result of the day and night encounters at Liebenau and Podol had been to give the Prussians complete command of the right bank of the Iser. The forces of Clam-Gallas were now concentrated at Münchengrätz, immediately on the left bank. He knew he would be attacked on the 27th with the whole available force of the two Prussian armies; he knew that against such a force he could not defend Münchengrätz: his object therefore, it cannot be too strongly insisted upon, was not, as Prussian partisans have asserted, to fight a battle, but to offer with a strong rearguard a defence sufficiently resolute to secure for the remainder of his force an

He retreats on Gitschin.

uninterrupted march on Gitschin. And this, it will be seen, he accomplished.

Regarding the action of the 27th, then, it is not necessary to enter into detail. It was simply a combat fought by the Austrian rearguard to secure the retreat of the main body. When, then, about ten o'clock on the morning of the 27th, the Prussians began to move forward, the Austrians set fire to the wooden bridge over the Iser. After some delay the advanced cavalry of the Prussians found a ford by which some of them crossed. Bittenfeld, who commanded at this point, began then to throw a pontoon bridge for the rest of his troops. This bridge was not completed till one o'clock. Then, and then only, did his army begin its movement across the river. The main body of the Austrians had long before begun its march to Gitschin. The rearguard meanwhile had maintained a steady artillery fire on the advancing Prussians. When the pontoon bridge had been completed they fell back gradually, disputing every point, but not committing themselves to an engagement. Having done all that was possible they fell back on Gitschin. They lost in killed and wounded 193 men and 1000 prisoners. But those prisoners were mostly Italians,[1] who laid down their arms without fighting for a cause which was not their own. The Prussians lost that day 341 men killed and wounded.

In the days immediately before Wallenstein Gitschin had been a poor village, counting but 200 inhabitants dwelling in wretched cabins. But the munificence of that warrior had made it a flourishing town. Its situation on the river Cydlina, which divides itself into two

[1] It is admitted that the Italian regiments showed no disposition to fight. Captain Hozier states that twenty-five of them laid down their arms to a Prussian lieutenant.

branches just below the town, and the fact that it possesses four flourishing suburbs, constituting the market of the district of the same name as the town, gave it considerable importance. It lies twenty miles to the east by south of Münchengrätz, and about twenty-nine from Königgrätz, in a prolongation of the direction from Münchengrätz. Three miles before the traveller from the latter place can reach Gitschin he comes upon a semi-circular road of broken hills, grown with patches of silver firs, and interspersed here and there with small villages made up of ten or twelve huts or cabins surrounded by orchards. It was on these hills that Clam-Gallas had drawn up the Austro-Saxon army. He had posted his right in and about the village of Eisenstadt; his left on the Annaberg, a hill on the south side of the road leading from Sobotka to Gitschin; his centre on the heights of Brada; his reserves in Gitschin. To compensate as far as was possible for the inferiority of the Austrian musket to the needle-gun Clam-Gallas had directed that the groups of fir trees I have mentioned should be occupied by skilled marksmen, each having two soldiers with loaded muskets in attendance. It will be obvious that this arrangement, though assuring a continuity of fire, could only be carried out by the sacrifice of numbers. The Austrian guns had been skilfully arranged so as to bring a cross-fire on the enemy advancing along the main road.

It was late in the afternoon of the 29th of June when the corps of General von Schmitt approached the left of the Austrian position. The galling fire which opened upon him from an unseen enemy as soon as he arrived within range proved to him that he had to contend with an army well placed and resolute to defend. In vain did he send his skirmishers against the marksmen hidden

Combat of Gitschin.

by the clumps of firs. Their rolling fire, well directed and sustained by the cross fire from the Austrian guns, caused him very heavy loss. He resolved after a time to wait the arrival of reinforcements. These came up very soon, led by General von Werder. This able commander, attacking then in considerable force, compelled the Austro-Saxons to quit their cover. Then ensued one of the severest fights of the war, the foes standing opposite to each other, separated only by a ravine, and firing pointblank. Whilst they were thus engaged we must see what was happening in the centre and on the right.

There the Austro-Saxons occupied the hill of Brada and the range of low hills resting on the Eisenstadt, and in front of the village of Brada, at the foot of the slope of the hills on the further side the villages of Podultz and Diletz. Here also the Prussian attack made itself felt, just before the village clocks had struck five. On the two villages last named the Prussians threw all their infantry. The fight for them was very severe, the attacking party vying with the defenders in the ardour of their efforts. At length, about half-past seven, the Prussian attack relaxed. It even seemed to the hopeful Austro-Saxons that the enemy had been permanently repulsed, when an event happened which decided the fate of the day and enabled the Prussians to claim a victory.

Nothing had been further from the intention of the general-in-chief of the Austrian army, General Benedek, than to permit the several corps of observation he had despatched to the front to be overwhelmed by superior numbers and beaten in detail. We have seen how Clam-Gallas had obeyed the directions of his commander at Turnau and Münchengrätz, combating only for delay and avoiding a decisive action. But he had regarded the defence of Gitschin as so important that he had notified the day previous to General Benedek that unless he should receive orders to the contrary he should hold that place to the last extremity.[1] He was holding it with a fair chance of success, when at half-past seven a despatch from Benedek reached him, directing him to avoid all serious engagement and to fall back on the main army.

This despatch was the turning-point of the combat on both wings and in the centre. The retreat had to be made in the presence of an attacking enemy who would claim the movement as a victory. And so, indeed, it happened. The sullenness and steadiness of the retreating troops, commented upon with apparent admiration by Captain Hozier,[2] showed most clearly that the men falling back knew that they had not been beaten, that they had at least held their own, that they were retreating in obedience to superior orders. It is at least a firm belief in the Austrian army to this day that but for Benedek's order to retreat Clam-Gallas and the Crown Prince of Saxony would have repulsed the Prussians.

Such is the history, the true history, of the combat of Gitschin. It had been better, perhaps, for Austria had no despatch from Benedek interfered with the dispositions of Clam-Gallas. For, as I shall have to show, the easy abandonment of Gitschin made possible the junction of the second army with that of Prince Frederic Charles. To the movements of that second army I must now turn the attention of the reader.

It has already been stated that on the evening of the 19th of June the Crown Prince of Prussia, who com-

[1] For his conduct at Münchengrätz and Gitschin Benedek removed Count Clam-Gallas from his command, and caused him to be brought before a court-martial. The Count was honourably acquitted.
[2] Hozier's *The Seven Weeks' War*, Vol. I. page 248.

Movements of the Crown Prince. 145

manded the first army, received orders to move with one corps to Landshut, leaving a second at Neisse, and placing a third and fourth in such a position that they could either co-operate with him or join the corps left at Neisse, according as the Austrian movements might be developed. It was thought not impossible that Benedek might begin the war by threatening the flank of the Prussian army in Silesia. Austria, however, was not nearly so ready for aggressive warfare as was her rival, and the chief of the Prussian staff, knowing the advantage of such warfare to an army ready to move against an enemy whose preparations were considerably behindhand, had directed the Crown Prince on the 20th of June to intimate to the nearest Austrian commander that the two nations were in a state of war, and on the 22d had instructed him to invade Bohemia and to make for Gitschin.

The Crown Prince carried out these instructions. On the 25th of June he had moved his 1st corps to Liebau and Schömberg, the Guards to Schlegel, the 5th corps to a position between Glatz and Reinerz, the first brigade of the 6th corps to Glatz, the remainder of that corps to Patschkau, the cavalry division to Waldenburg, his own headquarters to Eckersdorf. He had in hand 125,000 good troops. His plan was to march by one or more of the six passes, all of them difficult, which lead from Prussian Silesia through the county of Glatz into Bohemia, and to effect somewhere about Gitschin a junction with the first army. After due consideration he resolved to march by the three roads which lead to Trautenau, Braunau, and Nachod; on reaching the last-named place, to make a move to the left with the whole army, using Nachod and Skalitz as the pivots, seize the railway from Josephstadt to Turnau, and thus come into

K

close communication with the first army. He began this movement on the evening of the 26th of June.

On that date General Benedek's army was disposed in the following manner: the 4th corps was at Lanzow, the 10th at Pilnikau, the 6th at Opocno, the 3d at Königgrätz, the 8th at Tinist. It will thus be seen that the projected movement of the Crown Prince was not without danger, and that had the Austrian commander been well served by his intelligence department it was quite possible for him to concentrate the five corps named and smite the heads of the Prussian columns as they emerged from the passes.

But apparently he was not well served. The leading division of the 5th Prussian corps secured Nachod on the evening of the 26th, almost without firing a shot, as the Austrians had there but two squadrons and two light guns. On the 27th the 1st Prussian corps, commanded by General von Bonin, marched on Trautenau, an industrial town on the Aupa. It so happened that the only Austrian troops in the town were some dragoons of the regiment of Windischgrätz and a handful of jäger infantry, far too few to defend it. They made no attempt to do so. The dragoons, however, engaged outside the town in a short hand-to-hand encounter with the Prussian cavalry. They renounced this when they saw the enemy's infantry hurrying up at the double, and fell back, accompanied by the handful of jägers, unpursued.[1]

But there was to be fighting that day. It happened that the 10th Austrian corps, commanded by General von Gablenz, whom we have already met in the Danish

---

[1] There is absolutely no truth in the story that Trautenau was defended, or that the entire Windischgrätz regiment was routed by the Prussian cavalry. The account in the text is based on letters written at the time, and on the assurances to me of men who served there. *Vide* Hozier, Vol. I. pages 264, etc.

war, had despatched his 1st brigade towards Trautenau when he heard of the Prussian advance, arranging to follow with his main body as soon as possible. The brigade arrived too late to save Trautenau, but it took a position on a hill called the Capellenberg, to the south of the town. Here it was attacked by Von Bonin's corps, and being pressed hard, fell back across the wooded hills which line the course of the Aupa. Finding the pursuit more harassing than he had hoped, Bonin contented himself with taking possession of the village of Hohenbrück and the heights towards Rognitz, and at three o'clock halted to rest. He had scarcely done so when Gablenz joined his 1st brigade, and assuming the offensive, drove the Prussian corps first from Hohenbrück, then from the Capellenberg, and pressing still forward, compelled the Prussians to evacuate Trautenau. For the second time[1] in the war the muzzle-loaders, well led, had beaten the needle-gun.

Gablenz did not pursue the Prussians beyond Trautenau. Leaving a brigade there as a rearguard, he marched nearly south-eastwards and bivouacked at the little town of Neu-Rognitz, intending to move thence the next morning to Deutsch-Prausnitz, to come there in touch with a brigade sent to reinforce him. Meanwhile the Prussian Guards, ignorant of the day's proceedings at Trautenau, had reached that same evening the village of Eypel, on the Aupa, and the town of Kosteletz, five miles to the south-east of Eypel. During the night the Prince of Würtemberg, who commanded them, received information of the defeat of the Prussians, and resolved to avenge the affront by attacking Gablenz. Early then the following morning he sent out patrols to bring him information as to the whereabouts of the

[1] Langensalza was the first victory.

Austrian general. The patrols did their work in a very slovenly manner, for they informed the Prince that Gablenz was marching from Königinhof to Trautenau. The Prince thereupon recalled the division Hiller which he had despatched from Eypel towards Trautenau and waited for further information. Two hours later he learned the true state of the case, viz., that Gablenz was marching from Neu-Rognitz on Deutsch-Prausnitz. He then made dispositions to attack him from three points on his line of march.

I have stated that the object of Gablenz in marching to Deutsch-Prausnitz was to give the hand to Fleischacher's brigade of the 4th Austrian corps, which he had received information had been sent hither to reinforce him. But mistakes sometimes occur in war, and very often those mistakes are fatal to success. It happened that on this part of the Bohemian frontier there are two villages called Prausnitz: the one bearing the prefix of 'Deutsch,' the other that of 'Ober.' Both villages are generally spoken of in the neighbourhood as simply 'Prausnitz,' and it is probable that that name without the prefix was used in the instructions given to General Fleischacher. This at least is certain, that he marched on Ober-Prausnitz, and was not near the battlefield during the entire day.[1]

Gablenz was close to the village of Soor when he became aware of the vicinity of the Prussian Guards. He instantly made soldierly arrangements, ranging his artillery on the hills between Neu-Rognitz and Burgersdorf, extending his right wing to Prausnitz, and stretching his left towards Trautenau to give a hand to the rear brigade he had left in that town. The position was a difficult one, for the task set him was to repulse an enemy

[1] Yet Captain Hozier writes of him as though he took part in the action.

greatly superior in numbers until he should extricate his brigade.

Had the brigade Fleischacher but moved on the proper Prausnitz it is probable that the Prussian attack would at least have been repulsed, for from the positions they occupied they could not attack Gablenz without exposing their flank and left rear to an enemy in Deutsch-Prausnitz. But, not menaced in those quarters, they attacked the position occupied by the Austrians with so much vigour that, in spite of a heroic defence, Gablenz was driven from position to position, until he was forced to abandon the hope of saving the brigade in Trautenau. Dearly did the Prussians pay for their success. They stormed one after another the Austrian positions, but it was 'at an awful sacrifice; men fell every moment, and officers went down so quickly that hardly a company reached the summit commanded by its captain.'[1] But the end came at last. Gablenz fell back slowly and unpursued to Neu Schloss; the brigade in Trautenau, cut off from the main body, fell back into the town, and yielded it only after a desperate defence.

This success made the future movements of the two Prussian corps easy. On the 29th the Guards occupied Königinhof, on the left bank of the Elbe, expelling thence the small Austrian garrison, whilst the corps of Bonin occupied Pilnikau. There we must leave them whilst we follow the movements of the other corps of the second Prussian army.

The 5th Prussian corps had been directed to make its way through the defile which leads from Glatz to the town of Nachod. A strong defence to their march ought to have been made here, for the position is very defensible; but, as already stated, no preparations had been made,

[1] Hozier, Vol. I. page 272.

and the Prussians encountered only the slightest resistance in taking possession of Nachod and its castle. But the 4th Austrian corps, commanded by General Ramming, was at Skalitz, eight miles from Josephstadt, on the railway line towards the frontier, and between it and Josephstadt was the 8th corps, commanded by the Archduke Leopold. Benedek had instructed Von Ramming to smite the Prussian force as it issued from Nachod in the direction of Skalitz, and the Archduke to support him.

It was about ten o'clock of the morning of the 27th when General Ramming attempted to carry out these instructions. He had ranged his corps on the plateau of Wenzelsberg, a little to the west of the point where the Nachod defile debouches into the open country, his guns on the high ground pointing in the direction by which the Prussians must emerge. These were supported by two brigades of infantry in front, a third in reserve, whilst two regiments of cuirassiers were drawn up in the open, ready to prevent any attempt of the enemy to rally. The position was admirable in many respects; it would have been perfect if the Archduke had also occupied with his corps the village of Wisokow, situated on the railway at the point where the road from Nachod then joined it.

The Prussians were commanded by General von Steinmetz, the advanced corps by General von Löwenfeld, and the Crown Prince was with them. The surprise to the Prussians as the heads of their columns emerged from the defile a little after ten o'clock was complete. The leading files were smitten by the fire from the Austrian artillery, and as the debouchment from the defile was narrow and the defile itself crowded, there appeared for them to be no salvation. Löwenfeld was, however, equal to the occasion. Hastening as much as possible the debouching of his men, he led them to a wood, which

Combat of Nachod.

partly sheltered them from the enemy's fire, and kept them there till two regiments of cavalry had been able to emerge. He ordered these to charge the Austrian cuirassiers. They did so with great gallantry, but after a semblance of success were beaten back with loss. This skirmish cleared the way for the Austrian infantry, who now rapidly approached with the intention of driving the Prussian infantry from the wood. Had they succeeded in doing so they would have not only defeated the two Prussian corps but have captured all their artillery. But the Prussians held the wood splendidly. The Crown Prince, forcing his way through the crowd, encouraged them by his words and by his example. They still held the wood as reinforcement after reinforcement emerged from the defile, but from it they could not debouch as the Austrian cuirassiers were in the open eager to overwhelm them as they might attempt to advance. The Crown Prince recognised that unless he could force back that cavalry the day was irretrievably lost. Just then the 8th regiment of dragoons and the 1st Uhlans emerged from the pass. Explaining to these that the fate of the day depended on their efforts, he ordered them to charge. They obeyed with alacrity, and, with the enormous advantage of assailing horsemen who were stationary, whilst they came on with the full impetus of weight and moral power, they forced the cuirassiers from their position, and giving them no time to rally, effectually cleared the way. Then Steinmetz, who had come up with the artillery and infantry, dashed forward with both arms, and seizing the village of Wisokow, which ought to have been but was not occupied by the Austrians, made the position of Ramming at Wenzelsburg untenable, and compelled him to retreat hastily on Skalitz. Vainly did the cuirassiers attempt to retrieve the day. At Skalitz the

Archduke Leopold made a great bid for victory. Steinmetz had pressed forward, and his force engaged with that of the Archduke in fierce encounter. For long the victory remained doubtful, but after some hours of combat Archduke Leopold was forced to retire, first from Skalitz, and then, pushed by the victorious enemy, from a fresh position he had taken behind the Aupa.

But there was to be one more combat for the possession of the passes. We have seen how Von Bonin's corps and the Prussian Guards had, on the 29th, occupied Königinhof on the Elbe. As the Crown Prince had resolved to unite his army at that important place before commencing operations in concert with the first army he directed Von Steinmetz to march the same day, the 29th, in that direction.

Benedek, meanwhile, recognising the importance of the mission confided to General von Ramming, had despatched the 4th corps, commanded by General Festetics, to support him. Festetics had been at Lanzow on the 26th, and had marched thence with three brigades towards Dolau the same night to support the 6th corps. On the 29th he was at the little village of Schweinschädel, three miles from, and to the west by south-west of, Skalitz. He was attacked there by Steinmetz, and after an artillery combat of three hours fell back on the fortress of Josephstadt. Steinmetz then resumed his march, and took a position at Gradlitz, two miles to the east of Königinhof. There also arrived on the 30th the 6th corps, which had followed the 5th through the defile of Nachod.

The Crown Prince had now concentrated in the vicinity of Königinhof all the corps of the second army which he had led into Bohemia. His 1st corps was at Arnau, where was the bridge across the Elbe. There

Why the Prussians were Victorious. 153

also on the 30th communication was established with with the first army, then at Gitschin.

Of the operations so far it may be remarked that the Prussians had, and the Austrians had not, observed the great principle of bringing the greatest numbers to bear on the decisive point. In the action of Nachod, if the 8th Austrian corps, instead of being left in reserve, had occupied the village of Wisokow,[1] the 5th and 6th corps of the Prussian army must have been crushed. It would not have been difficult then to overwhelm the army of the Crown Prince and afterwards successfully to deal with that of Prince Frederic Charles.

[1] The statement by Hozier that the village of Wisokow was occupied by the Austrians is erroneous.

CHAPTER IX.

THE BATTLE OF KÖNIGGRÄTZ.

BOHEMIA is a country rich in strong defensive positions. Notwithstanding the reverses recorded in the last chapter Benedek might have concentrated his army, amounting on the 30th of June to 205,000 men, in a position which would have made the work of the invader difficult and dangerous. Such a position would have been presented had he occupied the right bank of the Elbe, his right resting on Königgrätz, his left, in the direction of Chlumetz, on the ponds of the lower Bistritz, in the Altwasser district. In such a position he could have bade defiance to any enemy, whilst, even supposing he were to be beaten, his retreat was secured. Benedek, however, selected a more forward position. This I shall now proceed to describe.

Immediately beyond the village of Sadowa, coming from the west, the road from Horitz to Königgrätz crosses the river Bistritz by a stone bridge. Higher up, as far as Miletin, and lower down, as far as Nechanitz, the river of itself would be only an insignificant hindrance to an advancing enemy, but it flows in a broad marshy valley, liable to constant overflows, which submerge the roads and the bridges. On the left bank of the Bistritz—between it, the Trotinka, and the Elbe—the country is irregular and hilly. The hills and the chains of hills are separated from one another by ravines,

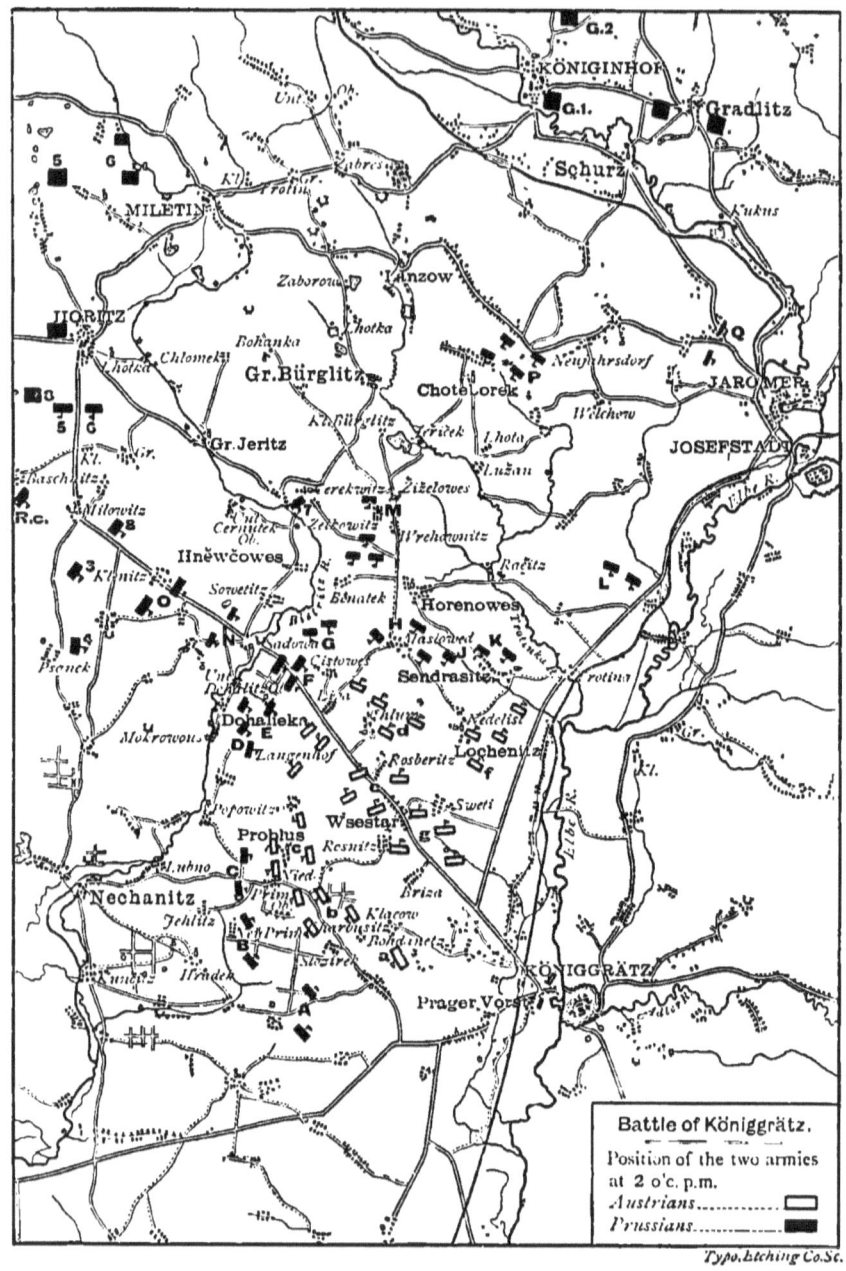

Benedek's Position. 157

which make excellent covered places for troops, especially for troops not required for immediate action. The country abounds likewise in woods, forests, and parks, especially in the neighbourhood of Nechanitz and Prizm. Irregular as is the hill-land, a soldier viewing it from the right bank of the Bistritz or from the summit of the hill of Dub, would draw a correct impression as to its general character. To him it would appear a large amphitheatre, whose highest point on the main road traversing it towards Königgrätz was the village of Chlum. From this village branched country roads northwards to Gross-Burglitz and thence to Horitz, southwards by way of Prolus to Nechanitz.

It was this tract of country, covered in front by the Bistritz, that Benedek had chosen in which to concentrate his army.

To the right and left of the highway between Sadowa and Chlum, the key and centre of his position, he had posted the 4th corps of his army. To the right of that corps, towards Horzenoves and the Trotinka, the 3d and 2d corps; to the left, and in touch with the 4th corps, and extending towards Nechanitz, the largely increased corps of Gablenz, now formed of two corps, the 8th and the 10th, recently blended: then the army corps of the Saxons. In the reserve, somewhat to the right of Chlum, stood at Rosberitz the 1st and 6th corps: in rear of them the cavalry divisions.

The actual front of this position from the Trotinka, just beyond Horzenoves, by way of Chlum and Neu-Prizm to Hradin, was about 15,000 paces, just over seven English miles. Its front was thus very strongly occupied, there being twelve men to a pace.

The position, naturally strong against a front attack, and occupied by a numerous infantry, had been further strengthened by science. Benedek had taken especial care to arrange his formidable artillery, 600 guns, in such a manner as to bear with tremendous force on an enemy approaching from Sadowa or from the north. With this view he had ranged his guns about Chlum and Lipa, on three natural terraces, the one above the other, pointing towards Sadowa, but capable of being turned in a northerly direction. That the line of fire in the Sadowa direction should be free and unincumbered, he had caused to be cut down the clumps and copses which lay between, and of the trees so cut down he had formed abattis, which, unseen from the distance, would obstruct an approaching foe, especially when exposed to the tremendous fire he could command.

The position was undoubtedly a strong one, but in the actual circumstances of the case it had its drawbacks. The first of these has reference to the distance between its extreme right and Königinhof, the headquarters at the moment of the army of the Crown Prince. Now, from Königinhof to Horzenoves, the extreme right of Benedek's position, is 18,000 paces, just over eight and a half English miles. Supposing, as the Austrian commander had the right to suppose, that between the 30th of June and the 3d of July there had been communications between Gitschin and the extreme right of the Crown Prince's position, and knowing, as he undoubtedly did know, that that prince was but three hours' march from the right of his position, he must have been aware that he was always liable to a flank attack. Allowing for delays in starting and in progress on the part of the Crown Prince's army the march would not take more than six hours. The supporting corps would arrive at short intervals later. Benedek's resolution to await attack from an army in front in a position exposed to a flank attack a few hours after the commencement of the front attack is then inexplicable. The idea that he hoped to defeat the first army before the second could arrive is incapable of being sustained. It vanishes before the stern logic of facts; for when he had repulsed with heavy loss the attack of the first army he, not then aware of the close proximity of the second army, made no effort to improve his advantage. Another action on the part of Benedek increased enormously the chances of misfortune rendered possible by the near vicinity of the Crown Prince. On the very morning of the battle he removed from his post, and placed under arrest his chief of the staff, General von Henekstein,[1] and appointed in his place General Baumgarten. Had Baumgarten been a heaven-born general, he could not have mastered in half-an-hour all the arrangements made the previous day by his predecessor. But he was a man not credited with capacity. His sudden appointment to the most important post in the army could then rarely fail to be most unfortunate. So, in the sequel, it proved.

Let us turn from the examination of the Austrian position to the action of the army which, on the morning of the 3d of July, is marching to assail it.

During the 1st of July the King of Prussia, from his headquarters at Gitschin, gave the following instructions to the leaders of his corps and divisions.

From the 4th corps the 8th division, that of General Horn, was to march so as to take at two o'clock the following morning a position at Milowitz; the 7th division, that of Fransecky, to cross the Bistritz at Gross-Jersitz, and reach the castle of Cerekwitz at the same hour. The 5th and 6th divisions, commanded by General von Manstein, were to take a position in reserve to the south of Horitz, the 5th forming the right, the 6th the

[1] He also placed under arrest Count Clam-Gallas and General Krismanic.

left wing, the latter being to the east of the road leading from Horitz to Königgrätz.

At the same hour on the 3d the 2d army corps was to take a position to the right of Horn's division—one division at Brschikstan, another at Pschanek. The reserve cavalry corps, saddled before daybreak, was to be ready at daybreak at Baschnitz, round which it had bivouacked. The reserve artillery was to move to Horitz, that of the 3d army corps to occupy the road to Miletin, that of the 4th on Libonitz, on the Gitschin road.

General von Bittenfeld was to march on the 1st, with as many troops as he could make available, as early as possible from Smidar to Nechanitz. The 2d army corps was to be in touch with Bittenfeld's corps on its left, the division Fransecky (at Cerekwitz) in touch with the 2d army corps, and the latter, it was hoped, in touch with the army of the Crown Prince, who had been requested to extend his right to Gross-Bürglitz.

The King of Prussia had arrived at Gitschin the afternoon of the 1st of July and assumed command of the three armies. On the 2d he held there a council of war to which all the army commanders were invited. At this it was resolved that the following day, whilst Prince Frederic Charles should send a reconnaissance towards Königgrätz, the Crown Prince should despatch a strong detachment towards Josephstadt with the view to cut off that fortress from communication with Benedek's army. Circumstances occurred, however, now to be described, which prevented the carrying out of these plans.

Whilst Prince Frederic Charles was attending the council of war held at Gitschin on the 2d two officers whom he had despatched to reconnoitre came upon a party of Austrian cavalry on the road leading from Horitz to Königgrätz, on the Prussian side of the Bistritz. The two officers, though hotly pursued, managed to escape, one with a slight scratch, and reached the camp in safety. The information he brought led Prince Frederic Charles to believe that Benedek would attack him on the morrow before he could effect a junction with his cousin. He therefore resolved to anticipate the enemy by advancing to engage him in front beyond Horitz, whilst Bittenfeld should assail his left flank. He at the same time despatched an officer to the Crown Prince—the distance being a three hours' ride—to inform him of his intentions and to ask his co-operation. It is a fact worthy to be noted that the Crown Prince and his chief of the staff, General von Blumenthal, positively declined to accede to the request of Prince Frederic Charles, possibly because they did not credit the report of an Austrian advance. It became necessary, then, for the King to intervene. The arrival of Count Finkenstein with a direct message from the sovereign naturally met with a promise of compliance.

That same night Prince Frederic Charles gave to his army the order to advance on the positions assigned to them in a previous page. He had under him 87,000 fighting men proved in action during the campaign. He still clung to the idea that Benedek would attack him. Even when, at half-past five on the morning of the 3d, his army had taken the positions assigned, without seeing or coming in contact with Austrian troops, he did not discard the idea. To test the theory further, he at that hour advanced Horn's division to Dub, and the divisions of the 2d corps to Unter-Dohalitz. Still no enemy appeared. Horn then received the order to advance from Dub to Sadowa. As he approached that place the fire from the Austrian guns posted at Lipa gave him the intimation that at last he had come upon the enemy. Whether that

L

enemy was a strong rearguard or the main body seemed to him at first doubtful, but a short reconnaissance left no doubt on his mind that he had the entire army of Benedek before him.

Prince Frederic Charles resolved to attack them without a moment's delay. His idea was to rivet the attention of the Austrian centre by a strong artillery fire, whilst Von Bittenfeld, on the Prussian right, and the Crown Prince, from the side of Königinhof, should act on their wings. At eight o'clock, then, he despatched Horn's division direct on Sadowa and the bridge over the Bistritz, its artillery in front; to its right, the 4th division on Unter-Dohalitz; to its right again, the 3d division that of Werder, on Dohalitzka and Mokrowous. At the same time he directed Fransecky, then with the 7th division at Cerekwitz, to march on Benatek, thence to move southwards only when the battle should be engaged in front between Sadowa and Mokrowous. Of the 3d army corps—the 5th and 6th divisions should march at once in order to support the 8th, 3d, and 4th divisions, then at Horitz.

Whilst these troops are marching to carry out their orders it may be profitable to take a last glance at the positions occupied by the troops now about to be attacked. The Austrian centre, where their guns were massed, lay in front of Lipa and Chlum, the latter the highest point of their position. How the guns were ranged and how the approaches were defended by abattis has been already told. The right flank extended to the village of Sendrasitz, with a brigade pushed on to the Trotina, a tributary of the Elbe. The left centre occupied the villages of Problus, Nied, and Ober-Prim, whilst the left rested on the wood and castle of Hradek, with an advanced guard at Nechanitz. The centre, supporting the artillery at

The Battle begins. 163

Lipa and Chlum, consisted of the 10th corps about Langenhof, the 3d corps near Cistowes, and the 4th corps, to its right, at Maslowied. The right wing counted the 2d corps and the 2d division of cavalry, the left centre consisted of the Saxons. In support stood the 8th corps, with the reserves, massed about the villages of Rosnitz, Wsestar, and Smeti.

The artillery fight began a little before eight o'clock and became very serious half an hour later. In the fierce combat the well-posted guns of the Austrians had all the advantage. The morning was wet and misty, and their guns, carefully placed, found their target with far greater certainty than could those of their freshly arriving enemy. When the fire was becoming very hot the Prussian King arrived on the ground and took the command. He very soon had experience of the correctness of the Austrian aim, for whilst he was seated on his horse a shell burst in the midst of a party of cavalry close to him and killed four of the men. Shortly after this event the rain, which had been falling heavily all the morning, suddenly ceased and the atmosphere cleared. Still, so well posted were the Austrians that, though their fire continued fiercely, the Prussian staff could see but little beyond the smoke. The actual position occupied by their infantry remained an unsolved problem. The dips in the ground and the small woods and the copses hid this arm from view. Something, it was felt, must be done to compel this unseen enemy to display his forces. About nine o'clock, then, the King ordered Horn's division and the two divisions of the 2d army corps to cross the Bistritz with their infantry, and Fransecky's division, the 7th, to press forward against Benatek. In obedience to these orders the three divisions first named crossed the Bistritz. Their men soon found themselves entangled in the wooded hills which rise on the southern bank of the river beyond the ground liable to swamps. They managed, however, to emerge and take position beyond the parks of Sadowa and Dohalitzka, on the hills which stretch from that village to Mokrowous. From these an artillery fire was opened; but, although the ammunition waggons were twice replenished, the Prussian leaders could not see that much impression was made on the enemy. Meanwhile Fransecky had marched his division against Benatek, well supported by cavalry. He was unable, however, to win ground quickly. Perseveringly he pressed forward, nevertheless, overthrew an Austrian cavalry regiment, capturing the colour; drove, after a very fierce struggle, the infantry from the wood between Benatek and Maslowied, and despatched thence a brigade, the 13th, towards Sadowa to extend a hand to Horn. But the splendid defence of the Austrians made his operations slow, and his losses very heavy. The fight for the wood, above referred to, was considered one of the most fiercely contested combats of the war.

With equal fury was the wood between Sadowa and Dohalitz contested and won. But the winning of these woods involved the keeping of them, and this the Prussians, exposed to a tremendous fire from an enemy most advantageously placed, found a very difficult task. At last the 2d army corps, which had occupied the wood of Dohalitz, could endure it no longer. Dashing from their cover, they rushed with fury against the Austrian positions at Lipa and Langenhof. But the artillery fire from the former place, and that from the infantry of Gablenz in the latter, mowed them down, and they fell back after having experienced terrible losses.

In the minds of some at least of the Prussian leaders

the conviction must have begun to enter that unless the Crown Prince should appear they were beaten. Not only up to this time, nearly midday, had they made no impression on the true Austrian position, but the very successes of Fransecky, brilliant in themselves, had not contributed to the attainment of their main object. For Fransecky, in his zeal for combat, had pressed too far forward, forgetting that his main object should have been to incline more to his left, so as to come in touch with the troops, now momentarily expected, of the Crown Prince.

Nor, whilst the fighting had been thus unprofitable on their left and in their centre, had the Prussian right accomplished much more. General von Bittenfeld had brought his troops into action about ten o'clock; had set the 15th division, that of Canstein, across the Bistritz at Nechanitz, with orders to move on Hradek; the 14th, following it, to drive the enemy from Problus; the 16th, with the reserve cavalry of the Elbe army, to support those movements, then to move by Charbusitz to Brzisa. The Austrian and Saxon defence on these points was splendid, and though the Prussians eventually made way it was but very slowly, and their advance did not affect the main attack and defence.

For in the centre Horn's division, and the two army corps co-operating with it, had suffered tremendous losses, and it had been found necessary to push the 9th brigade of the 3d army corps beyond Sadowa to keep the enemy in check. It was now midday. The artillery of the 5th division, which had been sent forward with the 9th brigade, covered itself, according to universal testimony, with glory. To its splendid exertions the Prussians attribute the fact that the Austrians were prevented from taking advantage of their repulse—for repulse it had been. However that may be—for the view is not shared by the

Austrians—the Prussian artillery was holding its front position when the information reached the King that the extreme left of Fransecky's division had come in touch with the Crown Prince marching from Königinhof. To the movements of that prince I must now ask the reader's attention.

The Crown Prince had received the King's orders to march to co-operate in the attack on the Austrian position about four o'clock on the morning of the 3d of July. He at once issued the following orders to his generals.

The 1st corps, that of Bonin, was to march in two columns from Arnau and Böhmisch-Prausnitz, the right column by Gross-Tretin, the left by Zabrzes, to Gross-Bürglitz; the reserve cavalry division was to follow them. The corps of Guards received orders to march from Königinhof in the direction of Jericek and Lhota. The 6th army corps was to move on Welchow, despatch thence a detachment to observe Josephstadt, whilst the remainder should push on to the Trotinka, cross it, and form the left wing of the second army. The 5th corps was to remain halted until the others should have been two hours on the way, and was then to march to take post at Choteborek, constituting there the reserve. The baggage trains were left where they had been.

A glance at the map will show that, according to these dispositions, it was the corps of Guards which would first come into action. From Königinhof, where they were, to Jericek and Lhota was just about seven English miles, say, having regard to the rain and the hilly country, three hours' march. From those places to Horzenowes would be another full hour, or in the event of the ground being contested two hours. Thus, to produce any influence on the fight, the Crown Prince must reckon on a period of five hours from the time of setting out.

The Prussian Guard Corps push on. 167

The roads were difficult for the Guards. The rain had saturated the clayey soil, and it was ascent and descent the whole way. The corps had received its orders at six, and it was past eleven before its leading columns reached the height of Choteborek. From this point a view of the battlefield was possible. To the eager troops it seemed as though the main fight, evidently of a very severe character, was taking place between Sowetitz and Sadowa. The other portions of the battlefield, down the Bistritz, were hidden from them by the intervening hills. Choteborek was too distant from the Austrian position to allow them to exercise thence any influence on the battle. The corps was therefore moved along the ridges of the hills which, on the right bank of the Trotinka, rise between Zizelowes and Cerekwitz. For this purpose the Trotinka was crossed at two points, Jericek and Luzian. From the height of Zizelowes a solitary tree in the distance indicated the point upon which the troops were to direct their march. The 1st division pressed onwards in that direction, and at midday reached a position whence their artillery fire could be brought to bear with effect. They accordingly unlimbered and opened fire on the Austrian corps, which had taken its position between Maslowied, Horzenowes, and, on its extreme right, at Racitz. After an artillery combat of considerable duration the infantry of the 1st division of the Guards, followed by the hussars and dragoons of the same corps, advanced. After a manful resistance the Austrians fell back to take a new and stronger position on the high range between Maslowied and Sendrasitz.

Whilst the 1st division of the Guards was preparing to attack this new position, the 2d, which had followed in its track as far as the height of Zizelowes, had seen thence the solitary tree, and had begun to march in its direction, had moved somewhat to the right in order to take its proper place relatively to the 1st division, and had taken the direction of Lipa. Whilst it is marching thither we have time to note that a portion of the 6th army corps, accidentally moving on lines parallel to that taken by the 1st division of the Guards, had formed on the left of that division; that the 12th division, marching early in the morning from Gradlitz, and crossing the Elbe by a pontoon bridge at Kukus, had taken a position of observation against Josephstadt, to remain thus until it should be relieved by the left wing of the 5th army corps, that of Steinmetz; that the 11th division, that of Zastrow, warned at six o'clock to move from Gradlitz, had crossed the Elbe by the bridges of Schurz and Stangendorf, the latter from its state of decay requiring much repair, and after a very trying march had reached Welchow; that, hearing there the sound of firing, borne by the wind from the battlefield, it had pressed hurriedly on, reached about midday the banks of the Trotinka, in the vicinity of Racitz, and had joined there in the attack on the right wing of the Austrian defenders, the centre and left of which were being assailed by the Guards at Horzenoves, an attack which, we have seen, had resulted in the taking by the Austrians of a new position at Maslowied and Sendrasitz.

The Prussians now prepared to attack this new position. The 1st division of the Guards, formed on the heights to the south-east of Maslowied, fronting the central positions held by the Austrians at Chlum and Rosberitz; to its left was the 11th division, facing Nedelist; to its right, the 2d Guard division faced Lipa; the 7th division, that of Fransecky, was still fiercely fighting between Benatek and Sadowa; the 1st army corps, that of Bonin, was approaching Benatek, and would soon be in a position to support the 7th division with its right, the Guards with its left.

It was now two o'clock. Up to that time the Prussians had made no real impression on any point of the Austrian position. In the centre the defenders had decisively repulsed the Prussian attack: the left of the 1st army, the troops led by Fransecky, had suffered very severely; its right, under Von Bittenfeld, had effected but little, and was checked in its further advance. There were wild spirits on the Austrian staff who urged Benedek to change by a general advance the repulse into a rout. The correspondent of the *Times*, Mr W. H. Russell, who witnessed the fight from a commanding position on the Austrian side, wrote that at this period the battle seemed won by the Austrians, and that it seemed to require only the assumption of a forward movement to render it decisive. Benedek, however, though he believed in ultimate victory, was not prepared to risk his army in a forward movement which would expose his right flank to troops marching from the direction of Königinhof until he should receive some authentic information of the movements of the Crown Prince. It speaks badly for the efficiency of the Austrian staff that no such information reached him.

The Prussians, too, were not without anxiety. The story told to prove that there all was confidence tells really the opposite tale. The story is that Bismarck offered his cigar case to Moltke at this period of the action, and that Moltke turned the cigars about to select the best, a proof, it is added, that at this crisis of the battle he was sufficiently confident of the issue to care specially for his palate. But, independently of the fact that confirmed smokers will, under all circumstances, pick out the cigar which suits them, there remains this other fact that Bismarck was anxiously watching for some sign of Moltke's opinion. He at least showed anxiety.

Between two and three o'clock there was, except on the Austrian right, a pause in the struggle. Both parties rested; the troops of the first army to gain renewed strength for the decisive struggle; those of the second to recover the dash their fatiguing march had somewhat impaired; the Austrians because they were no longer attacked in front, and because Benedek had resolved not yet to change his defensive into an offensive attitude.

On the Austrian right, however, the contest had continued. There, at its extreme point, the 'Schwarz-Gelb' brigade had been posted at Trotinka, a village at the point where the rivulet of the same name flows into the Elbe. They were assailed by the greater part of the Prussian 12th division, and after a very severe contest compelled to fall back on Lochenitz, from which also they were driven.

This unforeseen retrograde movement, causing the threatening by the Prussians of his extreme right, induced Benedek to order a movement which caused the loss of the battle. In a previous page[1] I have shown that whilst the Austrian guns were posted on Lipa and Chlum they were supported by 'the 10th corps about Langenhof, the 3d corps at Cistowes, and the 4th corps, to its right, at Maslowied. The right wing counted the 2d corps and the 2d division of cavalry.' No sooner had the information reached Benedek that his right was seriously menaced than he sent orders to his 2d and 4th corps to move in that direction, to occupy the line from Chlum to Nedelist. This they proceeded to do. Their places were not taken as they should have been, for either by a mistake or the miscarriage of orders the 3d corps was left at Cistowes, where also was General Fischbacker's

[1] Page 162.

brigade of the 4th corps.[1] These movements left the guns on Chlum and Lipa without support.

The Prussian Guards, we have seen, were facing Chlum when they halted at two o'clock. Had they at once marched forward to the attack it is possible that the result of the battle might have been different; but, we have seen, whilst they were halting to rest and order their forces, Benedek, possibly concluding that the Crown Prince was advancing down the Elbe to cut him off from Königgrätz, had denuded Chlum. When, then, between three and four o'clock the 1st division of the corps of Guards marched against Chlum, and the 2d, supported by battalions from the 1st army corps, moved on Lipa they found their task easy. The gunners, unsupported by infantry, could make no stand against the finest troops of the Prussian army, attacking in numbers vastly superior. The Prussian Guards seized Chlum, the key of the Austrian position, then turning south-eastward attacked Rosberitz, where Benedek had placed his reserves. The fight at this village was most fierce. The reserve artillery of the Austrians, placed advantageously, thundered on the advancing left wing of the Guards' division and caused them enormous losses. Whilst the fight was at its height Benedek brought up strong infantry columns from Langenhof and Wsestar, and these forming rapidly, drove the Prussian Guards from the positions they had almost won.

Just then, when it had seemed to the anxious mind of Benedek still possible to effect an orderly retreat, there came unexpected assistance to the Prussian Guards. The Prussian general, Von Mutius, who commanded the 11th division of Zastrow's corps, had reached Nedelist,

[1] This neglect is generally attributed to the fact, previously mentioned, that the Chief of the Staff had been appointed that very morning.

intending to halt there until he should be reinforced by the 12th division of the same corps. But when the sound of increasingly heavy fire from Chlum and Lipa reached his ears he pressed forward, and marching by Smeti, found himself suddenly on the right flank of the Austrian defenders of Rosberitz. His flank attack, made immediately, and when the Guards were again attacking Rosberitz, compelled the Austrians to evacuate the place. Soon the retreat of the defenders, always increasingly pressed, became more and more pronounced. By five o'clock the highway from Sadowa to Königgrätz was completely lost to them.

Whilst the Crown Prince is engaged in urging his troops, consisting now of all the divisions of his army, with the exception of the 5th and a brigade of the 6th army corps, along this highway, it is necessary that we should turn for a moment to the King and the first army.

We left the King and Prince Frederic Charles at midday, just listening to the report that the extreme left of his army had come in touch with the extreme right of that of the Crown Prince. The distance, however, was still great, and it was only at two o'clock that King William had satisfied himself that the Prince was pressing forward with the haste the situation demanded. Meanwhile he had ordered up, as a measure of precaution, his reserves to a point facing Cistowes and Lipa. Then, from the elevated plateau of Dub, he directed his anxious glances towards the north-east. Gradually he began to notice that the Austrian guns from Chlum and Lipa were directing a portion of their fire in the same direction. Neither the King nor the able staff which surrounded him could be quite certain that this change of direction indicated the advance of the Crown Prince, for it was quite possible that Fransecky might have made his footing so good that the Austrians were endeavouring to check him. Wisely, however, the King resolved to assume the first conjecture as representing the truth, and he informed his corps and divisional commanders accordingly. At two o'clock there was no longer any doubt. An hour later there followed the attacks on Chlum and Lipa. No sooner was it seen from the height of Dub that these positions had been forced than the King was pressed on all sides to send his cavalry to press the retreating enemy. King William then placed himself at the head of the reserve cavalry corps, and rode to the front from Sadowa. Everywhere he encountered signs of victory. Everywhere shouts of applause greeted him. He did not stop until he reached the fortress of Königgrätz, upon which and upon Pardubitz and Hohenmauth, the Austrian army had fallen back. He had reason to be content. He had won the battle which was to give to Prussia the much desired preponderance in Germany, and more even than that.

For to Benedek, after Chlum and Lipa and Rosberitz had been stormed, the conviction was clear that the day was lost. The unfortunate movement to the right of two of his corps, under the mistaken impression that the principal attack was being made there, had ruined him. But in the dark hour of his misfortune he behaved as an energetic and capable soldier. Covered by his cavalry, and but feebly pursued by the victorious enemy, he crossed the Elbe by the many bridges he had constructed between Königgrätz and Pardubitz, and fell back on Hohenmauth, breaking the bridges behind him. His losses had been heavy, consisting of about 18,000 killed and wounded, 19,300 prisoners, 161 guns, and five standards. The Prussian loss in killed and wounded amounted to nearly

10,000. Though in numbers the three Prussian armies had surpassed the enemy the Austrians had more than once been superior on the decisive points. The three Prussian armies counted 230,984 men, that of the Austrians 205,000. Of the battle I will only venture to remark that one fault lost it. It is at least possible, that if the Austrian commander had kept his two infantry corps massed about Chlum he might have repulsed the tired troops of the Crown Prince. But it was not to be. Of the part taken by the needle-gun in this battle, there is but little to record. The first phases of the fight brought the artillery on both sides to the front. Even in its later phases, the cannon and the bayonet charge did the principal part, and, as we have seen, there was practically no pursuit; the victors had been thoroughly exhausted.

Of the subsequent movements of the armies engaged I shall write in the next chapter. But I shall not delay till then to record that there were few superior officers in the beaten army who failed to realise that the defeat was a decisive one, and that the paramount influence of Austria, exercised for nearly 600 years [1] in the affairs of Germany, had departed for ever.

[1] Rudolph of Habsburg was elected Emperor of Germany in 1273, and acquired Austria in 1278.

CHAPTER X.

THE BATTLE OF CUSTOZA—THE CAMPAIGN IN BAVARIA
—THE MARCH OF THE PRUSSIANS ON VIENNA—
THE ARMISTICE OF NIKOLSBURG AND TREATY OF
PRAGUE.

IN writing a history of the re-founding of the German Empire the writer is constrained to bear in mind and to give prominent importance to the decisive events which chiefly tended to accomplish that main object of Prussian policy. Of these the battle of Königgrätz was not only one, but the most important one. It had been decided almost before the Main army had begun to move. One event had preceded it, the battle fought by the Austrians against the Italian allies of Prussia. But as this battle and the combats of the Main army at Kissingen and elsewhere constitute mere side issues, but little if at all affecting the main issue, I shall be pardoned if I devote to the consideration of these less space and less detail than I have given to the decisive battle of Königgrätz.

The first of the side issues to be noticed is the battle of Custoza. When Italy had, in the manner described, resolved to make common cause with Prussia against Austria, and had even refused the offer of Venetia, made to her too tardily by the Austrian Emperor, because she considered herself bound by honour to carry out her engagements with the northern German power, she formed two armies, one, the principal, under the maker of the treaty with Prussia, General La Marmora, to attack the line known as the Verona-Peschiera line; the other, led by General Cialdini, to cross the lower Po into the Venetian territory. To defend the Austrian Italian territories the cabinet of Vienna had placed the Archduke Albert, son of the illustrious Archduke Charles, with the 5th, 7th, and 9th army corps, an infantry reserve of four regiments, constituting a total of 73,000 men and 272 guns, between Pastrengo and San Bonifacio, in such a position that he could easily operate against an enemy on either bank of the Adige. The Archduke was forty-nine years old; had been brought up at the feet of Radetzky; had seen many combats, but had never commanded in chief in war.[1]

King Victor Emanuel had, on the eve of the breaking out of hostilities, joined and taken command of the principal army, which counted 146,000 men and 228 guns. He had resolved to cross the Mincio as soon as he should hear that hostilities had broken out in Germany. This information reached him on the 23d of June. Accordingly, he at once ordered the passage of that river.

The news that the Italians had crossed the Mincio reached Archduke Albert at two o'clock on the afternoon of the same day. Divining that it was the intention of Victor Emanuel to march by way of Villafranca and Isola della Scala to cross the Adige, so as to give touch to the advancing troops of Cialdini, and finding his convictions confirmed by the reports of his officers sent to reconnoitre, the Archduke resolved to seize at once the high ground between Somma Campagna, Sona, and

[1] It was well understood that in his military combinations during this campaign the Archduke was mainly guided by the advice of his very capable chief of the Staff, the Freiherr Franz von John.

M

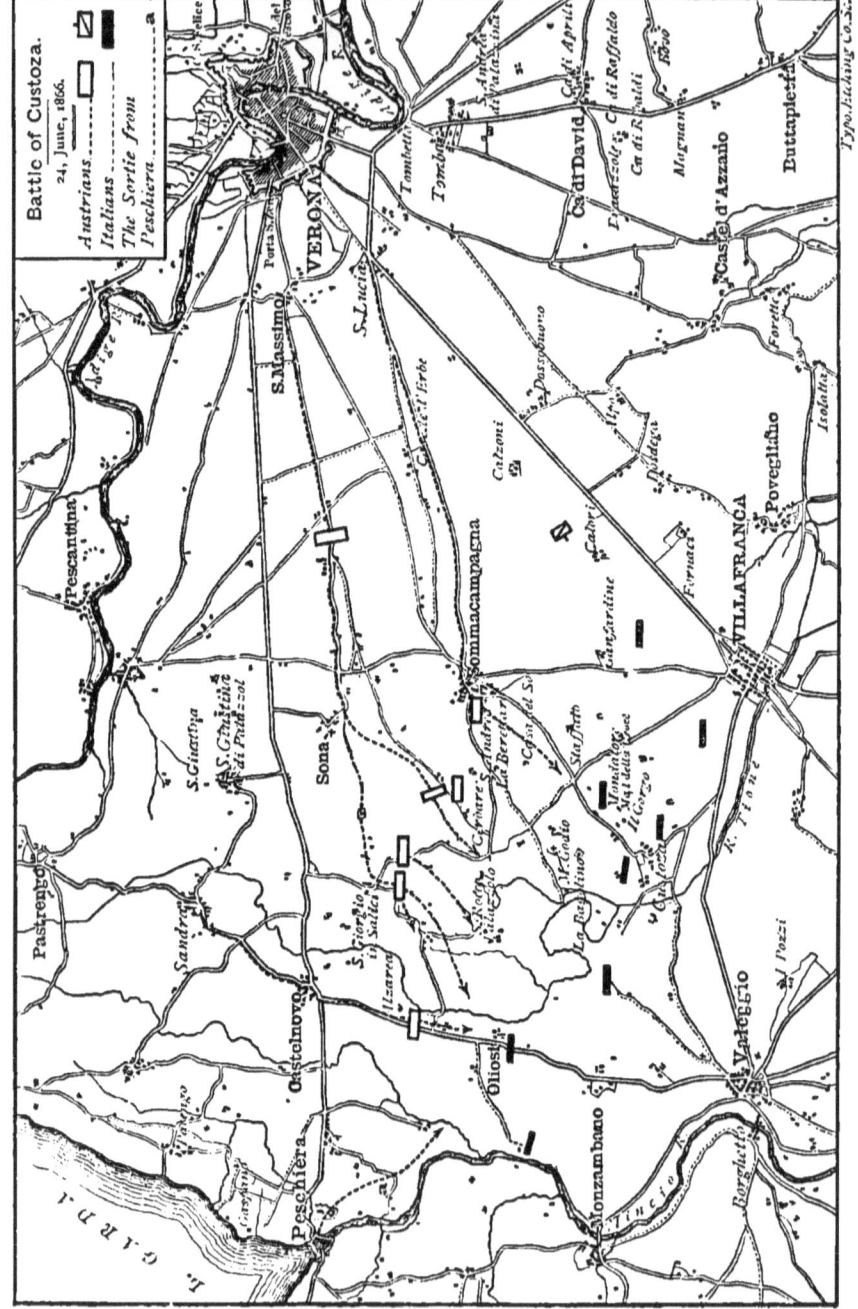

The Austrians take the Initiative. 179

San Giustina on the one side, and Valeggio, Monzambano, and Peschiera on the other, thence to assail the left flank of the Italian army on its march to the Adige. Having given the necessary orders, the Archduke, guided by the Freiherr von John, rode the same evening to San Massimo. Further informed there by his scouts, he directed the occupation very early the following morning of the line formed by Sandra, San Giustina, Sona, and Somma Campagna, and the making from the last named, which was to be the pivot, of an inclination to the left to bring the army on to the line formed by Castelnuovo, San Giorgio in Salice, Zerbare, and Berettara. He had present with him for these operations only about 57,000 men and 272 guns, the remainder having been used to occupy Peschiera and other fortresses.

The main Italian army was more considerable in numbers. Yet in the march he had undertaken the King had not been able to bring them all upon one line. In the action about to be forced upon him he could not utilise more than 90,000 men and 192 guns. It is necessary, however, to add that at one period of the fight the garrison of Peschiera made a demonstration in favour of the Austrians, a fact which should diminish the proportions indicated by the above figures.

At three o'clock in the morning of the 24th of June, after a night of storm and rain, the Austrian divisions marched to take up the positions assigned to them. The first concussion between the two armies was caused by the encounter of the Austrian 5th army corps on its march on Castelnuovo with the reserve cavalry division of the Italian army, the division of the Crown Prince Humbert, and the division Bixio. The fight here was very severe, and lasted nearly the whole day. Meanwhile General Cerale commanding the advanced guard of the Italians, had been attacked about seven o'clock by the Austrian reserve division near Alzarea, and forced back into Oliosi. The Austrian attack upon this village was very severe. The Archduke for a time directed the operations here in person, bringing up a brigade of the 5th army corps to support his reserves, whilst he directed two other brigades to gain possession of San Rocco di Palazzuolo. He succeeded likewise, whilst the fight here was progressing, in completing the communications between his several corps and divisions. After a strong Austrian cannonade Oliosi was set on fire, and Cerale had to evacuate it and fall back, contesting every inch of the ground, on Montevento. Thither he was followed by his persistent enemies, and so severely wounded that he had to make over command to the next officer. But he also fell, and the troops, hotly attacked, were left for a time without support.

For, whilst this division was being hardly pressed, other Austrian troops had completely occupied the attention of the remainder of the Italian army. At length, however, the division Sirtori came to the support of the Cerale division by taking an alignment to its immediate right. But it was in vain. At two o'clock the Austrians stormed Montevento. For a moment the progress of the victors was stopped by the sudden appearance on the field of the brigade of General Pianelli, left on the right bank of the Mincio, but which had been attracted by noticing the desperate plight of the Cerale division— but it was only for a moment. By three o'clock the left wing of the Italian army had been completely driven from the field.

Meanwhile the fight had been raging with great fury on the heights of the eastern bank of the Tione. Here the 9th Austrian corps had received orders to maintain itself at Somma Campagna. When, then, at eight o'clock in the morning of the 24th, its commander, Field-Marshal-Lieutenant Hartung, observed one Italian division pressing on by way of Madonna della Croce, and another across Monte Torre, he occupied Casa del Sole and Berettara strongly with his artillery. Just then he received orders to attack Custoza with his full strength. He did so, but the division Eugia, supported on its right by the division of the Crown-Prince Humbert, offered a very determined resistance. Against the latter the Archduke detached two divisions of cavalry. These charged repeatedly, but the squares formed by the Italian footmen were not broken. They were fighting under the eye of their Prince, himself constrained to take shelter in their midst.

Whilst the fight at this point was being vigorously carried on the division Brignone, consisting of two brigades, the one led by General Gozzani di Treville, the other by Prince Amadeus, came into the fight at a point between the divisions Eugia and Sirtori. These brigades had been originally designed to be the reserve of the two army corps now engaged. They had crossed the Mincio the previous evening, and on their march on the morning of the 24th to Valeggio had received orders to cross the Tione to Custoza. There La Marmora himself led them into the fight. Advancing from Custoza to Monte Godio, they were assailed by the 7th Austrian corps. But the men led by La Marmora were the picked soldiers of the Italian army—the grenadiers of Sardinia and Lombardy—and here, attacked by superior numbers, they displayed a courage and conduct not to be surpassed. Though other Austrian troops were brought against them, they maintained themselves on Monte Godio till past midday, then, having lost both their commanders, wounded, they were forced to fall back to Custoza.

The retreat of these brigades, coupled with the defeat of Cerale's division, already described, had the effect of restricting the Italian line of combat. They held now La Bagolina, Staffalo, and Custoza. On these points they still offered a stern resistance. But the Archduke Albert was now able to bring the greatest numbers to bear on the decisive point, and his troops, always making way, succeeded in rendering those positions untenable. At five o'clock the Italians, outflanked on their left and pressed in front, began to give way. They fell back, however, in excellent order; nor was it until seven o'clock in the evening that the Austrians entered the long-defended Custoza.

I have given more space to this battle than I had intended to bestow upon an event which I have described as a side issue, because, whilst the soldiers on both sides displayed courage and conduct, the triumph of leadership was with the Austrian leaders. They had the fewer troops, but their generals kept them well in hand, and maintained throughout the fight the connection between all the parts of his army. Pressing them on their front, they rolled them up by a strong attack on their left flank. In the leadership of the Italian army this latter quality was conspicuous by its absence. There was no unity of action. Each corps and each division seemed to fight for its own hand. Thus the Austrians, inferior as a whole, were superior at every decisive point, and thus they won the day. In Austria, the credit of the victory is given to the Chief of the Staff, General von John, and it was towards him that the hopes of every Austrian were turned when the news was spread that Benedek had been beaten at Königgrätz.

Turn we now to recount very briefly the campaign in

The Bund Army. 183

Bavaria. The Diet had on the 14th of June decreed the assembly of the army at Frankfort. It was to be composed of troops from Würtemberg, Baden, the Grand Duchy of Hesse, Saxony, Nassau, and Austria; and to be placed under the command of Prince Alexander of Hesse, an officer who had served with distinction in the wars waged by Austria. The decree was very generally responded to, and on the 18th of June Prince Alexander had under his orders 55,900 men.

Bavaria meanwhile had put into the field her own national army, consisting of 52,000 men, under the command of Prince Charles of Bavaria, a veteran in his seventy-first year, who since 1815 had not seen a shot fired. This prince directed likewise the movements of the 8th Federal corps, that of Prince Alexander of Hesse. The army of Prince Charles occupied the valley of the Upper Main, and he had his headquarters at Bamberg.

Prince Charles began his campaign by losing an opportunity which, if he had taken it, might have materially affected the fortunes of the war. In the seventh chapter I have told how the King of Hanover, pressed by superior forces in front, and his line of retreat occupied by a division 9000 strong, had sent pressing messages to the two princes, Alexander and Charles, to disengage him by a prompt advance. A glance at the scene of operations will show that had Prince Charles acted with vigour, had he detached a strong force into Thuringia, drawing to himself the King of Hanover on the one side and Prince Alexander on the other, he would have met the Prussian invasion with vastly superior forces, and had he been as capable as his admirers believed him to be, would have driven them back far into Prussian soil. But, instead of doing this, he replied to the message of the King of Hanover in a manner which could not fail to be read as insulting,[1] and detached by ordinary marches a brigade of cavalry to Meiningen—a perfectly useless proceeding. His punishment was to be sharp and immediate. I may add that no punishment was more richly deserved.

The capitulat on of the Hanoverian army on the 28th of June left the several Prussian divisions which had pursued that army to its destruction free to act against the Federal forces on the Upper Main and at Frankfort. Their leaders acted with a celerity and a dash which left nothing to be desired. Joined under the command of General Vogel von Falkenstein, they numbered 53,000 men. What their position would have been if Prince Charles had opened a way for the retreat of the Hanoverians may be judged from the fact that in that case they would have had to meet an army 125,000 strong. As it was they had before them two armies, each at least equal in strength to their own. Success for them, then, was a question of leadership.

On the 1st of July Von Falkenstein had collected the divisions Manteuffel, Goeben, and Beyer at Eisenach. His object was to press forward so as to interpose between the army of Prince Charles on the Upper Main and that of Prince Alexander at Frankfort. Prince Charles, scenting the danger, had transmitted orders to Prince Alexander to join him by way of Hanau, Fulda, and Hünfeld, whilst he moved with his army into the Fuldathal; pushing two divisions forward to Dermbach, and a strong cavalry division to the left to assure the junction with the 8th corps (Prince Alexander's). On the 4th of July, this cavalry division came in sharp contact at

[1] Hozier's *The Seven Weeks' War*, Vol. II. page 9. 'Prince Charles only replied that an army of 19,000 men ought to be able to cut its way through.'

Combats at Dermbach and Kissingen.

Hünfeld with the advanced guard of the Prussian division, Beyer marching by the highroad to Geysa, whilst Goeben was bending towards the left to take the Bavarians at Dermbach, and Manteuffel was following as a reserve to both. The Bavarian cavalry, thrown into disorder by the artillery fire of Beyer, fell back rapidly. Meanwhile Goeben had caught the two Bavarian divisions at Dermbach, had attacked them vigorously, but had made little impression upon their superior numbers. Towards evening he drew off. Both sides claimed the victory, but there can be no doubt that the advantage rested with the Bavarians, for they had repulsed a formidable attack. The next day the entire Bavarian army moved southwards to effect a junction with Prince Alexander. To prevent or to neutralise the effects of this junction Goeben pressed on by way of Fulda, and caught the Bavarian army at Kissingen on the 10th. The fact that the Bavarian army was spread over a distance of twenty-five miles, whilst he was supported at a lesser distance by two divisions, gave Goeben an advantage of which he made the fullest use. The Bavarian troops in the town and on the neighbouring heights were indeed well placed, but the vigour of Goeben's attack bore down all opposition. His men forced their way into the streets, drove the Bavarians from the town and from the heights behind it, and compelled them to retreat on Hasfurt. Schweinfurt, and Würzburg on the Main. On the same day the division Beyer, after a sharp combat, had occupied Hammelburg, twelve and a half miles from Kissingen, and that of Manteuffel had driven the enemy from Waldasechach and Hausen. Prince Charles, after the retreat from Kissingen, had established his headquarters at Schweinfurt. To hinder a junction between him and the Federal army Von Falkenstein made a sudden dash on

Aschaffenburg. On the 13th of July he smote, at Fronhofen and Laufach, a Hessian division sent thither by Prince Alexander, and on the 14th, in front of Aschaffenburg, defeated an Austrian division of the same army. The Prussians then stormed the town. The consequence of this success was the evacuation of Frankfort by the Federal army, and the entry therein, on the 16th of July, of General Von Falkenstein. Biberich and Darmstadt followed the example of Frankfort in submitting to the Prussians.

In consequence of the forward march of the three Prussian armies which had fought at Königgrätz from Bohemia the King had deemed it necessary to appoint a Prussian Governor-General of that kingdom, and had selected for the post the victorious general Vogel von Falkenstein. Manteuffel replaced him in command of the main army, increased now to a strength of 65,000 men. Meanwhile the Bavarian and the Federal armies had succeeded in approaching each other near Würzburg. They might easily have effected a real junction, but to delay this as much as possible Manteuffel marched against the Federal army, crosssed on the 24th of July the river Tauber, in the face of the Hessian division at Wertheim, of the Würtembergers at Tauberbischofsheim, and of the Badeners at Werbach. Whilst one of his divisions stormed Hochhausen and Werbach with great resolution another forced its way into Tauberbischofsheim. Here the fight was very severe. The Würtembergers were commanded by Von Hardegg, a capable officer, and five times did this brave man lead forward his troops for the recovery of the village. But the Prussians would not quit their hold. The Federal army then fell back upon a strong position at Gerchstein, linked on its right to the Bavarian army at Helmstadt and Uettingen.

End of the Campaign. 187

Manteuffel attacked this position on the 25th. He sent Goeben against the Federal troops in Gerchsheim, Beyer against the Bavarians at Helmstadt, holding in reserve the division Fliess, who had succeeded to its command. If there had been the slightest unity in the counsels of the allies, or the least pretence to leadership on the part of any one of their commanders, it had been possible to inflict a severe blow on the assailants, for two Prussian divisions were attacking posts strongly held and supported by a powerful army. But the imbecility which had characterised the movements of Prince Charles of Bavaria was never more manifest than on this occasion. The Prussians gained a footing in the villages attacked, the enemy falling back. And although the following morning Prince Charles talked loudly of attacking, second thoughts prevailed, and he resolved to retreat across the Main. But the Prussians gave him no rest. On the 26th they threatened his rearguard at Helmstadt. He succeeded, however, in taking his army across the Main at Würzburg, and occupied a position to the east of that town. The indefatigable Prussians followed him close, and on the 27th opened a fire against the fortress of Marienburg, on the hill opposite Würzburg. Such was the position when the information reached the combatants that an armistice had been concluded and that operations were to cease.

A German writer, Heinrich Blankenburg, who has written an account of the war of 1866, has stated that 'if a laurel branch could be awarded to Prince Alexander of Hesse, Prince Charles of Bavaria ought to have received a crown of poppies.'[1] That they both had splendid

[1] See also Malet's *Overthrow of the Germanic Confederation by Prussia in 1866*. The detailed account of the operations of the Main army in this book leaves nothing to be desired.

fighting material was proved four years later in France. But, combating in their own territories against half their number—that half led, however, by men who knew their own mind—they gave a living proof to the world that an army of lions can do nothing when their leaders are incompetent. 'How not to do it' was stamped upon all the manœuvres of Prince Charles and his associates.

How was the armistice referred to in this page brought about? We left the army of Benedek retreating from the field of Königgrätz on the evening of the 3d of July. We have seen him taking the road leading to Olmütz, whilst Gablenz, with the 10th corps, the three heavy and one light cavalry divisions, took the road direct to Vienna. The rearguard was formed of the 8th corps and the Saxons, and remained one march behind the main army. The Prussians were not in a condition to follow Benedek before four o'clock on the afternoon of the 4th, so that the Austrian commander had a start of nearly twenty-four hours.

The effect in Vienna of the results of the battle made itself felt at once. Benedek was removed from his command, though authorised to hold it pending the arrival of his successor, the victor of Custoza; Venetia was ceded to the Emperor of the French in the hope that this act of renunciation would procure a cessation of hostilities in Italy; the army which had fought at Custoza was ordered to Vienna; Benedek was directed to send the three generals he had placed under arrest on the morning of the battle to Vienna to be tried.

It is unnecessary, in a work of this character, to note in detail the marches of the beaten and victorious armies in their progress eastward. It must suffice to state that on the 7th of July the 3d and 5th corps of the Austrian army were sent by railway to Vienna; that Archduke

Albert assumed the command-in-chief on the 12th; that he took a position at Floridsdorf, on the north bank of the Danube, three miles from the city, and there intrenched himself; that he called to him the army still remaining under Benedek, and which that general had caused to halt at Olmütz. When Benedek attempted, on the 14th of July, to obey this order, the King of Prussia was at Brünn, and the Austrian commander found the 2d army was so disposed as to bar the direct road from Olmütz to Vienna. In attempting, on the 14th, to break out in that direction, he received a very severe slap at Tobitschan. But, on the 16th, he made his way to Pressburg, across the Little Carpathians. It was only by dint of hard marching over terrible roads that he accomplished this task. The Prussians, meanwhile, had pressed on by the direct roads, and on the 18th of July their King fixed his headquarters at Nikolsburg, in Moravia, fifteen miles from Vienna, having under him 194,000 tried soldiers, and, supporting them in the second line, 49,600 men ready for immediate action.

Perhaps no one in all Europe had been so disappointed at the short duration of the war as the French Emperor. Instead of there being an exhaustive contest, draining the resources of the two nations, and rendering both anxious to obtain the services of an ally or a mediator, this war had been practically decided just a fortnight after it had broken out. Determined, however, to exercise if possible some influence in German affairs, Napoleon III. had despatched to the headquarters of King William, as soon as he had heard the result of the decisive battle, an agent to urge the agreement to an armistice for three days. The King of Prussia had agreed to the proposal on certain conditions, but the Emperor of Austria had declined to accept conditions, which, he stated, were advantageous only to Prussia. The war therefore continued. But the King of Prussia had scarcely set foot in the castle of Nikolsburg when he was approached by Count Benedetti, the French ambassador, who had arrived there before him, with fresh proposals for an armistice. The King forwarded the proposals to Vienna, with the expression of his willingness to treat.

The position of Austria was at the moment very critical. Her second army occupied an intrenched camp in front of Vienna. Benedek, with the greater portion of the first army, was at Pressburg, in communication with the Archduke, yet forty English miles distant from Vienna. Immediately behind both was Hungary, not yet reconciled to the House of Habsburg, the feelings of her people liable to be roused by the formation at Neisse, in Silesia, of a Hungarian legion, under the famous Klapka, ready to cross the Jablunka pass into Hungary, and to urge a general outburst against Austria. A defeat at Floridsdorf; the intervention of the Prussian army between that place and Pressburg, difficult though not impossible; the possibility of a rising in Hungary —all these were dangers which had to be considered. They were considered, and the Emperor finally resolved to accept an armistice which would disclose to him whether the terms upon which Prussia would insist constituted a danger greater than those which a continuance of the war would involve. He despatched a reply to that effect on the evening of the 21st, and on the following day negotiations were begun.

Before the five days had passed preliminiaries were agreed and signed. These were to the effect (1) that, with the exception of the Venetian territories of which the Emperor of Austria had already disposed, the dominions of the Austrian Emperor should remain intact; (2) that the Emperor of Austria should recognise the dissolution of the German Federation, agree to a new arrangement of the ties which should unite Austria to Germany, promise to recognise the North-German Federation and a South-German Federation about to be formed, and not to interfere with either; (3) that the Emperor should transfer to the King of Prussia his rights over Schleswig and Holstein;[1] (4) that Austria should pay to Prussia a war indemnity of 40,000,000 thalers, of which one-half should be in cash—15,000,000 to represent the value of Austria's cession of the Elbe duchies, and 5,000,000 the cost of provisioning the Prussian army so long as it should remain in Austrian territory; (5) that, at the express desire of Austria, Prussia would leave the kingdom of Saxony in the state as to territory in which it was at the beginning of the war, reserving to herself the right to make special provisions with that kingdom regarding the war indemnity it should pay and the terms on which it should enter the North-German Federation, Austria promising to recognise all the territorial changes Prussia might see fit to make in North Germany.

The sixth article provided for the agreement of the King of Italy to the above terms; the seventh for the ratification of the treaty within two months; the ninth for the duration of the armistice for two months from the 2d of August.

It may be convenient here to add that the above terms were the basis of the definitive treaty which was signed at Prague on the 23d of August following.

[1] To this, at the instigation of the French Emperor, was added a clause, absolutely illusory in practice, providing for the cession of the northern districts of Schleswig to Denmark if the people of those districts should by a free vote express their desire to be so united.

Such was the treaty which terminated the war of 1866 between Austria and Prussia. The reader will not fail to note that whilst the second article excluded Austria from the rest of Germany, and gave to Prussia the right to make her own terms with the several kingdoms and principalities which, up to 1866, had regarded Austria as their head, and which had adhered to her in the quarrel forced by the North on the South; it accorded likewise to Prussia, in the fifth article, the power to annex Hanover, electoral Hesse, Nassau, and Frankfort, for, although those places were not mentioned, Austria renounced her right to interfere in any way with the territorial dispositions Prussia might choose to make. And, as was to be expected, she made without scruple those which contributed to her own advantage.

But the advantages derived by Prussia from the war were in reality far greater than a casual reader might gather from a perusal of the above analysis. What they were I propose now briefly to consider.

The war of 1866 had been designed deliberately by Count Bismarck for the effecting of two purposes: the one the driving of Austria out of Germany, the other the forming of a new federation of all the other States of Germany, of which Prussia should be the dominant power, the sole controller, the supreme arbiter. The first object had, we have seen, been secured for her by the treaty of Prague. To realise the other without further fighting it was necessary to obtain the assent of the French Emperor. The eyes of that potentate had not even then been fully opened to the fact that, during the many conversations between himself and Bismarck preceding the war, the latter had completely cajoled him. He still hoped, it might almost be said he still believed that as a return for all that he had done for Prussia;

for the influence he had exercised in cementing the alliance with Italy; for his coldness towards Austria, he might receive some of the coveted spoil. He was soon undeceived. When, during the negotiations at Nikolsburg and Prague, Bismarck mooted to him his project for uniting all Germany, the Austrian provinces excepted, under the leadership of Prussia, the Emperor absolutely refused his concurrence. Then, hoping still to gain something, he proposed a counter project, greatly limiting the power Prussia was anxious to obtain. Bismarck, knowing well with whom he was dealing, rejected his project, throwing out, however, a hint that it might be possible for France to indemnify herself by annexing Belgium. For a moment the Emperor seemed to hesitate. Then, further considering Bismarck's new plan, and thinking he detected in it an element which he could work to the advantage of France, he withdrew his opposition. It was finally arranged, with his approval, that whilst Prussia should not be prevented from annexing Hanover, Electoral Hesse, Nassau, and Frankfort, she should have power to extend to the States south of the Main the right of entering into some kind of national arrangement with the northern league.

In the next chapter I shall have to show that it would have been better for Napoleon III. had he kept entirely aloof from the negotiations between Prussia and the Southern States of Germany. For we shall see how, by his interference, adroitly used by Bismarck, he succeeded in placing in the hands of the King of Prussia the most powerful weapon against France which had been forged since the time of Charlemagne.

CHAPTER XI.

NAPOLEON III. AND BISMARCK — FOUR YEARS OF SMOULDERING IN PARIS AND BERLIN—THE HOHENZOLLERN CANDIDATURE — KING WILLIAM AND BENEDETTI AT EMS—EXCITEMENT IN PARIS—THE BERLIN FICTIONS RENDER WAR INEVITABLE.

ON the very eve of the war the French Emperor had declared alike his conceptions of the reasons for its breaking out and the conclusions to which it pointed. The aspirations of Italy and Prussia, he declared, were natural and just. The former required the completion of its geographical position, an end which would be obtained by the cession of Venetia. Prussia wished to remedy the faulty geographical arrangements which impaired her military action, and to introduce an improved Federal system into Germany. These ends would be accomplished, he declared, by a rearrangement of territory in the north of Germany, and by the creation of an effective union between the secondary German States. As to Austria, by the cession of Venetia to Italy, her strength in Germany would not be impaired. Such a solution of the war, he added, being one of internal arrangement only, would not impose upon France the necessity of rectifying her frontiers.

Such were the professions of the French Emperor before the war. As was usual with all declarations

Position of Napoleon III.

emanating from the same source, the spoken word concealed the secret thought. What that thought was has been too often stated in these pages to require repetition. It was confided to Bismarck at Biarritz and at Paris, and again, by the French ambassador, at Nikolsburg and Prague; and Bismarck, so long as the passive attitude of France was essential to the carrying out of his plans, had encouraged the Emperor to believe that something would come of it. But as soon as he had completed, signed, and sealed the arrangements recorded at the close of the last chapter, Bismarck had no further use for Napoleon III. He had got from the alliance all he wanted. Thenceforward he would have, as he understood thoroughly, to prepare for a struggle with the country the sovereign of which he had cajoled, smoothed with fair promises, and was now about deliberately to throw over.

The position in which Napoleon III. found himself in the autumn of 1866 was one especially galling to a man who for so many years had endeavoured to pose, and who to a very great extent had succeeded in posing, as the arbiter of the continent. He had done much during the fifteen years of his reign. He had largely aided in humbling Russia, had made Italy, had worked hand in hand with England, had increased the territories of France on her south-eastern border, and had made himself a sleeping partner with Bismarck in the attempt to enlarge Prussia. Careful, even prescient, in four of these undertakings, he had absolutely given himself away in the fifth. Whilst Bismarck had been making preparations he had trusted entirely to chance. His best troops were still in Mexico, and the army which remained in France was not ready for war. He had not only hoped, but had regarded it as an absolute certainty that the war would be long, and that it would finally end by leaving in

Germany two great powers, the North and the South, antagonistic to each other; Austria, strengthened possibly by the cession of Silesia ; Prussia, by the incorporation of Hanover; France compensated by the cession of the Rhenish frontier. But he had made not one preparation to realise these dreams. When the war closed so suddenly he was soon to learn that he counted for nothing in the settlement which must follow. He was Samson shorn of his locks. The Delilah of Berlin was now supreme. Delilah's will was law. And that eminent personage had resolved that the French Samson should speedily learn that intrigue, without force to back it, was an impotent factor in the face of a Prussia just emerging victorious from a bloody war, and with her resources rather improved than impaired.

For no sooner had the arrangements with Austria and the States of Southern Germany been completed, than Prussia proceeded to complete the work of incorporation within her own dominions of the territories she had won. Their resources, their troops, were now hers, and by the increased strength which they gave her she was far more powerful than was the Prussia which entered upon the war of 1866.

I have said that the position in which Napoleon III. found himself in the autumn of 1866 was especially galling to a man whose intrigues for fifteen years had resulted in so many brilliant successes. It was soon to become positively humiliating. Without at the moment the power to enforce his demands he continued to urge Prussia, as a compensation for her own increase of territory, to make to France some concessions—at the expense of Germany or of Belgium. Nothing could have better served the purposes of Bismarck than the making of these demands. That eminent statesman had had some

Fatal Effect to France of Napoleon's Intrigues. 197

difficulty in persuading Bavaria and the other States similarly situated to agree to certain territorial arrangements which Prussia regarded as essential. When their resistance was at its greatest Bismarck received the proposition from the French Emperor, presently to be more completely described, to concede to France some portions of Bavarian territory. Instantly German pride took fire. Not only did the minor States drop all their objections, but by a series of secret treaties they entered into an offensive and defensive alliance with Prussia, and engaged to place their entire forces at the disposal of the King in the event of a war with France. Thus the union of Germany, not consummated by the actual war, was brought about by the intrigues of Napoleon III.

A greater fault it was impossible for any ruler of France to commit. But it was by no means a solitary mistake. Napoleon's negotiations regarding the cession of Belgium to France had in the times preceding the war been carried on by conversations, which it was possible to deny, with Bismarck himself, or through secret and unauthorised agents who could be disavowed. But the disappointment engendered by the result of the war of 1866 led the Emperor to bolder and more compromising measures. The French Ambassador at the court of Berlin had been, since November 1864, Count Vincent Benedetti, the able representative of a Corsican family. In his intrigues regarding cessions of territory Napoleon III. had, up to the time of the conclusion of the war of 1866, gone behind the back of Benedetti. So ignorant was that minister of those intrigues that, just before the outbreak of the war, he had reported to his master the details of a conversation he had held with Bismarck, to the effect that Count Bismarck, to assure himself of French neutrality, though he would rather retire from public life than cede the Rhenish frontier, had declared that he believed it might be possible to obtain the King's sanction to the cession of the district of Trèves, which, with Luxemburg and parts of Belgium or Switzerland, would give France such an improved frontier as would satisfy her. But Benedetti added that Bismarck was the only man in Prussia who would willingly make any cession of territory whatever, and that the public demand for any such cession on the part of France would rouse a general feeling of indignation against her. The absolute ignorance of the French ambassador of the plottings of his master is proved by the fact that he concluded his despatch by stating that he had abruptly closed the discussion, not wishing to leave on the mind of Count Bismarck the impression that any scheme involving the cession of Belgian or Swiss territory would be countenanced at Paris.

The war then broke out. Almost immediately on its conclusion, whilst the late combatants were negotiating at Nikolsburg and Prague, Benedetti, obeying his master's orders, demanded the cession of the Bavarian Palatinate, of the portion of Hesse-Darmstadt west of the Rhine, including Mayence, and of the strip of Prussian territory on the Saar which had been taken from France in 1815. According to Bismarck, Benedetti supported this demand with a threat of war in case it should be refused, but this is most improbable. There can be no doubt, however, that Bismarck categorically refused the demand. Benedetti then started for Paris to report in person the result of his conversation. His return produced a ministerial crisis. The minister for foreign affairs, Drouyn de Lhuys, had been of opinion that the dignity of France required that such a demand, if made, should be supported by arms. As the Emperor, however, could not bring himself to declare war for a purpose which would expose him to the denunciation of Europe, Drouyn de Lhuys resigned, and Napoleon III. bade Benedetti to return to Berlin, and endeavour to obtain, in the place of the frontier on the Rhine, the cession of Belgium. Of the circumstances which followed his return the following account will, I believe, bear investigation.

Englishmen who took a deep interest in the outbreak in 1870 of the war between France and Germany will not fail to remember that, in the July of that year, Bismarck endeavoured to gain the sympathies of Europe by publishing, amongst many other matters, an account of a proposal made to him in the autumn of 1866 by Count Benedetti, on behalf of the French Emperor, to obtain the sanction of Prussia for the incorporation of Belgium with France. Bismarck supported his statement by a draft treaty, in the handwriting of Benedetti, which contained (1) the recognition by France of the conquests made by Prussia during the war; (2) the promise of the King of Prussia to facilitate the acquisition of Luxemburg by France; (3) the promise of the Emperor not to oppose a Federal union of the Northern and Southern States of Germany to the exclusion of Austria; (4) 'The King of Prussia, in case the Emperor should enter or conquer Belgium, will support him in arms against any opposing power'; (5) there should be a treaty offensive and defensive between the contracting parties.[1]

There can be no doubt that such a proposition was made by Benedetti; but there can be as little that the circumstances accompanying it were far different from those which Bismarck would have had the world believe. He had often dangled before the French Emperor the

[1] The text of this treaty was published in the *Times* of July 25, 1870.

project of the annexation of Belgium. It had been a card kept in his sleeve to show but not to play. He had shown it at the time of the negotiations of Nikolsburg. That he ever intended to play it is quite another matter. For some years prior to 1866 he had been accustomed to cajole Napoleon, and he believed he could continue to cajole him until he should be able to dispense with his aid, or be prepared for the action which he even then said would be necessary for the complete consolidation of Germany. To him, then, the talk about the cession of Belgium was an old story.

It was not so with Benedetti. I have already shown that on this point the ambassador had never been admitted into the confidence of his master. He knew nothing of the hints, the innuendos, the whisperings of Biarritz and Paris. He had, we have seen, slighted Bismarck's proposal, when, only shortly before, that statesman had alluded to the possibility of France indemnifying herself at the expense of Belgium, not wishing, he said, to leave on the mind of the German statesman the impression that the Emperor would even listen to such an idea. In this respect his recent visit to Paris had undeceived him. He had found his master 'hungry' for some sort of compensation, caring not at all at whose expense that compensation should be. Doubtless he had repeated to his master the words used by Bismarck on the occasion just referred to, and he had returned to Berlin with express injunctions to bring Bismarck to book on the subject of Belgium.

At the historical interview, then, Benedetti had begun by referring the Prussian foreign minister to the conversation previously held, and had added that the Emperor his master was prepared to negotiate on the basis which had been then suggested by his listener. Bismarck, far from showing surprise or indignation, at once assented to the principle, and proceeded to sketch out verbally the draft treaty referred to in the preceding page. From the dictation of Bismarck Benedetti wrote the draft. Further, in his report to his master, Benedetti stated that he had found Bismarck keenly anxious to extend the federating principle to the German States south of the Main, and most anxious for the support of France in carrying out the plans he had formed in that respect; that he seemed to be perfectly sincere with regard to Belgium. At a later period Benedetti wrote that the negotiation only failed because the Emperor required that the fortresses in Southern Germany should be held by the States to which they belonged. Before that point could be settled General Manteuffel, who had been despatched to St Petersburg to negotiate an intimate union with Russia, returned with the treaty between the two powers signed and sealed. Then the assistance of France became unnecessary. The negotiation regarding Belgium was dropped, and the French Emperor was relegated, in the mind of Bismarck, to the position of a sucked out orange.

The enemies of the Emperor Napoleon III., in France, have said, and said truly, that 'every error which it was possible to commit had been committed, in 1866, by that prince.' He was now to reap the fruits of his miscalculations and his intrigues. It is certain that towards the close of the year 1866 his eyes were opened to the fact that from the first to the last Bismarck had fooled him. He had been beaten at every point. He had previously assisted to build a united Italy to the south-east of France. Now against his interests, against his most cherished wishes, he had assisted in forming a united Germany on his north-east frontier. Nor had his humiliations ended there. The termination of the civil war in America had brought him a summons from the United States government, courteous, it is true, but still a summons, to withdraw his troops from Mexico. The latest moment to which he could defer acting on the mandate of the United States was the spring of 1867. Doubtless the bringing back to France of 25,000 trained troops was in itself an advantage, but it was a humiliation to move them at the dictation of a foreign power. Napoleon had to forfeit the word he had plighted to the prince he had induced to proceed on an adventurous mission to Mexico. His reputation suffered enormously in consequence, and he, who for the first fifteen years of his reign had been accepted as the most astute of princes, began to be regarded as a vacillating dreamer, without honour, and without practical ability. He was growing prematurely old, he was suffering from a disease which incapacitated him from hard work, and his supporters were falling from him. His failures, his loss of prestige, his declining health were producing an uneasy feeling in the country. The Emperor himself began to be anxious as to the future of the dynasty of which he had been the second founder. To rehabilitate himself and his family in the eyes of Frenchmen he must do something. Seeking for a sensation, his eyes turned on Luxemburg, a territory connected with the crown of Holland, but whose fortress, the strongest in Europe, was garrisoned, up to 1866, as a part of the German Federation by Prussian troops. For the transfer of this duchy, possessing 998 square miles, to France the Emperor entered into negotiations with the King of Holland.

The bargain was struck. Before, however, the transfer could take place Bismarck, who had been privy to and had not objected to the Emperor's plan, suddenly informed the Emperor that it could not be. True it was

Bismarck prevents Acquisition of Luxemburg. 203

that during the negotiations of the previous year he had himself suggested the cession of Luxemburg to France. True it was that since 1866 Luxemburg had not been included in the North German Federation. But its fortress was garrisoned by Prussian soldiers. It could not be taken by France until the Prussian garrison should have departed. Bismarck was resolved that for the purpose desired by the Emperor Napoleon they should never depart. Accordingly he gave it to be understood at Paris that the annexation of Luxemburg to France was impossible. And, to give emphasis to his declaration, he published about the same time the treaties Prussia had made with the Southern States of Germany, treaties which bound them to place their armies at the disposal of Prussia in the event of a war with France.

The action of Bismarck in thus denouncing an arrangement which he himself had in the preceding year cordially recommended, and to which he had given his private approval, was the first outspoken proof that he had broken absolutely with Napoleon III. He wanted nothing more from France. He knew that, in the interests of Germany, not yet thoroughly consolidated, it would be necessary to have recourse once more, and that within a measurable distance, to his favourite nostrum of 'blood and iron,' and he regarded the proposed cession of Luxemburg to France as a question which would sufficiently excite the German mind to make them regard it as an aggression on the part of France at all costs to be repelled. France, he was aware, was not ready for war. The German army could be mobilised certainly within a fortnight. Despite all that he had said, all that he had promised, under circumstances which no longer existed, was it politic, he asked himself, if it could be prevented, to allow a neighbour with whom it was logically certain that Germany would within a brief period be at war to possess herself of the strongest fortress in Europe, possessing a strategical position of vital importance, on the Franco-German frontier? It was this last consideration which decided him to urge his master, who was bound by no promises, to refuse the assent of Prussia to the transaction.

It was at this crisis that Austria reappeared on the scene. The Emperor Francis Joseph, though terribly disappointed at the result of the war which had been forced upon him, had on its conclusion wisely resolved to put an end to that internal quarrel which at a critical period of the war had alienated from him the thorough support of his Hungarian subjects. On the 30th of October 1866, therefore, he had called to the Foreign Office Count Beust, formerly minister to the King of Saxony, and had given him *carte blanche* to come to an understanding with the Magyars. Beust gave to the task all the powers which had given him a European reputation. He first made a commercial treaty with France, then after discussions with the chiefs of the several parties he convoked an extraordinary Diet for the 2d of February 1867. On the 7th he announced autonomy for Hungary. On the 17th the Emperor nominated a separate ministry, with Count Andrassy as president for Hungary. All went well: the enthusiasm was tremendous, the reconciliation perfect. On the 7th of June the Emperor and Empress were crowned at Pest King and Queen of Hungary.

The bases of this reconciliation having been known early in the year it can easily be understood why Austria, notwithstanding her humiliation in the autumn of 1866, should step forward in the spring of 1867, endowed with a new life, and assume her proper position in European politics. She confined herself to making the practical

The Luxemburg Question settled. 205

suggestion that Luxemburg should be united to Belgium, and that France should be indemnified by a small district of Belgian territory. This was an arrangement which would at the same time have satisfied the *amour propre* of France and have been accepted at Berlin. At the critical moment, however, the person who would have benefited the most from the transaction, the King of the Belgians, nipped it in the bud by declaring that he would cede no territory to France. Napoleon III., incensed at the double dealing of Bismarck, resolved then to take up the glove thrown from Berlin, on such grounds as would secure for him the sympathy of Europe. There was no question but that Prussia had no right to garrison the fortress of Luxemburg. The connection of the province of that name with Germany had been a matter of past history. The great bulk of the people of the province not only were not Germans, but they had no sympathy with German ways. Hence Napoleon III. was within his right when he insisted that the Prussian garrison should evacuate the fortress (March 1867), and made preparations to enforce his demand. Prussia refused to withdraw her troops. Then the government of St Petersburg stepped in with a proposal that the question should be settled by a conference of the powers at London. This was agreed to with certain restrictions by the two powers chiefly concerned. The conference assembled at London on the 7th of May. On the 11th its deliberations were completed and an agreement was signed. By this Luxemburg was declared neutral territory under the guarantee of the powers. Prussia was to withdraw her garrison, and the King of Holland undertook to demolish the fortifications of the fortress and to maintain it as an open town. These conditions were duly carried out.

If the result was a slight diplomatic triumph for France, and in a military sense a real gain—for it deprived Prussia of a fortress which in the event of a war with France she might have utilised with great effect—yet it made clear to the mind of Napoleon III., perhaps for the first time, the extent to which Bismarck had fooled him. No man likes to be duped, and there are few who would not have displayed a sense of annoyance more openly than did the French Emperor. But, with a great many faults, Napoleon possessed the gift of reticence, and from this time forward he set himself to the task of building up alliances which would help France in the future. It was for this object that in August of the same year, accompanied by the Empress, he met the Emperor and Empress of Austria at Salzburg, and in November received the same Emperor at the Tuileries. At the same palace the Austrian ambassador, Prince Metternich, became a *persona gratissima*. He threw himself heart and soul into the French project. The wish of France and Austria was to regain for the latter her position in Germany. The one obstacle in the way of this policy was the resistance of the Hungarian ministry. It was because Austria had ceased to be, in the sense attributable to the term, a German power, that Hungary had obtained an equal position in the counsels of the empire, and she had neither interest nor inclination to recover for the joint Empire a position which would not fail to diminish her own influence. Yet, notwithstanding this, the intimacy between the emperors and their ministers became more and more consolidated, and resulted in mutual promises of support in the event of war with Prussia. So intimate indeed did the relations become that in the winter of 1870 the Archduke Albert, the victor of Custoza, visited Paris, and a French general

The French Emperor's Policy regarding Rome.

visited Vienna for the purpose of arranging a plan of campaign in the event of war.

Nor was Napoleon III. less intent upon gaining Italy. But for the unauthorised attempt of Garibaldi to seize Rome in November 1867 it is probable that a clear understanding between the rulers might have been arrived at. But the battle of Mentana, the insolent language of the very worst of the Napoleonic generals, Du Failly, the declarations of M. Rouher in the French Assembly, and the French reoccupation of Rome, produced a coolness which long prevented a cordial understanding. Eventually, however, the Austrian minister, Count Beust, intervened, and through him an arrangement was arrived at, of which the French Emperor was cognisant, to the effect that, in the event of war between France and Prussia, Austria and Italy should act together defensively.

It will thus be seen that when the year 1870 dawned France had still but shadowy alliances to depend upon. Her continued occupation of Rome prevented, and would always prevent an offensive and defensive alliance with Italy, whilst the opposition of Hungary would operate equally to deter the Austrian Empire from undertaking a war for the obtaining of objects to which Hungary was opposed. The position of France may fairly be described as a position of isolation, supported only by the good wishes of the Emperor of Austria and his court and of the King of Italy.

Meanwhile Bismarck had been engaged in strengthening the position his policy had gained for Prussia in 1866. In the three-and-a-half years which had elapsed since the war he had established a customs parliament for all Germany, the precursor he hoped of a National Assembly representing the States to the south as well as those to the north of the Main. He had assimilated the military systems of Bavaria, Saxony, Würtemberg, and Baden to the system of Prussia. His eminent colleague, the war minister Von Roon, had brought to the organising of the new German army all the talent which had made the Prussian army the most formidable in Europe. The defects which the campaign of 1866 had made apparent had been remedied; new weapons, improvements on the needle-gun, had been introduced into the armies of the several States, and, above all, Von Roon had devoted his earnest attention to ensure rapidity of mobilising. In a contest with France the greatest advantage would accrue to the nation whose army should be first in the field. The direction of the State railway system had been governed by the necessity of quick concentration on points deemed to be formidable close to the French frontier. By the beginning of 1870 Germany was as ready for immediate war as she was likely to be for a long time to come.

In some respects, it must be borne in mind, war had become almost a necessity, certainly very desirable, to ensure the perfect union of Germany. The assimilations to which I have referred had not been accomplished without considerable friction. The secondary States had not become reconciled to the system of 'climbing down' in favour of Prussia, of adopting habits till then foreign to them, of coalescing completely with the people they had fought in 1866, to the sole advantage, it seemed to them, of the rulers of that people. They had not yet thoroughly realised that their interests and the interests of Prussia were absolutely identical. It was felt at Berlin that war and only war could remove this feeling: a war for the same interest, against a common enemy, waged, the Berlin clique would take care to impress upon the world, for the defence of the threatened Fatherland. Such a war would obliterate all the petty feelings which combined to produce friction, would remove all jealousies, would, if successful, give to every German State a common renown, and by the introduction of a union complete in name as well as in fact, would satisfy those sentimental aspirations which since 1848 had animated every German heart.

Of the ruler of Prussia, King William, I do not speak. He, I believe, was a thoroughly honest man. He would never knowingly have countenanced intrigue. But, in the hands of the clique, of which Bismarck, Von Roon, and Moltke were the ruling spirits, the king had no chance. He had to be 'managed.' The mode in which he was made to believe that it was the ambition of France, rather than the determination of the 'clique,' which brought about the war of 1870, has now to be described.

Despite the checks he had received since 1866, Napoleon III. still continued to assert, as though it were a power not to be questioned, the prestige of France. It seemed to him the one chance of maintaining his position. He had become very anxious regarding the future of the dynasty he had founded. It had been impossible to conceal from the quick-witted people over whom he ruled the nature and extent of his diplomatic failures. The United States and Prussia had alike forced him to eat the leek, and neither he nor France had digested the food. He was, I must repeat, prematurely old; was suffering from a painful disease, and had long ceased to take that personal interest in the details of State affairs, which had been conspicuous in the earlier days of his reign. In the general elections of May 1869 Paris, Lyons, Marseilles, and other large centres of industry had declared with no uncertain voice against his system of personal government. In the new parliament of May 1869 the various elements which, on a crisis would vote together, constituted an actual majority. Before the formidable array of eminent statesmen who led the various sections of this coalition Napoleon III. gave way. On the 17th of July he modified, in a constitutional sense, the principle upon which his cabinets had theretofore been formed. In August and September, in concert with the Senate, he introduced the principle of ministerial responsiblity. In his speech from the throne on the 29th of November following, he declared himself in favour of liberty, but of liberty based on order; and on the 27th of December he appointed his first constitutional ministry, with a leader of one of the liberal parties, Emil Ollivier, at its head. On the 28th of March 1870, the new ministry laid before the Senate its scheme for a new constitution, to be submitted eventually to the entire nation for sanction. On the 20th of April the constitution was agreed to by the Senate, and on the 8th of May following, the people of France were asked to record their votes for or against the new constitution and the liberal reforms instituted since 1860. The voting was very decisive in favour of the new measures, 7,350,142 recording their assents, and only 1,538,825 dissenting. But the secret gratification of the Emperor was short-lived. When the votes were analysed, it was discovered that more than 50,000 soldiers and sailors had voted against the scheme. The effect of this discovery was to renew in the mind of the Emperor all his mistrusts, and to incline him once again to a policy of adventure.

No long time passed before an opportunity occurred, as he believed, for asserting the prestige of France and gaining a diplomatic victory. For nearly two years the virtual dictator of Spain, General Prim, had been en-

The Hohenzollern Candidature. 211

deavouring to persuade a member of one of the great families of Europe to accept the throne vacated by the departure from the country of Isabella II. He had encountered refusal after refusal. In the summer of 1869 he had sounded a member of the Sigmaringen branch of the Hohenzollern family, Prince Leopold, brother of the present King of Roumania, on the subject. It may be said in passing, that, in opening this negotiation, Prim had no desire to offer an insult to France; for although Prince Leopold bore the name of Hohenzollern, the connection with the ruler of Prussia dated very far back, whilst he was more recently related through the Beauharnais family with Napoleon III. On the other hand, it must be admitted, the friendship of the Sigmaringen branch with the ruling family of Prussia was intimate; the prince's father had been the first prime minister to King William; and it was he, it is believed, who first suggested to the king the appointment of Bismarck to the post of prime minister.

The overtures of General Prim in 1869, secret as they were, very soon reached the ears of the French Emperor, and Benedetti was instructed in the summer of 1869 to inquire at Berlin as to their existence. The reply of Count Bismarck, given on his word of honour, was that the candidature had never been suggested at Berlin. This reply was considered satisfactory, and the project remaining for twelve months undiscussed was regarded as abandoned.

However, in the spring of 1870, it was again renewed, secretly as before, but so effectually, that on the 3rd of July, Paris was startled by the announcement that Prince Leopold of Hohenzollern-Sigmaringen had agreed to accept the vacant throne of Spain, provided the Cortes should confirm his election thereto. Naturally enough, a storm of indignation broke out in Paris. The popular mind, sufficiently excited against Prussia by the manner in which, since 1866, she had persistently thwarted the attempts of French statesmen, eagerly seized the occasion to declaim against the new effort of her neighbour to plant an enemy on the throne of a country peopled by men of the Latin race. The Government, guided by the foreign minister, the Duke of Gramont, fresh from his embassy to Vienna, radiant with the hopes there conceived of a firm alliance between France and Austria, declared to the legislative body, on the 6th of July, that the attempt of a foreign power to place one of its princes on the throne of Charles V. imperilled the interests and the honour of France. This imprudent declaration, which had been drawn up at a council of ministers presided over by the Emperor, rendered the maintenance of peace difficult. It was calculated to inflame alike the two nations, and to render it difficult for the King of Prussia to recede. The one chance of avoiding war was to induce Prince Leopold to resign.

That Napoleon III. wanted war is not for a moment to be supposed; but, for reasons presently to be assigned, he was in a state of mind which might easily cause him to drift into it. It is difficult to suppose that he could have been altogether deceived as to the readiness of the Prussian army for war, the state of unpreparedness of his own. As proof of the former, he had before him the reports of the French military attaché at Berlin, Colonel Stoffel. Of the latter there was abundant evidence at hand, if he had chosen to search for it. But, for some time past, the Emperor had ceased, as I have said, to take personal interest in the details of the several offices of State. He appointed officers whom he thought he could trust, and he believed whatever they chose to report to him. His war-minister, Marshal Lebœuf, was a man who especially enjoyed his confidence. Only one year younger than his master, Lebœuf had the reputation of being an excellent officer. After two years' service on the general staff, he had been appointed in 1832 to the artillery; had served on the general staff in the first expedition against Constantine (1837), and had remained in Africa till 1841; had then served in France in responsible positions until, in 1852, he was promoted to be Colonel. He had served with distinction in the Crimean war, first as Chief of the Staff of the artillery, then as Brigadier-General commanding the artillery before Sebastopol. At the close of the war he was nominated chief of the artillery of the Guards, with the rank of general of division. At Solferino he commanded the artillery, and it was his skilful attack on the Austrian centre which decided the day. In September 1866, he had been employed by his master to hand over Venetia to the Italian plenipotentiaries. In January 1869, he had been nominated commander of the 1st army corps, then having its headquarters at Toulouse; and, on the death of Marshal Niel the following August, had accepted the portfolio of war-minister. He had thus a good record, and a considerable reputation. But history is full of examples of the manner in which great reputations wither when tested by the necessity of action. In the council of ministers of the 6th of July above referred to, Lebœuf had solemnly declared that the French army, whether as regarded its numbers, its arms, its organisation, and its supplies, was ready for war. The contrary was the truth, and no one ought to have known it better than Lebœuf.[1]

---

[1] 'He was neither a great organiser nor a strategist, but had ever shown himself to be an energetic corps-commander and a brave soldier.' Brockhaus, *Conversations-Lexikon*, Vol. IX.

If Lebœuf was regarded as the hand of the French ministry, the Duke of Gramont, at this crisis, was its head. The prime minister, Ollivier, had allowed himself to be seduced, against his better judgment, by the assurances of the one and the confidence of the other. Gramont was all for war. He believed that at the first success of the French arms Austria would strike to recover her lost ascendency in Germany. Napoleon, personally averse to war, was yet anxious regarding his dynasty. A pusillanimous policy, he felt, would endanger the succession of his son. War might regain for him his vanished popularity, might recover for him the prestige lost in 1865-6. He was himself, he thoroughly well knew, unfit to command an army, but he had in Bazaine a general, tried in war, capable, he believed, of rivalling the famous strategists of Germany. Possibly to his enfeebled mind war presented better chances for the future than did peace, especially peace without honour. The French people, especially the mob of Paris, were strongly in favour of war.

If such was the position in Paris in the early days of July 1870, what was it at Berlin? That is a matter which well deserves the consideration which I am about to bestow upon it.

There were three men in the Prussian capital who knew that war with France, sooner or later, was inevitable; who knew that a successful war would cement the union with the south which the Austrian war had begun; who knew that no better occasion for war, provided France could be induced to declare it, would be likely to arise than that provoked by the Hohenzollern candidature; who knew that, whilst Germany was ready, France was unprepared ; who possessed the means, if France should hesitate, of lashing the French people to fury and of exciting the German people to indignation; the means, also, of securing the sympathy of Europe—at least for the moment. These three men possessed the power to control the situation, for whilst one, Von Roon, had trained the army, another, Moltke, had complete mastery over the military situation; the third, Count Bismarck, the author of the war of 1866, had resolved to complete the work then achieved by a final demonstration of the efficacy of 'Blood and Iron' to solve political differences. Their one difficulty lay with the King. William I. was too honest, too upright, to sanction measures which could not bear the light of day. But William had been imbued with a thorough distrust of Napoleonic aims and Napoleonic policy, and a means might, through that channel, be found of 'managing' him.

Such being the situations at Paris and Berlin, it remains for us to record the events as they followed.

We have seen how the French minister for foreign affairs, the Duke of Gramont, an ardent partisan for war with Prussia, had obtained the control of the French cabinet. On the night of the 6th of July he had despatched directions to Benedetti, still representing France at Berlin, to proceed at once to Ems, where the King was taking the waters, and to demand that, as the only means of averting war, he should direct Prince Leopold to revoke his acceptance of the Spanish crown; further, that he, the King, should give an assurance that the candidature should not be renewed. Benedetti obeyed, saw the King on the 9th, represented to him the excitement which the news of Prince Leopold's acceptance had caused in Paris, the consequent danger of the situation, the advantage of the continuance of peace between the two countries, the impossibility of maintaining it if the candidature were maintained. He concluded by explaining, in a manner at once courteous and deferential, the requirements of his cabinet. The King, who had received from Berlin an intimation of the demands which Benedetti would make, and who was probably really concerned at the results which had followed Prince Leopold's acceptance of the Spanish crown, had, before the interview, taken such measures as he thought would ensure that prince's renunciation, and, with it, the maintenance of peace. He was able, therefore, whilst asserting his position as the Head of the Hohenzollern family, to assure the French ambassador that he had already entered into negotiations with Prince Leopold and his father, and that he expected shortly to receive a favourable reply from Sigmaringen. Had the matter rested with Benedetti, the incident would have been practically at an end. The ambassador recognised that the King had made a serious and spontaneous effort to avoid war. In reporting the details of the interview to Gramont, he laid stress on this point, and suggested that a display of a little moderation on both sides would gain for France a diplomatic triumph without the dangers of war.

This despatch produced in the highest circles in Paris a revulsion in favour of peace. Napoleon III., never an earnest advocate for war, now openly joined the party which was struggling for peace. On the 11th there was a pause in the military preparations. Gramont, however, still maintained his warlike attitude. He replied to Benedetti's despatch in the spirit of a madman. And although, on the 12th, it became known in Paris that a telegram from Prince Leopold's father had been received at Madrid, withdrawing the prince's candidature, Gramont took advantage of it only to press upon his ambassador the obtaining from the Prussian King guarantees against its renewal. But, except by Gramont and the few extremists, peace was regarded as assured. The prime minister, Ollivier, announced to the Legislative Chamber the withdrawal of Prince Leopold's candidature, and congratulations were exchanged on all sides. But Gramont was apparently resolved to force on war. In an interview with the Prussian ambassador at Paris, Baron Werther, he sketched a letter which he proposed King William should write to the Emperor. In this the King was to state that, in sanctioning the candidature of Prince Leopold, he had meant no offence to the French nation, and that in associating himself with the withdrawal of that candidature, he desired that all misunderstandings between the two governments should cease. Baron Werther promptly despatched this proposition to Ems.

This despatch placed in the hands of the war party at Berlin the weapon it required. To them it was a power to influence and control the King. On the morning on which it reached Ems, Benedetti, before its arrival, had seen the King, and had received from him a promise, that as soon as the expected letter from Sigmaringen should reach his hand, he would send for him. A little later arrived the express from Baron Werther with Bismarck's comments thereupon. Its contents deeply offended the King. So much so, indeed, that when an hour later, the letter from Sigmaringen arrived, he contented himself with sending an aide-de-camp to Benedetti with a message, to the effect that a letter had been received from Prince Anthony withdrawing his son's acceptance, and that the matter was at an end. Benedetti requested the aide-de-camp to inform the King that his instructions compelled him to ask for a guarantee against the renewal of the candidature. The aide-de-camp delivered the message, and returned with the answer that the King gave his entire approval to the withdrawal of the candidature, but that he could do no more. Benedetti then begged for an audience. The King replied, that as he had said his last word an audience was useless. The negotiations between the King and the ambassador were conducted with the most perfect courtesy, and the following morning the two exalted personages took leave of one another at the railway station with the usual marks of respect.[1]

Still peace was possible. The peace-party at Paris was gaining ground. The King of Prussia had indeed declined to give the guarantee demanded by Gramont, or to sign the letter which that nobleman had dictated, but the withdrawal of the candidature had been absolute. From the transaction the French had obtained all the glory. They had won a diplomatic triumph. Had the matter rested there, the Hohenzollern candidature would have caused no war. This was felt alike at Paris and at Berlin. If nothing had emanated from Berlin, the war party in Paris must have succumbed. There was no material left whence to evoke a war-cry. France had demanded the withdrawal of the Hohenzollern candidate, and the Hohenzollern candidate had been withdrawn. There was surely nothing left to fight for.

If this fact was patent to the thoughtful politicians of Paris, still more evident was it to the triumvirate at Berlin. There was, then, they felt, to be no war. The opportunity was slipping from their hands. Unless they could do something to rouse to passion-heat the subsiding excitement of the Parisian mob, the chance was gone never, under such favourable circumstances to return.

[1] The third volume of that painstaking and brilliant work, the *History of Modern Europe*, by the late Mr Fyffe, contains full and accurate particulars of the events which preceded the war of 1870-1.

Bismarck applies the Match to the Flame. 219

But the brain of the statesman who had annexed Hanover and driven Austria out of Germany was equal to the occasion. A few hours later a telegram was officially published at Berlin, stating, in such terms as to convey the impression that the French ambassador had rudely attempted to force his presence on the King, that the latter had thereupon refused to receive the ambassador, and had informed him by an aide-de-camp that he had nothing more to communicate to him. This telegram was sent to the representatives of Prussia at most of the European courts, and to her agents in every German capital. Inspired paragraphs, stating in broader language the same facts in an exaggerated form, appeared in all the important German newspapers, and were despatched to the Paris papers by their correspondents. It was circumstantially stated in these that Benedetti had forced himself on the King on the promenade at Ems, and that, in the presence of a large company, the King of Prussia had turned his back on the French ambassador. The authors of these paragraphs thoroughly understood the peoples they were really addressing. To the German people it meant that the French ambassador had insulted the Prussian King; to the French, that the Prussian King had deliberately insulted France in the person of her ambassador.

In France, which Bismarck had gauged to the core, these demi-official paragraphs were as the application of a match to gunpowder. It was neither the vapourings of Gramont, the waverings of the Emperor, nor the persuasive powers of the Empress, which caused the war of 1870; it was the paragraphs dictated at the Foreign office of Berlin. The effect they produced in Paris was precisely the effect which their author intended they should produce. They reached the French capital on the

14th. On that day the Cabinet met, for the first time, at eleven o'clock, before the fictions manufactured at Berlin had arrived. At that Council the peace-party, prominent among the members of which was the Emperor, had a decided majority. But when the midday post came in, bringing the manufactured stories of the insult offered to the French ambassador at Ems, there occurred, as the astute wire-puller at Berlin had calculated, a complete revulsion. For the second time that day the Cabinet met, and at this, though the Emperor still declared for peace, great agitation prevailed. It broke up, having decided only to call out the reserves. But, upon the excitable population of Paris, the story of the insult had a deeper and wider-reaching effect. Crowds assembled in all the public places; strong bodies of men paraded the streets, calling out for revenge, and for a march on Berlin. It was partly to the influence of those demonstrations, ever increasing in number and turbulence, partly to the earnest solicitations of many of those about him, that the Emperor at last give way. Shortly before midnight a third Cabinet Council met, and at that it was resolved to declare war.

The reader will not fail to note, that the immediate cause of the Franco-German war of 1870, was the concocted story of the insults which had not been offered to the French ambassador at Ems; and that that story was manufactured at Berlin for the purpose of exciting France to war.

The next day the Prime Minister, Ollivier, announced to the Assembly that France had declared war against Prussia, and demanded supplies for carrying it on. The Assembly contained a large number of sensible men, many of them, like M. Thiers, life-long opponents of the Empire. Yet it was soon seen that the madness which had seized the people in the streets had infected also the legislators. Not one voice was raised against the war because it was, in itself, unjust. Thiers simply objected to it as inopportune, and declared the occasion badly chosen. Of all the members only ten voted against the granting of the supplies.

The Prime Minister, Ollivier, carried away either by the popular enthusiasm, or by the conviction that further resistance to the cry for war was impossible, declared that he entered on the war with a light heart,[1] whilst the War Minister, Lebœuf, when asked if the army was ready for war, replied gaily that not even a button was wanting to the men's gaiters.

But war has been declared. In the next chapter we shall consider the number of the combatants on both sides, their resources, their leaders, and their modes of operation.

[1] 'They' (Ollivier and many of his colleagues) 'discovered when it was too late that the supposed national impulse which they had thought irresistible was but the outcry of a noisy minority. The reports of their own officers informed them that in sixteen alone of the eighty-seven departments of France was the war popular. In the other seventy-one it was accepted with hesitation or regret.' (Fyffe, Vol. III. page 421.)

CHAPTER XII.

THE FRANCO-GERMAN WAR—THE NUMBERS AND RESOURCES OF THE COMBATANTS—THE LEADERS ON BOTH SIDES—AUSTRIA AND ITALY—SAARBRUCKEN, WÖRTH, SPICHEREN.

AT midnight, on the 14th of July, France had resolved on war with Prussia. On the morning of the 15th, the order was issued for the mobilisation of her forces, and for their concentration on the Prussian frontier.

The French field army, called at the outset the 'Army of the Rhine,' consisted nominally of 336,000 men with 924 guns. It was considered that, of these, 300,000 would be available for the initial operations.[1] The infantry of the army was provided with a breach-loading weapon, called after its inventor the Chassepot. The Chassepot was a weapon in all respects superior to the famous needle-gun, which was still the weapon of the Prussian army. Attached likewise to the divisional artillery was a machine gun called the Mitrailleuse, from which great things were expected. But this gun had been manufactured with a secrecy which, whilst it prevented foreign inspection, had withheld also the knowledge of its mechanism from the soldiers who were to work it. In the field, therefore, it proved a failure.

Since the Crimean and Austrian wars, whilst the armies of the other European States had advanced in

[1] The actual number reached only 250,000.

efficiency, the French army had deteriorated. The reason was that favouritism rather than merit had been made the road to court favour. The officers who had pointed to the training of the Prussian soldiers, as indicating the necessity for the adoption of similar modes for the French army, had been laughed at and left in the cold. The consequence was, that for ten years prior to the war of 1870, the French army had received instruction only of the most superficial character. It had been considered sufficient if the soldiers were brought to the point of making a good show on the parade ground. Little more had been required of them. Field training and musketry training had been alike neglected. The officers had ceased to study, and the Government had taken no pains to instruct them. What was more vicious still, the alienation between officers and men, which had been noticed even in the war of 1859, had widened. The officers generally had ceased to take the smallest interest in the comfort of the men in camp or in quarters. These matters were left to the non-commissioned officers. Needless to add, they were not always properly attended to. The consequences are thus stated by an English critic, from whose exhaustive work I shall be obliged often to quote:[1] 'Save in the guard and Algerian regiments alone the commissioned ranks had but little knowledge of or sympathy with the privates, the privates little respect or affection for their officers.' It may be added, that the system of drill was so devised as to give no play to the reasoning powers of the officer. He was a machine and nothing more.

Other causes had combined with those mentioned to weaken the morale and power of endurance of the French

---

[1] *The Battle of Spicheren*, by Brevet-Major C. F. R. Henderson. (Gale & Polden's Military Series.) Gale & Polden, London and Chatham.

soldier. Amongst these may be mentioned the origin of the second Empire. The reviews in the plains of Satory in 1850-1, when the soldiers were regaled with 'sausages and champagne,' the attempts made to debauch the officers, the subservience displayed by the Emperor to the men, whom he regarded as the basis upon which his authority rested, his constant endeavour to make them comfortable rather than efficient, had led to a feeling of contempt for a Government which seemed afraid to command. Then, again, the service in Algeria had, with its wild licence, tended to relax the bonds of discipline; whilst the fatal Mexican expedition, far from having upon the men the hardening effect which service in India has upon the British and Irish soldier, had made the French soldiers more exacting than those who had gone before them. 'A roof,' writes Henderson, 'had come to be considered an absolute necessity.' Thus it came about that, 'in the midst of summer and a thinly-populated country, the men of the army of the Rhine were encumbered with the useless addition of their canvas shelters.'[1]

Nor were the abilities of the leaders of the French army sufficiently marked to compensate for the deficiencies of the troops. Napoleon III. himself had, we repeat, convinced himself in the campaign of 1859, the only campaign in which he had led an army into the field, that he had not been gifted with the qualities requisite for the successful command of an army. Marshal Bazaine, who, in the opinion of the Emperor, possessed the qualities in which he was deficient, had for two years commanded the small army which had waged war in Mexico, but he had given there no proof of extraordinary capacity. His early service, from 1833 to 1849, in Algeria, passed mainly in the administration

[1] Henderson's *Spicheren*.

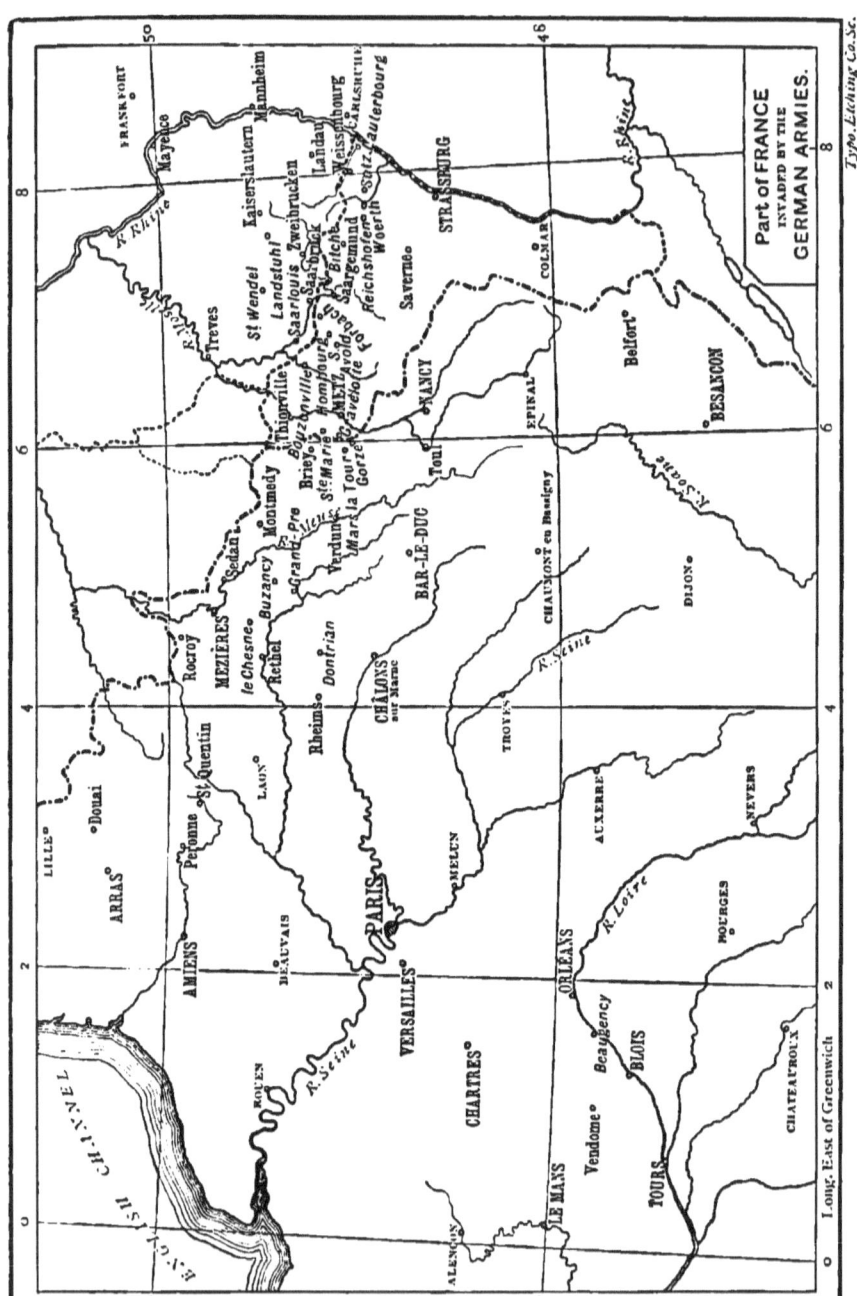

departments, had procured for him the character of being a clever intriguer, a match even for the Arabs on ground of their own selection, rather than of a brilliant officer. From 1850 until the breaking out of the Crimean war, he commanded a regiment in Africa. In that war he served as Brigadier-General until, on the 22nd of September, 1855, he was promoted to the command of a division. Appointed, after the war, to be Inspector, he gained a considerable acquaintance with the characters of the leading officers of the army. In the war of 1859 he again commanded a division, and distinguished himself greatly at the decisive storming of the churchyard of Solferino. In 1862 he accompanied the French expeditionary army to Mexico, first as commander of a division under General Forey, afterwards as commander of the entire force. His greatest merit in this command lay in the fact that he was able to bring back his army, almost intact, to France. It will be seen that no solid public grounds existed for attributing to Marshal Bazaine the qualities of a great leader; and although the Emperor believed that he possessed such qualities, it is more than probable that his belief was influenced largely by the knowledge of Bazaine's unalterable devotion to his dynasty.

Next to Bazaine, in the opinion of the Emperor, before him in the opinion of Europe, stood Marshal M'Mahon, Duke of Magenta. His flank march on the 4th of June 1859 had combined, with the extraordinary inactivity of the Austrian commander, Count Giulay, to save the French army from defeat, and the French Emperor from capture, on that eventful day. That one exploit had given him a great reputation in France, but there is no ground for supposing that he was more than a brave commander, not to be intimidated by responsibility, yet unequal to the task of planning and directing a campaign. Still, when the war broke out, he was probably the best commander in the higher ranks of the French army.

It is unnecessary to say much about Marshal Canrobert, for the Crimean war gave our countrymen and the world an opportunity of judging the fitness of this brave soldier to command in chief. Of the other marshal, Lebœuf, I have already spoken. Of another general, high in favour at court, and whose operations were destined to exercise a fatal influence on the early stages of the campaign, General de Failly, it is only necessary to state, that, though wanting neither in ability nor courage, his moral nature had become so enfeebled that, for the purposes of war, he had become worse than incapable. General Frossard, on the other hand, who commanded the 2d army corps, was an accomplished officer. But even he was not equal to critical occasions.

Of the artillery of the French army it has to be said, that it was far inferior to that of the Germans, and known to be so by the French war department. In the matter of reserves, France had comparatively nothing.[1]

Far different were the composition and the state of preparation of the Prussian army; far different, also, those of her German allies; far higher the qualities of their general officers; far superior the discipline and morale of their troops; far more ready, in every single

---

[1] 'In the gigantic reserves of Prussia, Napoleon recognised an element of strength for which France had no equivalent. With the help of Marshal Niel, his most capable adviser, an act was passed for the formation of a national army; but, on the death of that minister, was tacitly repudiated by the Government preferring a small budget to a strong line of defence.' Henderson's *Spicheren*.

particular, to begin a war; far more thoroughly provided to carry that war to a successful issue.

The German infantry had been thoroughly organised on a system which gave to every officer the necessity of exercising independent action, and to the men the faculty of understanding the object of the manœuvre directed. Its cavalry had been specially instructed in duties of reconnaissance, of ensuring repose for the infantry, of collecting intelligence, of concealing the march of armies, of acting as a completer of victory, or as a shield in case of defeat. It had profited greatly by the lessons it had learned in the war of 1866.

The German artillery had likewise been greatly improved in efficiency of manœuvre since 1866. It was in all respects superior to that of the French.

Of the Prussian and south German leaders, I will only say that we shall meet again the men from whom we parted on the conclusion of the armistice of Nikolsburg. What was their task and how they executed it will be described in the pages that follow. In mere numbers, the King of Prussia had a great advantage over his enemy. For, whilst without any assistance from South Germany, and after allowing for three army corps which might be necessary to watch Austria and Denmark, he could begin the campaign with a force of 350,000 men, he was certain of the assistance of Southern Germany, and confident that unless the French should obtain considerable successes at the outset, neither Austria nor Denmark would stir a hand to aid them.

To counterbalance this superiority of numbers the French Emperor had cherished a vague hope that, in a war against Prussia, he might possibly count upon the ancient friendship for France of Bavaria and Saxony, and to a still greater extent upon Austria and Italy.

With regard to Saxony and Bavaria, he was speedily undeceived. Bismarck had done his work of amalgamation too well to allow of any hope that sentimental reminiscences would induce the minor powers of Germany to stand back from the defence of the Fatherland. To them the Prussian minister had made it abundantly clear that it was Napoleon III. who was the aggressor, and that his aim was to aggrandise France at the expense of Germany. But the case of Austria differed in all respects from that of her allies of 1866. By a course of fraud and falsehood, Prussia had in that year forced upon her a war which had not only deprived her ruling house of her immemorial ascendency in Germany, but had expelled her from the sphere of German influence. The Chancellor of the Austrian empire, moreover, Count Beust, was a statesman who had, as minister of Saxony, combated the policy of Bismarck, and who had brought to his more exalted post a strong desire to upset, if it should be possible, the settlement of the Treaty of Prague. Beust was therefore very much inclined to favour an alliance with France, if such an alliance could be made without endangering Austria. Doubtless he had discussed the matter with the Duke of Gramont, and possibly he had left on the mind of that too sanguine statesman the impression that Austria would accompany France in a war against Prussia with something stronger than mere sympathy. And if Napoleon III. had not been in so great a hurry; if he had allowed the incident of the Hohenzollern candidature to pass by; and if he had then worked steadily for alliances for a war which, he must have been aware, would sooner or later be forced upon him, such a combination might have been arranged. But for Austria, unprepared as she was for war, to throw herself suddenly into a struggle to which an integral part, a most important part, of her dual monarchy was opposed, was a matter not to be thought of. The clear foresightedness of Bismarck had provided for the possibility of such an occurrence. Austria could not move to the support of France without incurring the danger of an invasion from Russia, and Beust had good reason to believe that the one would entail the other.

These matters were discussed at a council held at Vienna on the 18th of July. It was there resolved that Austria should for the present remain neutral, unless Russia should take active part with Prussia; but that if the French should succeed in penetrating into Southern Germany in force, then Austria should join her with her whole army. In a despatch to Prince Metternich at Paris, Beust pointed out that to declare war immediately against Prussia would not fail to bring Russia into the field; but that if Russia were cajoled until Austria should be ready, and the circumstances of the war should be such as would render it advisable, Austria would then declare herself. He added that Austria had already agreed with Italy for a joint armed mediation, and he strongly engaged him to urge upon the French Emperor the securing of the sympathy and support of Italy by the evacuation of Rome.

Napoleon III. was indeed at this very time engaged with negotiating with the King of Italy to secure a triple alliance between the three powers. It was in consequence of these negotiations that the French troops evacuated the Papal States on the 2nd of August. The co-operation of Italy, as the co-operation of Austria, was made to depend upon the obtaining by the French troops of initial successes. It was not only understood, but was actually drafted in a treaty—the signing of which, however, was prevented by the rapid course of the war—that if on the 15th of September, France should be holding her own in Southern Germany, then Austria and Italy would jointly declare war against Prussia.

These conditititions made it clear that ultimate success in the struggle about to commence would accrue to the power which should obtain the first advantages.

That Germany—for it was Germany and not Prussia only which entered upon this great struggle—would obtain these initial advantages seemed almost certain. Count Moltke had for some time previous been engaged in planning for a war with France. So far back as 1868 all his arrangements for the formation of the armies to be employed, the points to be occupied, the nature of the transport, had been clearly laid down. These instructions had been carefully studied by the several corps-commanders and their staff. Not one matter, however apparently trivial, had been neglected. When, then, on the 16th of July, the King of Prussia gave the order for mobilisation, it required only to insert the day and the hour on which each body of troops should march. With respect to the armies of the States of Southern Germany, Moltke, anticipating that the French Emperor would throw his main army as rapidly as possible into Southern Germany, had recommended that the contingents from that part of the country should march northwards to join those of Prussia on the middle Rhine, to assume there a position which should menace the flank and rear of the invading army. This position would be the more practical, as in the event of the French not invading Southern Germany, the combined force, stretching from Saarbrücken to Landau, would be ready to invade France, and sever the communications with Paris of the French armies on the frontier. Count Moltke had calculated that the German troops

intended to cross the French frontier would be in a position to make their forward movement by the 4th of August. Pending the development of the French strategy with respect to Southern Germany, therefore, he thought it prudent to delay the march of the southern contingents, in order that no part of the army might be suddenly overwhelmed by a superior force. On the actual frontier he placed, then, only a few light troops, for the purposes of reconnoitring, and for checking the first advance of the enemy until supports should arrive.

The French Emperor had, indeed, been keenly alive to the advantages which would accrue to himself from a prompt invasion of Southern Germany. He designed to concentrate 150,000 men at Metz; 100,000 at Strasburg; to cross into Baden with these armies; whilst a third, assembling at Chalons, should protect the frontier against the German forces. The plan itself was an excellent one had he only been able to execute it, for, as we have seen, early success in Southern Germany would have meant the armed assistance of Austria and Italy. But the French army was in a condition more unready, one might truly say, of greater demoralisation, thus early, than its severest critics had imagined. Considerable forces were indeed massed about Metz and Strasburg. But the commissariat and transport departments were in a state of the most hopeless confusion. The army could not move. To remedy these evils time was wanted, and time was the commodity the generals could not command. Every day which evoked some little order out of chaos brought the Germans nearer to positions, the occupation of which would render impossible the contemplated invasion. The Emperor had quitted Paris for Metz, accompanied by the Prince Imperial, on the 28th of July, and had arrived there and taken the supreme command the same day. The day following he met his generals at St Avoid, and unfolded to them his plans. Since war had been declared he had lost many illusions. It had become clear to him that he was warring against the concentrated might of Germany; that he could not make the inroad into Southern Germany originally contemplated without exposing Paris to an attack from forces already occupying the country between Trèves and Mannheim; that he was bound to hold that line. Anxious, however, to assume the offensive, he dictated the following plan to his marshals. Bazaine with the 2d, 3d, and 5th armycorps should cross the Saar at Saarbrücken, covered on his left by the 4th corps, which should make a show of advancing against Saarlouis, whilst M'Mahon, pushing forward from his position near Strasburg, should cover his right. The Emperor had some reason to believe that the Saar was weakly held.

But his own generals showed him that his plan was impossible. They represented to him that instead of the 300,000 men whom, in the delirium of the Paris enthusiasm, he believed he would find available for his purposes, he had at the utmost 186,000; that in every requirement for moving the army was deficient; that there was scarcely a department which was not disorganised. He was compelled, therefore, to renounce his plan for decisive offensive action. He came to that resolve most unwillingly, for Paris was behind him, ready to rise unless he should make some show of advancing. It was to reassure the excited spirits of the capital, rather than to effect any military result, that, on the 2nd of August, he moved with 60,000 men in the direction of Saarbrücken. The garrison of that place consisted of something less than 4000 men with six guns. The Emperor attacked it with the corps of Frossard, eighteen battalions and four batteries. These compelled the slender German garrison to evacuate the place, but Frossard, though the bridges across the Saar were not defended, made no attempt to cross that river. The soldierly manner in which the Germans had covered their retreat had left on his mind the impression that they were more numerous than they were, and that there was a larger force behind them.

Still, for the only time in the war, the Emperor was able to send a reassuring telegram to Paris. The young prince, upon whom the hopes of the nation would, he hoped, rest, had undergone the 'baptism of fire.' French troops had made the first step in advance.

Soon, however, it became clear to him that the enemy had concentrated along the line of the frontier, and were about to make their spring. Moltke, in fact, from his headquarters at Mayence, was, by means of solitary horsemen employed in profusion, keeping himself thoroughly well acquainted not only with the movements of the French but with their vacillation, their irresolution, their want of plan. The sudden appearance from unexpected quarters of these horsemen conveyed a marked feeling of insecurity to the minds of the French soldiers, and these feelings were soon shared by their chiefs. It was very clear to them that an attack might at any moment come, though from what quarter and in what force they were absolutely ignorant. This ignorance increased their vacillations, their uncertainties. Orders and counter-orders followed each other with startling rapidity. The soldiers, harassed, began to lose confidence; the leaders became more and more incapable of adopting a plan.

Suddenly, in the midst of their vacillations, of their marchings and counter-marchings, the true report reached them, on the evening of the 3d of August, that a French division, the outpost of M'Mahon's army, had been surprised and defeated at Weissenburg by a far superior force. Napoleon at once ordered the 5th corps to concentrate at Bitsche, and despatched a division of the 3d to Saargemünd. These orders were followed by others. Those of the 5th of August divided the army of the Rhine into two portions, the troops in Alsace being placed under M'Mahon, those in Lorraine under Bazaine, the Emperor retaining the Guard. Those of the 7th directed the 2d corps to proceed to Bitsche, the 3d to Saarguemund, the 4th to Haut-Homburg, the Guard to St Avoid. These instructions plainly signified the making of a flank movement in front of a superior enemy. With such an army as the Emperor had, inferior in numbers, many of the regiments as yet incomplete, all his resources behind him, and these becoming daily more available, his one chance was to concentrate in a position commanding the roads behind it, and yet adapted for attack if attack should be necessary. As it was, without certain information as to the movements of the Germans, anxious to move, yet dreading to do so, until his regiments should be completed, the French Emperor was confused and helpless. He forgot even to transmit to the generals on one flank the general directions he had issued to those on the other. Bazaine, for instance, was left on the 5th in ignorance of the Emperor's intentions with respect to M'Mahon; on the 6th none of the subordinate generals knew that the flank march was contemplated. Frossard, who had fallen back to Spicheren, considered his position so insecure that he suggested to Lebœuf that he should be allowed to retire from the Saarbrücken ridge. He was ordered in reply to fall back on Forbach, but no instructions were given him as to the course he should pursue in the event of his being attacked, nor were the contemplated movements of the Emperor communicated to him.

In every order that was issued there was apparent the confused mind of the issuer.

Turn we now to M'Mahon and the movements of himself and his generals. When the war broke out M'Mahon was in the vicinity of Strasburg with 45,000 men; General Douay with 12,000 men at Weissenburg. The same confusion prevailed here as at Metz. The orders given to M'Mahon were of the vaguest description: Douay had no instructions at all. Yet, in front of him, the German hosts had been gathering. The commander of the left wing of the German army, the Crown Prince of Prussia, had, in obedience to the instructions he had received, crossed the frontier river, the Lauter, on the 4th of August, with an army composed of the 2d Bavarian and 5th Prussian army, numbering about 40,000 men, and marched on Weissenburg. As his advanced guard approached the town, it was met by a heavy fire from the French garrison. The Crown Prince resolved at once to storm the place. Douay had placed his troops in a strong position, a portion of his men occupying the town defended by a simple wall; the bulk, formed on the Gaisberg, a hill two miles to the south of it. Against this position the Crown Prince directed his chief attack. The contest which ensued was most severe, the assailants and the defenders vying with one another in determination and courage. But the odds in favour of the former were too great to permit Douay to hope for ultimate success. After a resistance of five hours' duration the Germans carried the Gaisberg. Douay himself was killed; but his surviving troops, though beaten, were not discouraged. They successfully foiled an attempt made by the Germans to cut off their retreat, and fell back on the corps of M'Mahon, which lay about ten miles to the south of Weissenburg.

The same day on which the Crown Prince had attacked

and carried Weissenburg, another German army corps, that of Baden-Würtemberg, a part of the third army, under the command of the Crown Prince, had advanced on and occupied Lauterburg. That evening the entire third army, consisting of 130,000 men, bivouacked on French ground. Meanwhile M'Mahon, on hearing of Douay's defeat, had marched to Reichshofen, received there the shattered remnants of Douay's division, and, with the Emperor's orders under no circumstances to decline a battle, took up a position on the hills of which Wörth, Fröschweiler and Elsasshausen form the central points. He had with him 47,000 men, but the 5th corps, commanded by De Failly, was at Bitsche, seventeen miles from Reichshofen, and M'Mahon had despatched the most pressing instructions to that officer to join him. These orders, however, De Failly did not obey.

The ground on which M'Mahon had retired offered many capabilities for defence. The central point was the village of Wörth on the rivulet Sauerbach, which covered the entire front of the position. To the right rear of Wörth, on the road from Gundershofen, was the village of Elsasshausen, covered on its right by the Niederwald, having the village of Eberbach on its further side, and the extreme right of the position, the village of Morsbronn, to its south-east. Behind Wörth, again, distant a little more than two miles on the road to Reichshofen, was the key to the position, the village of Fröschweiler. From this point the French left was thrown back to a mound, covered by a wood, in front of Reichshofen.

On the 5th of August the Crown Prince had set his army in motion, and had rested for the night at Sulz. There information reached him regarding the position taken by M'Mahon. He immediately issued orders for the concentration of his army, and for its march the

Battle of Wörth. 237

following morning towards the French position, the village of Preuschdorf, on the direct road to Wörth, to be the central point of the movement. But the previous evening General von Walther, with the 5th Prussian corps, had reached Görsdorf, a point whence it was easy for him to cross the Sauerbach, and take Wörth in flank. Marching at four o'clock in the morning Walther tried this manœuvre, and at seven o'clock succeeded in driving the French from Wörth. M'Mahon then changed his front, recovered Wörth, and repulsed likewise an attack which had in the meanwhile been directed against Fröschweiler by the 11th Prussian and 5th Bavarian corps. For a moment it seemed as though he might hold his position. But between eleven and twelve the enemy renewed his attack. Whilst one corps again attacked and carried Wörth, the 11th Prussian corps, aided by sixty guns placed upon the heights of Gunstett, assailed his right. They met here a most stubborn resistance, the French curassiers charging the advancing infantry with the greatest resolution. So thoroughly did they devote themselves, that they left three-fourths of their number dead or dying on the field. But all was in vain. The Prussians steadily advanced, forced their way through the Niederwald, and threatened Elsasshausen. Whilst the French were thus progressing badly on their right, they were faring still worse in the centre. The Germans, having seized Wörth, stormed the hilly slopes between that place and Fröschweiler, and made a furious assault upon the latter, now more than ever the key of the French position. For whilst Fröschweiler was their objective centre, their right was thrown back towards Elsasshausen and the Niederwald, their left to Reichshofen. Whilst the 11th Prussians were penetrating the Niederwald, preparatory to attacking Elsasshausen on the further side of it, the 5th Prussian corps with the 2nd Bavarians were moving against Fröschweiler. It was clear then to M'Mahon that further resistance was impossible. Still holding Fröschweiler, he evacuated Elsasshausen, and drew back his right to Reichshofen. The safety of his army depended now upon the tenacity with which Fröschweiler might be held. It must be admitted, in justice to the French, that they held it with a stubborn valour not surpassed during the war. Attacked by overwhelming numbers, they defended the place, house by house. At length, however, they were overpowered. Then, for the first time, the bonds of discipline loosened, and the French, struck by panic, fled, in wild disorder, in the direction of Saverne. They reached that place by a march across the hills the following evening. On their way they fell in with one of the divisions of the corps of de Failly, and this served to cover the retreat.

Though their defeat, considering the enormous superiority of their assailants, might be glorious, it was doubly disastrous, inasmuch that it followed those perturbations of spirit alluded to in a previous page, which had done so much to discourage the French soldier. A victory at Wörth might have done much to redeem past mistakes. A defeat emphasised them enormously. It was calculated that, inclusive of the 9,000 prisoners taken by the Germans, the French lost 24,000 men. The loss of the victors amounted to 10,000. They captured thirty-three guns, two eagles, and six mitrailleuses.

The Emperor was deeply pained by the result of the battle. To keep up, if possible, the spirits of his partisans, he wired on the evening of the 7th to Paris, with the news of the defeat, the words, "tout se peut rétablir." He was mistaken. Whilst the Crown Prince was crushing M'Mahon at Wörth, there was occurring close to the scene of the

Prince Imperial's baptism of fire, an event which may be regarded as one of the decisive events of the war.

The second German army corps, commanded by Prince Frederic Charles, had taken the position assigned to it, between Mannheim and Mayence, on the 29th of July. Thence it was directed to concentrate on the line Alsenz-Grünstadt, twenty-six miles beyond Mayence. The advance beyond that line presented some difficulties, for, between it to the north-east, and Neunkirchen-Zweibrücken to the south-east, there lay a spur of the Vosges, some forty miles in breadth. Across this spur were only rugged roads, and although two of these, on the proper right of the Prussian army, were traversable by troops, the remainder merged into one road at Kaiserslautern, half way through the hills, and so continued as far as Homburg, twenty-three miles to the front. Time therefore would be required before the corps which composed the second army could deploy on the line of Neunkirchen-Zweibrücken. More than this; the French were known to be at Forbach, and a rapid advance by them from that place would necessarily throw the second army on the defensive. The new line, moreover, was but twenty miles distant from Forbach and Saargemünd, both occupied by the French. It was impossible then for the Germans to entangle their force of 120,000 men in the spur they hoped to traverse until the intentions of the French at those places should be known. A rapid advance from them by an energetic and skilful commander, made when the army was so entangled, could scarcely fail to cause them disaster.

However, on the 1st of August tentatively, and on the 2nd with greater rapidity, the second army committed itself to this undertaking. It was engaged in it when, on the 3rd, information reached Prince Frederic Charles that the

French had advanced from Forbach and Saarguemund and seized the heights of Saarbrücken. To the clear head of the director of the movements of the German armies it soon became evident that the enemy contemplated no further forward movement, and he wired the same evening to the Red Prince to push on so as to deploy the second army in front of the belt of forest near Kaiserslautern—*i.e.*, on the line of Neunkirchen-Zweibrücken—whilst the 1st army should advance upon Tholey, and the 3rd upon Weissenburg. The Red Prince carried out these instructions, and, from the 4th, had his army in position ready for action. On the night of the 5th his five army-corps and the Guard occupied Neunkirchen, St Wendel, Zweibrücken, Homburg, Kusel, Landstuhl, Otterberg, and Münchweiler, in touch with the first army on its right. It was the intention of Moltke to make a grand advance of both armies, together 320,000 strong, into Alsace, as soon as the advance of the 3rd army into Lorraine should make itself felt. Yet this plan, owing to the action of the commander of the first army, General von Steinmetz, was not carried out in the manner he had contemplated.

Under the impression that the French army was about to attack the Prussian second army, Steinmetz had resolved on the 3rd, in order to facilitate the advance of that army, to draw to himself the attention of the enemy's forces. With this view he proposed to advance into the line Saarlouis-Hellenhausen; thence, the following day, to push forward reconnaissances in force up the Bouzonville, Boulay, and St Avoid roads. Orders received that night modified these arrangements, and, on the 4th, the first army concentrated towards Tholey. It remained in that position on the 5th. But, on the 6th, Steinmetz, warned to evacuate the Wendel-Saarbrücken road, to leave it free for the advance of the second army, pushed forward with the view of taking a position within a day's march of the Saar, so as to strike the flank of the French should they make an attack on the second army. Pushing on, the advanced guard of the 14th division of his army proceeded to occupy the heights of Saarbrücken, whence the French had retired. There they deemed themselves secure. For although across the open fields in front of them were the hanging woods of the Spicheren heights, occupied by 28,000 men and ninety guns, nothing betokened that those heights were strongly occupied. On the escarped Rotherberg some companies of French infantry were indeed visible, and small bodies were seen in the Forbach valley. From these appearances the Prussian general commanding the 14th division, Von Kamecke, judged he might have before him some 7000 men, no more.

Of the action which followed, my account must necessarily be condensed. Dealt with by the painstaking and gifted writer to whom I am so much indebted,[1] the story fills a small volume. To that volume I refer the reader who would desire to master every detail of the terrible fighting, and to criticise the leading on both sides on that eventful day.

'The Spicheren plateau,' writes the authority I have just referred to, 'is a salient of the great table-land of Lorraine, rising squarely between the valley of the Saar upon the one hand and Forbach on the other ; separated from the Saarbrücken ridge by the St Arnual Valley, the breadth of which amounts on the east, near St Arnual village, to 1000 ; on the west, between the Rotherberg and Reppertsberg to quite 2000 paces. The slopes of the plateau, save at the left-hand corner, where the Rotherberg juts out to the northward, are densely wooded, and on every side so steep and abrupt, that even an unen-

[1] Henderson's *The Battle of Spicheren*. Gale & Polden.

cumbered man finds it no light task to scale them. Between the oaks and beeches which clothe the cliffs from base to brow, the undergrowth flourishes in such luxuriance, as to present peculiar difficulties to the movements of a body of soldiers heavily equipped, and bound to maintain formation. The crest of the heights is about 300 feet above the valley.

'The Rotherberg, viewed from the Saarbrücken ridge, appears an insignificant height, and easy of ascent. But from the valley at the foot, where the verge of the main plateau is no longer visible, the famous spur stands out a formidable hill, the crest about 150 feet above the level. East, west, and north the fall is steep, and where, at the date of the battle, the red rock cropped out from the scarped hillside, it was sheer and precipitous. . . . The surface of the spur, 250 feet in breadth, is bare and undulating, rising gently to the south, and joined to the plateau by a somewhat narrower saddle.

'The Spicheren-Saarbrücken road, which, after crossing the valley from the Nussberg, winds round the eastern shoulder of the spur, supported on a log embankment, was practicable for artillery.'

On the morning of the 6th of August the three divisions which constituted the force of General Frossard were posted as follows : Jolivet's brigade of the 1st division was to the north-east of Stiring-Wendel ; Valazé's brigade was to the west of Forbach ; the 2d division was at Oetingen, three miles south of Spicheren ; the 3d division was at Spicheren. Very early that morning Frossard had received a telegram from Lebœuf, warning him that he might be attacked that day. Frossard threw up intrenchments at some commanding points, but did nothing further in the way of preparation. He had, however, several telegraphic communications with Bazaine, the gist of the latter's instructions being to the effect that he had ordered two divisions to support him ; but that if he were seriously attacked, he would do well to retire on Calenbronn. It apparently never occurred to Bazaine to ascertain the precise position of the 1st German army by a cavalry reconnaissance, though such a movement was very feasible. He had himself, whilst reconnoitring on the Saarlouis road that morning, been fired at by a detachment—a troop or two—of Prussian Hussars, but instead of following them up, he had simply suggested to Frossard the advisability of detaching a large force to watch that road.

Though Bazaine had recommended Frossard to fall back on Calenbronn in the event of a serious attack, he had, I have said, clearly intimated to him that he had posted two divisions to support him in case that course should not be feasible. Frossard had, at Forbach, large stores of provisions and matériel, and it was the reluctance to abandon these without a struggle, combined with the certainty he felt that he would be supported, that decided him not to move without fighting. He had one division on the Spicheren heights ; another was on the Rotherberg ; a brigade covered his left was at Stiring-Wendel ; another occupied the Pfaffen wood on his right. His position had a length of 4700 yards : the troops he disposed of numbered 27,000. The position, though it possessed some strong points, was not, taken altogether, a strong defensive position. It was broken ; unfavourable for counter-attack ; and it was only from the Rotherberg that the guns could play on the valley by which the Prussians must approach.

We left General Kamecke with the advanced guard of the 14th division of the Prussian army surveying the position I have indicated from the Saarbrücken ridge. He had with him, or close at hand, 10,750 bayonets. The occupation of the Rotherberg was necessary for the maintenance of the ridge on which he was standing. So far as he could trust to his eyesight, that hill was but lightly occupied. After considerable hesitation, then, he resolved to drive the French from it.

Shortly before twelve o'clock Kamecke directed his 27th brigade to drive the French artillery from the Rotherberg. The right attack made with great gallantry was met by the French, who, at this point, were considerably stronger than the assailants, with resolution. The fire from the Chassepots, the guns, and the mitrailleuses told with deadly effect, and it seemed at one time as though the Prussians were about to fall back. Two and a half hours of fierce fighting, however, saw them, 2000 strong, deployed along a front of 1400 yards facing the French, and depending for a further advance on the progress the attack might make on the other flank and in the centre.

During the same period, the left attack reached, after an hour's march, under fire the greater part of the way, the foot of the Rotherberg heights at the point where those heights had a sheer descent into the plain. Moving rapidly and in broken order through the thicket to their right, the assailants reached a point where the height seemed more accessible, and at once attempted it. Soon they came in contact with the defenders, and a little further they found themselves exposed to the fire from the troops on Spicheren. For a time they were in a very critical position. Far from being able to assist the right attack, their one hope was to be extricated from the trap into which their own daring had led them. To see how this was accomplished we must await the further developments on both sides.

Still believing that the French were in small force, and were bent on withdrawing, if they could, Von Kamecke determined to try the effect of a front attack with the two battalions and three batteries which still remained to him. Placing the batteries in a position to concentrate their fire on the defenders of the spur, he moved forward his infantry across the 1500 paces which intervened between his point of advance and Spicheren. Though exposed to a heavy fire, which thinned their ranks, the men pressed forward with great gallantry, and gained the shelter of the heights they hoped to storm, and whose abruptness at this point shielded them from the enemy's fire. But even then the general position (2.30 p.m.) was critical. The central attack could do no more than hold its own: the left attack had been repulsed in an attempt to extricate itself by a forward movement: the right attack stood fronting a superior force supported by one still stronger. For the first time, probably, the Prussian leader realised that he had led his men into a trap. It seems certain that if at this moment the French had, with their superior numbers at the decisive point, assumed the offensive, a great disaster would have occurred to the Prussians.

Unfortunately for the French, their commander, Frossard, was not at the point which was being assailed. He was in Forbach, imperatively detained there, he thought, by the necessity of being in constant telegraphic communication with Bazaine. It was his first command demanding independent action. He was embarrassed by the evidence which accumulated every hour that the force attacking his position veiled a much larger force; and, not possessing that 'divine afflatus' which characterised Napoleon, and Clive, and Frederic, and, in his best days, Masséna, he was afraid to commit himself to any bold or decisive[1] action. Content that his

---

[1] Henderson truly remarks: 'Had Frossard been gifted with a spark of Napoleon's genius, he would have re-enacted Rivoli and have destroyed one, if not both, of the hostile columns. (Page 153.)

generals had apparently repulsed the attack, he resolved to await the reinforcements expected from Bazaine. It is due to him to add, that he had a right to expect these, for at 2.25 he had received a despatch from his commander-in chief which left no doubt on his mind that 25,000 men were marching by good roads to support him. It would seem, however, that the generals to whom Bazaine had sent the order to advance displayed the most culpable indifference to the fate of the advanced corps of their own army, and made no effort to support their comrades.

Such was the condition of affairs at half-past two, the French holding their positions, the attacking Germans exposed to great danger, if a counter-attack were to be made in force; the two German armies, the 1st and 2d, hurrying to support their comrades; the French divisions detailed to support Frossard combining practically to leave him in the lurch. It was just at this moment that the officer commanding the French on the Rotherberg, General Laveaucoupet, resolved to attempt on a small scale the manœuvre which Frossard should have tried in force, to make a counter attack. At half-past two, then, he made a very resolute effort to turn the Prussian left. He had some success at first, but the opportune arrival of reinforcements to the threatened Prussian left checked him. Then it was that the Prussian leader, Von Kamecke, obeying a true soldierly instinct, resolved to make a bold effort to capture the Rotherberg. This, by a display of great daring, he succeeded, though at a great sacrifice of life, in partially effecting, that is, his men obtained a firm footing on that well defended hill.

Meanwhile, on their right, the French, recovering from their check, had succeeded in driving before them the Prussian left. But this occurrence, owing to the presence

French maintain the Fight on the Rotherberg. 247

of mind of the Prussian officers, was turned to their disadvantage. For whilst, owing to occurrences in the other parts of the field, the French were unable to pursue their advantage on their right, the Prussians, who had been repulsed on the left, guided by the sound of combat, dashed across the valley to reinforce their comrades. Pushing on under such cover as was to be found, they surprised the French, and compelled them to relinquish their hold on the trench they had so well defended.

At Stiring-Wendel the Prussian attack had made some progress, but, up to half-past three, nothing decisive had occurred. At that hour the French, reinforced to 6000, stood opposed to about 5000 Germans.

At three o'clock General von Goeben, commanding the 8th army corps of the Prussian army, arrived on the ground, and assumed the direction of the fight. He speedily recognised that the French were bringing all their available reserves to reinforce their troops on the Rotherberg, to drive from its crest the 1800 German troops, who, we have seen, had planted themselves on that important position. His object was to maintain that post, and his manœuvres were directed to attain that end. From half-past three till half-past four the fight on the Rotherberg was conducted with great fury, the Prussian advance being supported by the fire from the guns judiciously placed on the Galgenberg and Folster height. It was this fire, admirably conducted, which prevented the more numerous French infantry from dashing forward to sweep away the enemy's footmen as they ascended. Still they maintained their position, the slaughter being great on both sides. But between halfpast four and five the first battalion of the Prussian 12th regiment, arriving by successive companies in the very nick of time, forced the French to relinquish their hold on the spur which they had by a supreme effort almost gained, and to withdraw to a position higher up the cliff. The consequence was that, at five o'clock, the Prussians still held the edge of the Rotherberg, the north-west corner of the Gifert wood, the ravine separating the two positions, and, to the left, the ridge within the wood. The French line, extending across the spur and bending back at an angle, was still strongly held. In the other parts of the field the French had at least held their positions, but the Prussian reinforcements were coming up quickly. Amongst those who had arrived during the interval just mentioned was General von Zastrow, commanding the 7th army corps, and he, as senior officer, had, at half-past four o'clock, assumed the chief command.

The main object of contention was now the possession of the Gifert wood. To drive out the Prussians, now become somewhat superior in numbers, the French had here concentrated 9000 men. Then between five and six o'clock 'the front of the battle swayed backwards and forwards, ground being won and lost as fresh troops came up on either side.' The breadth of the wood at this point did not exceed 500 yards. The fighting was very close, the smoke blinding, and officers were forced to use their revolvers. In such a combat the superior training of the Prussians, the practice to which officers and men had been alike subjected to use their brains in difficult circumstances; the greater cohesion between the private and the officer; gave the assailants a great advantage. In that one hour's combat these advantages made themselves felt. Though equal was the valour, equal the determination of the French, that training and that cohesion just turned the scale, and at six o'clock the French yielded the crest and fell back in good order towards Spicheren, to hold a second position stronger than that which they thus renounced.

New French Position at Spicheren.

The front of the new position taken by the French commander rested on the Spicheren knoll, the right being made secure by a ravine. The left rested on the Spicheren wood. To eject the French from this was, at six o'clock, the intention of the German leader. It was the more necessary that he should succeed here, for on his right, at Stiring-Wendel, the French, strongly reinforced, were more than holding their own, and at one time it seemed as though one vigorous effort would have given them a position which must have compelled the Prussians to renounce the advantages they had gained on the Rotherberg.[1]

The effort of the Prussians was now, between six and seven o'clock, directed to the driving of the French from the Spicheren knoll, and, this having been effected, to the turning of their left flank by the Spicheren wood. But so vigorous was the defence, and so severe the fire of the Chassepôts, that their first attack on the knoll was repulsed with heavy loss. Then, a severe artillery fire, lasting over half-an-hour, from guns commanding the position, compelled the defenders to evacuate this post; but, at 6.45, 'the battle had come to a standstill; the French still presenting an unbroken front, and overwhelming with fierce bursts of musketry every effort made by the Prussians to break forward from the wood, and maintaining a constant and heavy shell fire on the border.'[2] The Prussian generals felt that a strenuous effort must be made to preserve the advantages they had gained; and that their

[1] Henderson writes (page 214), that notwithstanding their 'gallant stand against overwhelming odds, it is extremely improbable that the Prussian right could have long resisted the attack so energetically pushed by Generals Bataille and Vergé. Besides the troops that had stormed the copse, 6000 infantry, at least, the whole garrison of Stiring-Wendel were close at hand, and it is not too much to assert that one vigorous effort would have given the French the battle.'

[2] Henderson, page 220.

only chance was to attempt, whilst holding the enemy in front, a solid flank attack. This they made with six battalions and two batteries. These reached, by a path previously traversed by their comrades, the western brow of the Spicheren plateau; formed there at right angles to the French position, and driving back the light troops of the enemy, gained, after a severe struggle, a solid position on his left which threatened to 'pierce the very heart of the defence.' At the same time the front defence, rendered uneasy by this flank movement, had somehow relaxed; and it seemed as though a combined effort must give the Prussians the victory. But at this supreme moment the French infantry proved themselves worthy of the renown they have gained on many a hard fought battle-field. They had been fighting for seven hours: they had been compelled, after a terrible struggle, to yield some strong positions: but now, called upon by the general who had led them with skill and gallantry, General Laveaucoupet,[1] to make one final bid for victory, to charge with all their force the enemy in front of them, they responded with a vigour, a dash and a resolution which would have done honour even to those noble compatriots who had conquered Italy in 1796. Furiously they charged: with a great effort they drove back the enemy in front of them, but just as it seemed that they might redeem the day, the flank position gained by the six Prussian battalions in the manner described, forced them to relinquish their hold. Darkness was coming on; they could see neither the numbers nor the position of their enemy: they only knew that the further they advanced the more they would place themselves, if he were in force, in his power: they therefore in the most perfect order, relinquished the positions they had

[1] This general, one of the best on the French side, of the war of 1870, died, at an advanced age, whilst I was writing these lines.

won, and whilst their comrades repulsed the flank attack of the Prussians, they fell back unpursued on Spicheren. They had at least the consciousness that they had inflicted a very heavy loss on their enemy, that they had saved their honour, and that if the generals of their army had displayed one-fourth part of the energy evidenced by the Prussian Generals, they would have been victorious.[1]

Why was Frossard not reinforced? At nine o'clock he had telegraphed to his chief Bazaine that he had heard cannon-firing in front, and had suggested that Montaudon should send a brigade to Grossbliederstroff, and that Decaen should advance to Merlebach and Rossbruck. At 10.40 he had reported that the enemy had shown himself at the two places last named. At 11.15 Bazaine had replied that he had sent one division to Bening, another to Theding, and told Frossard to send a brigade to watch Rossbruck, adding, that if the attack were really serious, it would be advisable to concentrate on Calenbronn.

About this time Bazaine himself made a reconnaissance towards Carling, and was fired at by Prussian scouts.

At 2.25 Bazaine telegraphed that he had ordered Montaudon (by telegraph) to Grossbliederstroff. So far the movements he had taken coincided with the advice he had given to Frossard, to fall back on Calenbronn if he should be seriously attacked. But he stopped short at a point which, if pursued, would have given his orders life and vitality. He made no reconnaissance in the direction of Saarlouis, he despatched not a single staff officer to ascertain the position of affairs, he did not even take one step to ascertain how far his orders to the several generals had been obeyed; whether Frossard had fallen back on Calenbronn, or whether Montaudon or Decaen had advanced

[1] The Germans lost 223 officers and 4648 men: the French 249 officers and 3829 men.

to his support. He excused himself for these shortcomings by pleading the necessity of remaining in close communication with imperial headquarters—an excuse which cannot be accepted, and which places his conduct in striking contrast with that of the generals of the army opposed to him. It was not till five o'clock, having been since two o'clock without any news from the front, that he telegraphed to Frossard for some information: '*Donnez-moi des nouvelles pour me tranquilliser.*' At that moment Frossard and his men were fighting for their very lives. He gets, of course, no tranquillising news; but nearly an hour later he hears that Frossard's right has been forced to fall back, and receives a demand for succour. Instead of complying with this demand, he contents himself with recapitulating the position of the divisions he had ordered forward to support Frossard. A few minutes later comes the report that the battle, which had been very heavy, was dying away, and asking for a regiment. A regiment is at once sent forward in two trains to Forbach. Towards eight o'clock he hears of the retreat, and replies that he has done all he can, that he has only three regiments to guard the St Avoid position, and asks Frossard to explain the position he thinks should be occupied.

It would seem that, on further investigation, however much Bazaine's personal action is worthy of condemnation, his divisional generals were, perhaps, even more culpable. After half-past two o'clock Frossard left Bazaine in ignorance of his position, and made no effort to call up the commanders whom Bazaine had ordered to support him. Bazaine's order to Montaudon to move forward reached that general's division at three o'clock, but at the time Montaudon was away reconnoitring, and his division made no movement until his return at five. The troops did not reach their appointed position until seven. No

Culpability of French Divisional Commanders. 253

staff officer was sent to communicate with Frossard, nor did Frossard communicate with Montaudon. Castagny, who had been ordered at eleven to march on Theding, did set out at once in the direction of Spicheren. He marched, however, by a road which took him somewhat to the right of the true line. Consequently, after marching five miles, he lost the sound of the firing and halted. A little later, on the report of some peasants that the French had gained a victory, he returned. Again at five he advanced, but he did not reach Folkling, three miles from Spicheren, till nine o'clock. Metman's conduct is even less excusable. He reached Bening, in obedience to Bazaine's orders, at three o'clock. There he was seven miles from Stiring-Wendel. He heard the firing, and if he had only pushed on he would have reinforced the French at the very point where the Prussians were weakest, and where, even without him, the French, by a bold advance, might have gained the victory. But Metman did nothing. He made no attempt to discover the meaning of the firing. He appears, writes Henderson, ' to have forgotten that the chargers of even infantry adjutants have legs.'

The loss of the battle of Spicheren, then, is not attributable to the French soldiers, who behaved splendidly: it cannot altogether be attributed to Bazaine, although a Masséna, a Lannes, a Davoust, would have displayed on such an occasion a personal activity which could not have failed to ensure success. It is to be attributed to the want of energy, of confidence in one another of the French divisional commanders ; to their careless indifference, the result of bad training ; to their neglect of the most ordinary military precautions : in one word, to their inferiority, as divisional leaders, to those of the same rank in the Prussian army. But for the men, I repeat, it is difficult to say too much in their praise. They were indeed an army of lions. But there are circumstances, and Spicheren was one of them, in which it is impossible even for an army of lions to succeed.

After the battle, the French, as I have said, fell back unmolested. Their battalions were still intact; 'their retreat, so far from being a rout, was made in so leisurely a fashion that the bivouac fires of their rearguard were to be seen on the Pfaffenburg.' 'The Prussians,' writes the same author,[1] 'were so exhausted, and in such extreme confusion at every point, that a further advance would have been no less difficult to initiate than to carry out.'

[1] Henderson, page 241.

CHAPTER XIII.

COLOMBEY—VIONVILLE—GRAVELOTTE.

THE conviction that a serious defeat would imperil the dynasty was ever before the eyes of the French Emperor and his superior generals. On the day following the disasters of Wörth and Spicheren, Napoleon sent five telegrams to Paris, acknowledging the disasters and appealing to the patriotism of the citizens, whose cries, 'À Berlin,' had done so much to provoke the war. In the last of these messages he plainly told them that it was necessary that Paris and France should 'consent to make great efforts of patriotism.' In Paris the news produced an effect such as that which is caused on a human being by a smart blow on the temple. There was no demonstration: the faculties of the mob seemed stunned. The awakening from the delirium which had sent the masses into the streets to shout for war, had paralysed all their energies. In vain did the Empress issue a reassuring proclamation. In vain did the ministers, while declaring Paris in a state of siege, exhort the people to rise as they had risen in 1792. The population seemed bewildered, and it was only when the awakening was complete, that, instead of responding to the call, the masses and their leaders began to search for a victim. The first victim was the Ollivier ministry. In the chambers which had been specially convoked, contrary to the wishes of the Emperor, the minister who had declared war 'with a light heart' announced his resignation, and with it, the fact that, with the consent of the Emperor, General Cousin-Montauban, Count of Palikao, the general who had commanded the French troops in the Chinese war of 1860, had been entrusted with the formation of a Cabinet. It was the last Cabinet of the Second Empire.

To return now to the field.

After his defeat at Wörth, M'Mahon had led his defeated and disorganised army to Nancy, thence to Chalons, without attempting to avail himself of the many defensive positions offered by the Vosges mountains. The Crown Prince of Prussia, committing to General von Werder, with the Baden troops and the Prussian Landwehr, the task of besieging Strasburg, was therefore able to cross those mountains without opposition. It was the fear lest that prince should again be able to attack the French marshal before he should have had time to reorganise his forces that had directed his movements, and those of the corps commanded by De Failly, on Chalons, there to unite with the reserves organised at that place. There M'Mahon arrived with but 16,000 of his original army of 38,500 on the 16th of August, and there the same day the Emperor joined him, having left Bazaine at Metz with about 170,000 men. Of these 11,000 were cavalry, and he had 280 guns.

On the 12th of August the Emperor had, in consequence of communications from Paris, renounced the command-in-chief of the French armies in favour of Marshal Bazaine, and a day or two later had, as we have seen, set out to join M'Mahon at Chalons. His last instructions to Bazaine—if, indeed, under the circumstances, they can be called instructions —were to the effect, that he should fall back with his army behind the Meuse, to form a close touch with

M·Mahon at Chalons, and with the troops which were rapidly approaching, consisting of the garrison of Rome, of the troops sent originally on board the fleet, of the marines, and of the remainder of the 7th corps. To carry out this idea, which had his full approval, the French commander-in-chief directed his engineers, on the 13th, to throw pontoon bridges over the Moselle; sent the same day a portion of his military trains as far as Gravelotte; and set out on the 14th to carry out the plan indicated, leaving only one infantry division to garrison Metz. Had he succeeded, the war would assuredly have assumed a phase very different from that which actually occurred. But, on that very day, the 14th, the first Prussian army, commanded by Von Steinmetz, had taken a position on the east front of Metz. The patrols sent out later in the day reported to the several corps-commanders that the French divisions encamped on the right bank of the Moselle had begun to march away. One of those commanders at once put his troops in motion.

There were three French army corps encamped on the right bank of the Moselle, the 2d, the 3d, and the 4th. The second and fourth had already begun their march when the third, left as the rear-guard, was suddenly attacked by a portion of the 1st Prussian army near the chateau of Colombey. It happened in this wise. On hearing that the French were moving off, the happy inspiration entered the mind of General von Goltz, commanding the advanced troops of the 7th Prussian army-corps, to dash forward to hinder as much as possible their retreat. Quitting then with his troops, at half-past three, his bivouac at Laquenexy, and summoning the 1st corps and the 1st cavalry division to follow in support, Von Goltz dashed forward and attacked the

3d corps at the village of St Barbe. The 2d and 4th corps turned back to help their comrades; supports came up to the Prussians, and very soon a serious action, extending from St Barbe to Grigy, a length of nearly seven miles, was engaged. For seven hours the battle raged with varying fortunes, both sides fighting with great courage and great determination. At nine o'clock the Prussians desisted, and whilst the French then moved to carry out the plan they had begun that morning, the Prussians fell back on their original positions. For neither side could the battle be claimed, in itself, as a victory, but, judging from its results, it was fraught with enormous advantage to the invaders, for it lost to Bazaine most precious hours, and those hours, well used by his enemies, forced his army, as we shall see, into a trap whence, during the war, it never emerged but to surrender.

Serious as was the battle of Colombey, it did not prevent the French from continuing their retrograde movement. They spent that same night (of the 14th) in crossing to the left bank of the Moselle. On the morning of the 15th Bazaine had his five corps, the 2d, Frossard's; the 3d, Decaen's; the 4th, L'Admirault's; the 6th, Canrobert's; and the Guards, Bourbaki's; ranged on the left bank of that river, with the road to Verdun open to him. He at once set it in motion in two parellel lines. But either from a lingering reluctance to quit the vicinity of Metz, or because he had not realised the vital importance of quick movement, nor the possibility of rapid movement on the part of the enemy, he made progress at a rate so slow, that when he encamped that night the advanced-guard of his northerly column was at Doncourt; that of the southern column at Vionville; the headquarters, with the bulk of the army at Gravelotte.

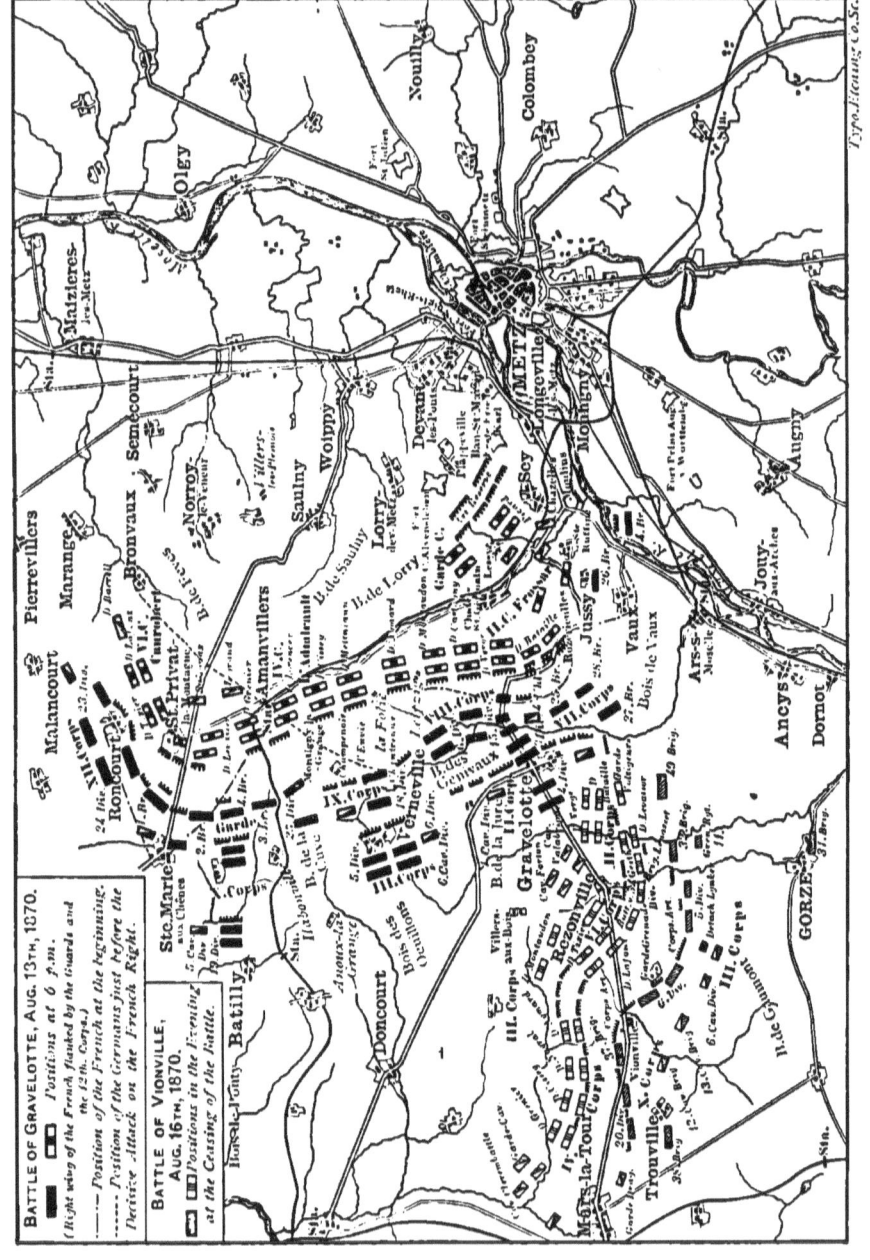

Great Energy of the Germans. 261

For the Germans, after the tremendous efforts they had made on the 14th to prevent the escape of their principal enemy, had become all the more determined to spare no pains still to detain him. For them the battle of Colombey had not been fought in vain. It had, as I have said, given the much required time to the second army to cross the Moselle. On the 14th, then, the following dispositions were made at the German headquarters. Of the first army, the corps of Manteuffel and two cavalry divisions were to remain on the right bank of the Moselle; the 7th and 8th corps, those of Zastrow and Goeben, were to cross that river to the south of Metz; the second army would follow their example. Following these orders on the evening of the 15th of August, whilst the French were resting in the positions I have mentioned, the 3d corps of the second army, that of Constantine von Alvensleben, began the passage, crossed the river, and pushing on in a northerly direction to gain the bye-road leading from Metz to Verdun, reached Gorze and Orville at three o'clock the following morning. Resting there but two hours Alvensleben resumed his march, followed by the 6th cavalry division towards Mars-la-Tour and Vionville. As he approached the latter place, the patrols he had sent to the front announced to him the presence of the advanced posts of the French, covering, they reported, a very large encampment. Recognising that he had succeeded in gaining a strong position on the enemy's flank, and that an attack even with his comparatively small force would, in the moral condition of the French army, hinder their forward march, Alvensleben resolved on an immediate assault. Riding with his cavalry to the front, he began the fight about seven o'clock with that arm alone. For two hours he sustained the combat against the superior numbers of the French infantry. The latter, who had wheeled round to meet their enemy, occupied Vionville with their right. Thence, to the left towards Metz, their line followed the crest of a range of hills, presenting a convex face to the Germans, who, it will be understood, were coming up from the south. The key of the position was Vionville, for, if the Germans could drive the French from that place, they would cut their communications with Verdun. The retention of Vionville became then the main question with the French, its capture the salient object of the Germans.

Bazaine was now thoroughly aware of the importance of pushing on to Verdun. He hesitated then to commit his army to offensive operations against the enemy on his flank, but continued to push his main force beyond Gravelotte, hoping to ward off the flank attack by the retention of the position I have described. But, at ten o'clock, the infantry of the 3d German corps reached the ground, and attacked Vionville with great fury. The French defended themselves with their usual gallantry, but whilst their leaders were distracted by two objects, that of escaping with the main body, whilst a portion of the army should ward off the flank attack, the Germans had for the moment but one object, that of taking Vionville. In this object they succeeded, after fierce fighting, at eleven o'clock. An hour later they had gained a position stretching from Flavigny to Tronville, and thence to the further end of the wood on its left, almost facing Mars-la-Tour. It was just at this time that Bazaine, accompanied by Frossard, rode to the field to strengthen his receding centre. He had just succeeded in doing this when information reached the German leader that Canrobert, who commanded on the French right, was forcing back the German left. To restore the battle there Alvensleben despatched General Bredow with his cavalry brigade. Bredow galloped up

The Battle of Vionville.

the slopes to the north of Vionville, deployed his men, and, charging under a very hot fire, forced the enemy to give ground.

It was now three o'clock, and whilst in the centre and on the left the battle languished, a second furious combat had commenced on the French right between the troops just arrived on both sides—the 3d and 4th French, and the 10th German, corps. After a fiercely contested encounter of three hours' duration, the superior numbers of the French prevailed, and the attack was slowly forced back. On their right, and in the centre, however, the Germans clung firmly to the positions they had gained. During the three hours' contest I have referred to, Prince Frederic Charles, who had now assumed supreme direction of the fight, had failed in an attempt to turn the French right beyond Mars-le-Tour; the French had then endeavoured to take full advantage of this failure, but their forward movement had been checked by the brigade of the dragoons of the Guard, whilst another cavalry brigade assailed their left wing. Then ensued a terrible contest between the cavalry of the two armies, not unequal in number, for there were twenty-two squadrons of the French against twenty-four of the Germans. It was the fiercest cavalry combat of the war. Five thousand men met in a hand-to-hand encounter, the more severe as each man felt that upon the issue depended the ultimate fate of the army of which he was a component part. After many alternations the French were forced back; then the Germans, to finish the day, made a combined attack on the heights of Rezonville. But there the defenders stood firm, and the attack was repulsed. When darkness set in, the Prussian advanced posts extended from the Bois des Oignons along the plateau of Rezonville as far as Yronbach. Both sides then rested from their labours.

The battle had been one of the bloodiest of the war. It had lasted twelve hours, and the losses on both sides had been enormous.[1] Both occupied during the night the positions they had maintained during the battle.

Bazaine telegraphed to Paris that the enemy had been repulsed along the whole line, and that the French held their positions. This, in a certain sense, was true : he had repulsed the German attack, and, though the road to Verdun was no longer available, he had still a way to the north open to him. On the other hand, the German attack had lost him another day. He could still, however, he hoped, beat back the enemy, and force his way out of the trap in which it was designed to detain him. He spent the 17th, then, in moving the right wing of his army across the north Verdun road to St Privat, on the road from Metz to Briey. His left, composed of the 2d corps under Frossard and the 3d under Lebœuf, he placed so that its extremest point should rest on a hill near the village of Rozerieulles, on the main road to Gravelotte. From this hill its right extended towards St Privat, so as to come in touch with the corps of L'Admirault, on whose right again, occupying St Privat, was Canrobert. Notwithstanding his heavy losses on the previous day, Bazaine still could reckon on a force but little short of 125,000 men.

Amongst the German generals who had attacked the French at Vionville, the expectation had been that the French, confiding in the superiority in point of numbers which they at the moment commanded, would become the assailants on the 17th. But when they saw that

[1] The French lost 879 officers and 16,128 men ; the Germans 711 officers and 15,079 men. The number of the French on the field amounted to 138,000, with 476 guns ; but of these only two-thirds were engaged ; that of the Germans to 67,000, with 222 guns. *Vide* note at end of chapter.

Bazaine was simply changing his position for one presenting greater capabilities for defence, they prepared for a decisive battle on the morrow. The day's rest enabled the King to call up the remaining portions of his second army.

At six o'clock on the morning of the 18th, the King, who had slept at Pont-à-Mousson, rode to the summit of the hill to the south of Flavigny. Thence he could see the second army, which had come up an hour earlier, marching in a northerly direction in perfect order, each of its corps complete in itself, each with its own leader, and its destination clearly imprinted on that leader's mind. The direction of the 7th corps was towards Gravelotte. It seemed to him at first that the French right wing had established itself at St Privat to cover the movements of its left and centre.

The King of Prussia had at his disposal 230,000 men; all well-trained soldiers; many of them flushed with recent victory. At ten o'clock, after some changes, necessitated by the fuller information he obtained as to the enemy's position, he directed the 9th corps on Vernéville and La Folie, opposite to the French centre (L'Admirault); the corps of guards in support on Amanvillers; the 12th corps on to the high-road to Briey. Soon it appeared to the attacking party that the French position extended to its right as far as a point opposite Vernéville, and that there was concentrated the extreme right of the French army. The position was covered by ditches and hastily thrown-up intrenchments. Not only was it a very strong position, but the fire from the chassepôts, commanding a longer range than the Prussian needle-gun, commanded the ground over which the German army must advance. The dispositions for attack were then so far changed, that whilst the first army should hold Gravelotte and detain the enemy at the nearest point to Metz, the second, inclining to its left, should drive the centre and right from the strong positions it had occupied.

It was close upon midday before the batteries of the 9th Prussian corps, suffering in its advance very heavy losses from the chassepôts, opened fire near Vernéville on the French centre. The French batteries replied with vigour, and, soon after, the French tirailleurs, taking advantage of the fact that the German batteries were unsupported by infantry, charged one of them, and captured two of its guns. At two o'clock, the other German batteries had been so much damaged, that they were no longer in a position to continue the fire, nor was the situation mended when the artillery of the 2d division of the same corps (the 9th) arrived at Habonville, and put in position, on both sides o fthe railway, its five batteries. Upon these the concentric fire of the French was now directed. The German batteries which had been playing since midday were now drawn to the rear pursued by the French tirailleurs, who, however, were repulsed. Reinforcements soon came up from the 3d corps and the Guards, and before long there was concentrated at Vernéville a front of 120 pieces of artillery, supported by infantry. The anxiety which had been very real at the German headquarters for the safety of this position ceased from this moment. The position indeed had been a dangerous one for the assailants. The German staff, with all its intelligence, had mistaken the French centre for its right. If Bazaine, on his side, had not made the mistake of massing too large a portion of his force close to Metz; had he placed the Guards on his right, instead of keeping them in hand; in fact, had he been a daring and not a timid commander, the Germans might have had to pay dearly for their mistake.

For, about two o'clock, the German leaders had begun to realise that the position which they had regarded as the French right, and had attacked in that belief, was really the French centre. The general commanding the 1st division of the Prussian Guards had seen his left strongly menaced at the moment he believed that he occupied a position immediately in front of the extreme right of the French line. The point whence he was menaced, a village called Sainte-Marie-aux-Chênes, was strongly occupied and capable of a good defence. It became necessary, therefore, to carry it at all hazards. But for this it was necessary to await the arrival of the corps of Saxons, then rapidly approaching.

At three o'clock the Saxons' batteries reached a position whence they could open on Sainte-Marie, and, as soon as their fire had made itself felt, the Prussian and Saxon infantry charged and carried the village. They were not allowed, however, to hold it with impunity. The French made many and well-sustained efforts to regain it, but the constant arrival of reinforcements gave the Germans the advantage, and they held the place to the end. Soon after, the 9th corps established itself in the farm of Champenois, opposite to the very centre of the French position: but although they made many efforts, some of them in considerable force, to break through the front of the French position, they were invariably repulsed, and suffered severely. At this point, up to five o'clock, the attack on the French centre had been practically resultless.

At five o'clock, however, all the divisions of the army of Prince Frederic Charles had taken up the positions prescribed to them. The King and his advisers had originally intended to await that event before making the attack general. But the sound of the heavy fire at Vionville, at midday, led them prematurely to believe the moment had arrived. The King ordered, then, the artillery of the right wing to open fire. In pursuance of this order sixteen batteries of the 7th and 8th corps, placed on the right and left of Gravelotte, began to play on the French position, and although the gunners were exposed to, and greatly suffered from, the fire of the French tirailleurs, these latter were dislodged by the German infantry, and the batteries mentioned were enabled to advance close to the western border of the valley of the Mance, thence to open a heavy fire upon the right of the French left.

In front of the left, and of the left half of the centre of the French position, stretching from a point on its left, where it almost touched the Bois de Vaux to another ust beyond the village of Champenois, was the wood known as the Bois de Génivaux. The French still held the centre of this wood, but the 9th German corps had penetrated into its extreme northern portion, and now the 29th brigade of the 1st division of the 8th corps, covered by the artillery fire referred to in the preceding paragraph, entered the right of it, and some fractions of it gained the stone and gravel quarries of the farm St Hubert (opposite the centre of the French left). During their advance the German artillery fire had at this point dominated that of the French, and the latter had concentrated their efforts to the defence of the farm of St Hubert, threatened by the fractions of which I have spoken. At three o'clock the Germans carried this farm. A very fierce attempt made by the victors supported by the 31st brigade, to carry the farms of Moscou and Leipsig, the former to the French right of St Hubert, the latter at a greater distance to the right of that, both situated on ground that had been cleared, was defeated with enormous loss to the Germans; but the 26th brigade succeeded in capturing Jussy, a farm to the Prussian right of the Bois de Vaux, at the apex of the angle of the left of the French position, the point, in fact, where the extreme left was thrown back towards Pappeville. The possession of this farm established the Germans, who carried it, on the direct road from Verdun to Metz at a point close to the latter fortress.

It will thus be seen that between three and four o'clock the Germans had made some progress on their right. But it was not progress of a decisive character; it had been gained at an enormous loss; and it left the French in very strong positions. But, such as it was, it inspired one at least of the German commanders, as we shall see, with confidence that he had only to advance to complete the victory. The same sanguine disposition did not prevail in the German centre, for the generals there, not yet supported by Prince Frederic Charles on their left, had a sort of dim consciousness that there were, in front of that left, masses of French troops with whom they would have to deal, and who, if they should promptly make a forward movement, would take them in flank, whilst they were seriously engaged with the French centre in front of them. In this respect they were right. Not one of the German leaders had even at four o'clock realised the commanding position occupied by the French right, and it had been in the power of the French general commanding there, Marshal Canrobert, to make the assault fatal to the assailants.

Prominent amongst the German generals who, at four o'clock, believed the battle to be gained, was General Steinmetz, the commander of the first army. He then at that hour gave the order to renew the attack on the French left with fresh troops. In obedience to this order the 7th corps proceeded to occupy the outer fringe (that nearest to the French) of the Bois des Génivaux, whilst four batteries, supported by the first cavalry division, advanced at a trot through the long defile of 1500 paces to the east of Gravelotte. But the French were ready for their foe. No sooner did the heads of the columns emerge from the defile than there opened upon them from the chassepôts and guns which commanded its mouth a fire so terrible and so concentrated that, in a moment, all the gunners of four batteries were killed, and it required extraordinary efforts on the part of the Germans to drag back the guns to the fringe of the wood. The German batteries which had been placed at the farm St Hubert suffered also greatly from the French fire, but they held the farm. The cavalry which had been sent in support of the four batteries had succeeded in deploying in the direction of St Hubert: but between them and the French there was no position they could charge. Realising this fact, and suffering greatly from the bursting of the enemy's shells, the cavalry retreated, having accomplished nothing, by the valley of the Mance.[1]

The retreat of the German cavalry encouraged the French infantry to the left-front of St Hubert to deploy and push forward to the farm of Point du Jour, driving back as they advanced, detached bodies of the enemy to the fringe of the wood. Their chassepôts even reached the spot where the general-in-chief of the Prussian army

---

[1] La Mance is a rivulet running from a point near La Folie, the centre of the French position, through the ground occupied by the 7th and 8th German corps, and thence, after making a curve to the south, entering the Moselle near Ars-sur-Moselle.

had taken post, and a ball from one of them killed the horse on which Prince Adalbert was mounted. Reinforcements enabled the Germans to win back their lost ground at this point, but they could make no impression on the main left of the French position, and at five o'clock both parties, thoroughly wearied, rested as if by mutual consent from their labours.

But the rest was not for long. It was nearing six o'clock when the Prussian King reached with his staff the hill to the south of the Malmaison farm. From this point could be seen the farms of Point du Jour, Moscou, Leipzig, and Montigny-la-Grange; but from Point du Jour to La Folie (the French centre) the smoke completely obscured the view; whilst, on the extreme French right, to the north, a distance of over four miles, the sound of heavy firing came with ever increasing vehemence. It seemed to the King, under these circumstances that, unless he was ready to admit failure, something decisive must be attempted. Accordingly he gave orders to Steinmetz to advance, and placed at his disposal the second corps, which, after a long march, had just reached the ground.

Accordingly, Steinmetz, taking with him all the available troops of the 7th corps, excepting five battalions left in reserve, crossed the valley of La Mance, and, joined as he marched by the battalions posted in the wood of Vaux, took the direction of Point du Jour and the quarries with the hope of driving thence the 2d French corps.

But there the French were ready to receive him. The 2d corps had but just been reinforced by the Voltigeurs of the Guard, and Bazaine had sent all the available reserves to support the front line. Upon the advancing Germans, then, there poured from the French position an artillery and infantry fire of the most murderous character. Steinmetz could make no way. But just then the 2d German corps, led by Fransecky, which had been marching since two o'clock in the morning, reached a point to the south of Gravelotte. Recking but little of the fatigue they had suffered, the gallant Pomeranians composing this corps manifested an irrepressible desire to be led instantly against the enemy. Yielding to their enthusiasm their generals led them beyond Gravelotte right up to the quarries and to within a few hundred feet of Point du Jour. Then between them and the French there ensued a furious hand to hand encounter. It was so dark that it was almost impossible to distinguish friend from foe. Firing therefore gradually ceased, though it was not altogether silenced till ten o'clock. Before that hour, however, the Germans had recognised that the French occupied on their left a position which was impregnable, at least for the moment, and their leaders resolved to persevere no further till the morrow.

Meanwhile, on the French right, to the right and left of St Privat, where Canrobert commanded, events were progressing which exercised a great influence on the general results. Canrobert's own corps, the 6th, and the 4th, under L'Admirault, occupied the villages of St Privat and Roncourt, the former just opposite the village of St Marie, the latter to the right of St Privat. Their left held the railway station of Armanvilliers. Opposed to them, on their proper right, were the Saxons, led by the Prince Royal of Saxony, and the Prussian Guards, commanded by the Prince of Würtemberg: but up to a quarter past five o'clock there had been no communication between the the two commanders. In fact, it was just at that hour that the Prince reached the village of St Ail, three-quarters of a mile, in the direction of Metz, from St Marie-aux-Chênes. At that time the Prince Royal of Saxony was engaged in concentrating his troops along the forest of Auboue, with the intention of marching thence to turn the extreme right of the French army.

Left, then, as far as the troops to his proper left were concerned, to himself, the Prince of Würtemberg despatched his fourth brigade against the farm of Jerusalem, immediately to the (French) left of St Privat. At the same time General Manstein, to whom had been consigned, at Habonville, the 2d brigade of the Guards, directed it upon Amanvillers, still further to the south of St Privat. Between these marched the Hessian battalions. Half an hour later there followed from St Marie, direct upon St Privat, the first division of the Guards. Whilst these troops are advancing we will proceed to note what had been the precautions taken by the French to ward off such an attack.

The main defences of the French position were St Privat and Amanvillers, the latter being the railway station on the line from Metz to Verdun. The distance between the two is about a mile and a quarter. Both these places were very strongly occupied. In front of them, especially of St Privat, the slopes leading to the valley, covered with brushwood and trenches, were guarded by infantry and artillery, so well disposed, that, up to the moment of the attack of which I am about to write, they had warded off every attack. Not a single German cannon-ball had reached either of the two main defences, St Privat and Amanvillers.

At five o'clock the Prince of Würtemberg made dispositions to attack the two main points noted. He directed the 4th brigade of Guards on the farm of Jerusalem, whilst General Manstein marched the other brigade

S

which had been assigned to him against Amanvillers. Between the two attacks marched the Hessians. Half an hour later the 1st division of the Guards was directed from St Marie-aux-Chênes towards St Privat. To march against this latter, which in itself was very strong, all the houses being of masonry, well armed, and full of soldiers, the Germans had to ascend a long slope formed of ridges and brushwood, every point of which was occupied by the French tirailleurs, so posted that each ridge as it neared the town commanded the ridge below it. There could scarcely have been a position better adapted for defence.

And most gallantly did the French defend it. 'The Guards who advanced to the attack suffered losses out of all proportion,' writes Moltke. 'In less than half an hour five of their battalions lost all their officers and the others the greater part of them, especially the superior officers. Thousands of killed and wounded marked the passage of those battalions, which, despite of their heavy losses, continued to advance. Their ranks, decimated, re-formed again and again, and even when they had as their leaders young lieutenants or even cadets, these brave soldiers held firmly together, and preserved all their moral force.'

Gradually the French fell back before their persistent advance. At a quarter past six the Germans had made good their way to within 600 paces of Amanvillers, and 800 of St Privat. From those points to the two places mentioned the ascent increased in steepness, and was almost without shelter. There, then, the exhausted assailants halted, taking advantage of the shelter-trenches which the French had abandoned. There, for the space of half an hour, extended on a line of 4000 paces, and having as a reserve at St Marie but four battalions, they kept at bay for half an hour the division De Cissey and the French cavalry, who attacked them repeatedly.

Why the French generals who commanded on the right did not employ a greater strength to accomplish a result which, followed up, would have gained for France a great victory over vastly superior numbers, can only be accounted for by the fact that the previous successes of the German had rendered them doubly cautious. They had, they conceived, only a sufficient number of men to defend the strong positions they occupied, and they knew not the weakness of the attacking enemy. Some recognition of the possibilities before him seem to have been aroused in the mind of Marshal Canrobert, for earlier in the day he had sent a message to Bazaine, earnestly entreating the despatch to his assistance of the French Guards. Had those Guards reached him, the result of the day would have been different. Bazaine, regarding the maintenance of a close communication with Metz to be absolutely essential, had but partially complied with his lieutenant's request. He had sent to him a division of the Grenadiers of the Guard, under General Picard. But Picard lost his way, and, though the distance was but five miles, did not reach Canrobert till too late. The fate of France had been in his hands, and he sealed it.

For, whilst Canrobert was too feebly endeavouring, with an insufficient force, to destroy the tired German soldiers who lay panting in the shelter-trenches at distances of from six to eight hundred paces from his two main positions, there were marching to assist the latter those Saxon troops whom I have described as having, a little before five o'clock, marched to their left to double up the extreme right of the French. About seven o'clock, two of their brigades appeared on the field of the fight to the left of the German Guards. Two others were reforming near the forest of Aubouc. Whilst they were thus occupied, the twenty-four batteries of the German artillery had opened a strong fire upon Roncourt (to the French right front of St Privat).

It became then, at this period, about seven o'clock of that August evening, clear to Marshal Canrobert, that the Germans with increased forces were about to make a very serious effort to force the positions he held. Regarding St Privat as the key of that position, the French Marshal resolved to concentrate his troops in and about that strong post. Whilst holding St Privat to the death, he would leave but a feeble body of men in Roncourt, and would throw back his right so as to occupy in strength the outer fringe of the wood of Jaumont. By this disposition he kept his troops well in hand, an advantage not to be despised when the hour of the day is considered. The consequence was that the Saxons, pressing on to Roncourt, occupied it with but slight opposition, and came in touch on their right with their battalions which had preferred to march direct on St Privat, and who, in their turn, joined on their right the troops of the Guards who, since a quarter past six o'clock, had been resting in the shelter-trenches.

No sooner had this junction been effected than a very fierce artillery fire from the twenty-four German batteries opened upon the posts occupied by the French. Under this fire the masonry houses of St Privat crumbled. It was, however, promptly answered by the French guns posted between St Privat and the forest of Jaumont, and which commanded the ground across which the Saxons were advancing. Other batteries posted to the (French) left of St Privat, and the tirailleurs, who covered the French front, opened likewise on the Prussian troops to the right of the Saxons a fire so severe and so continued that the

The Germans carry St Privat.

German advance on that side became possible only at the expense of enormous sacrifices.

Still it was possible, and the German soldiers, though losing men at each step, pressed forward with admirable courage. Soon they had reduced the distance to St Privat from 800 to 300 paces. Thence, joined by fractions from the 10th corps, they gave all along the line the last assault. The French defended themselves with the greatest resolution and tenacity, but their defences were in flames : gradually they were attacked on three sides : at last, driven back by vastly superior numbers, they had to choose between the fire of the houses and the enemy. Those who could not escape then surrendered. The few who could escape fell back on Amanvillers, which held out till three o'clock in the morning. During the night and the following morning the French right and centre fell back in disorder on their left, and thence into Metz. The road to Paris had been lost.

The loss of the battle of Gravelotte must be attributed to the errors of the French commander-in-chief. Bazaine wished to seize the road to Paris, and at the same time to maintain his hold on Metz. To accomplish this end, he should have made his right strong enough to destroy the German troops which might attempt to hinder its progress. This had been possible at a quarter past six o'clock. Bazaine had some glimpse of the possibilities before him when he detached General Picard and a division of the Grenadiers of the Guard to his aid. But the remissness of that officer, who, quitting Plappeville at three o'clock, had not accomplished the five miles which intervened at seven, rendered nugatory this feeble effort. It was this failure, combined with the heroic determination of the Germans to renew the battle at seven o'clock, which lost the battle of Gravelotte to the French. The latter had fought well, and against vastly superior numbers.[1] They had held their ground in the centre and on the left. It is possible that a more vigorous offensive on the part of Canrobert about a quarter past six o'clock might have prevented the after attack of seven o'clock, but even that is a matter for conjecture. This is certain, that the French soldiers fought nobly; that they were badly commanded; that their defeat was, under the circumstances, fatal.

The Germans lost 5238 killed (of whom 329 were officers), and 14,435 wounded (of whom 577 were officers). The French lost, in killed and wounded, 609 officers and 11,705 men.

[1] Von Moltke's enumeration of the numbers cannot be accepted. Because in the October following there were 173,000 soldiers in Metz, he calculates that there must have been 180,000 in the field at Gravelotte. The Germans, he asserts, numbered exactly 178,818 men. But he leaves out of this latter enumeration the whole of the German 2d corps, which, though it arrived late, joined in the fight; nor does he count the portion of the first German army which shelled Metz from the eastern bank of the river, and kept the Imperial Guard on the spot. The reference to the French numbers is still more absurdly incorrect. In the 173,000 of the garrison who surrendered in October, at least 60,000 were Gardes Mobiles, who took no part in the battle. Bazaine asserts that he had but 100,000 engaged; the Prussian staff reckon the French as from '125,000 to 150,000'; General Hamley, a high authority, states that the French were 'outnumbered by more than two to one'; Brockhaus' 'Conversations-Lexikon, a standard work, gives the respective numbers at 230,000 and 150,000. But it is certain that the entire French army under Bazaine at that time was somewhat under 125,000. We shall probably be correct in accepting 230,000 as the strength of the Germans, and in setting down the French, outside of Metz, at 110,000. It is absolutely impossible that they could have exceeded that number.

Vide a very interesting article in the *Academy* of December 19, 1891, by Judge O'Connor Morris, on this subject.

CHAPTER XIV.

SEDAN.

DURING the 19th of August the rest of the army of Bazaine entered Metz. The force had been cut off by the incapacity of its generals from all active co-operation in the defence of France. The Germans did all that was feasible to close the avenues of escape from the trap in which their enemies were now confined. Early the same morning their cavalry destroyed the rail communication between Metz and Thionville. Then, leaving the greater part of the 1st and 2d armies to blockade the fortress, the Prussian King detached from the latter three corps—the Guards, the 4th, and the 12th—and committing the command of them to the Crown Prince of Saxony[1] as a separate army, to be called the 4th, directed him to effect a junction with the 3d army, and to watch closely and follow the operations of the army then re-forming at Chalons under Marshal M'Mahon, with which was the Emperor Napoleon.

Including reinforcements, the army which remained before Metz, and which was commanded by Prince Frederic Charles, consisted of eight and a half army-corps; viz., the 3d army, composed of five and a

[1] The Crown Prince of Saxony enjoyed the reputation of being the only German general of royal blood who could dispense with the services of a chief of the staff. He was too capable to need an adviser.

half army corps; and the newly-enrolled 4th army, counting, as we have seen, three corps. Attached to it also were four divisions of Prussian cavalry, the Saxon cavalry division, and the South-German cavalry. These two armies, the 3d and 4th, delayed not an hour longer than was necessary to carry out the general instructions their general had received from the headquarter staff.

The task required the exercise of energy, quick and prompt decision, and accurate judgment. The new army of Marshal M'Mahon had it in its power to fall back on Paris, and to increase by an army of tried soldiers the garrison of the threatened capital of France. One of the hitherto possible obstructors to the siege of that city —the army of Bazaine—lay behind the walls of Metz. There remained, in the opinion of the German chiefs— an opinion not justified by events—only the army of M'Mahon. That destroyed, Paris must succumb. To remove that army from the path which led to Paris, or to destroy it, was then the task entrusted to the Crown Prince. Able as he was, he could scarcely have accomplished it but for the infatuation of the advisers of the Empress Regent, then exercising all the powers of the Emperor in the administration of affairs.

When, on the 28th of July, the Emperor had set out to join the armies on the frontier, he had committed the government of France to the Empress. I have told how, a few days later, the ministry of Ollivier had been forced by public opinion, dismayed by the earlier defeats of the French, to resign: how it had been succeeded by a ministry of which General Cousin - Montauban, Count of Palikao, had become Minister - President, Minister of War, and leading spirit. He it was whose advice, or rather whose orders, given in the name and

M'Mahon ordered to help Bazaine.

with the authority of the Empress-Regent of France, led the Empire to destruction. We shall see how.

After his defeat at Wörth, M'Mahon had fallen back with the disordered remnants of his army on Chalons, there to reorganise and strengthen it. Much progress had been made in both respects, when, after the result of the battle of Gravelotte had been known in Paris, he received instructions from the Count of Palikao to march with the four army corps at his disposal northwards towards the Meuse, and to give a hand to the beleaguered Bazaine. The Emperor, greatly suffering from the disease which finally caused his death, scarcely able to sit on a horse, and then suffering acute agony; his spirits depressed more even than by his sufferings by the misfortunes which had accompanied all the operations of the French armies, accompanied the army. But he accompanied it solely as a spectator. As Emperor he had no power to exercise, for he had transferred all his authority to the Empress-Regent; as General he was likewise powerless, for on the 12th of August he had resigned his command in favour of Bazaine. His great wish was to end his life gloriously.

M'Mahon set forth to carry out his instructions. He marched from Chalons on the 23d of August with four corps,[1] and quitting the grand route made his way across country as best he could to the village of Dontrien, on the bank of the river Suippe. The army rested that night on the banks of this stream, stretching from Auberive to Heutregiville. The next night the army bivouacked at Contreuve and the villages in the vicinity, having its head-quarters at Rethel. On the 25th it was evident that great uncertainty prevailed at head-quarters, for in

[1] The 1st, under Ducrot; the 5th, De Failly; the 7th, Douay; the 3d, composed of fresh levies, Lebrun; a total of about 135,000 men.

obedience to orders the army executed a change of front on its left, the 7th corps proceeding about five miles to Vouziers, the 5th and 12th remaining at Rethel, the first halting at Attigny. At midday the army was ranged on the left bank of the Aisne. It was clear that M'Mahon expected an attack, for a careful watch was kept on the route from Monthois, by which only an enemy could approach.

That same evening there arrived along that route, viz., the route of Monthois, the cavalry division Margueritte, 2000 in number, which had been ordered to support the 7th corps and to cover the left flank of the army. For some reason which was not apparent, this division was now brought into the very centre of the army. This movement caused a lively sensation in the camp, and the soldiers, always since the events which immediately followed the outbreak of hostilities, distrustful of their leaders, began more and more to question alike their abilities and their loyalty.

The following morning, the 26th, M'Mahon, leaving a brigade of the 2d division to watch the route of Monthois, directed the 7th corps to pass through Vouziers, cross to the right bank of the Aisne, then to halt and pile arms, whilst he despatched the 4th Hussars along the high road to reconnoitre. Some hours later, about half-past two, a despatch from General Bordas, whose brigade had been despatched to occupy Bugancy, a few miles distant, announced that he had encountered superior forces at Grand-Pré, and had been forced to halt there. The commander of the 7th corps, General Douay,[1] expecting to be attacked, at once made his men fall in, and marching forward a short distance ranged his division on two hills between the villages of Chestres and Falaise, sending an aide-de-camp to the Marshal with the informa-

[1] A brother of the General Douay killed at Weissenburg.

The Soldiers distrust their Leaders. 283

tion. The corps remained in eager expectation of combat till four o'clock, when the return of the 4th Hussars caused fresh excitement. They had seen nothing. Two hours later a fresh despatch arrived from General Bordas with the information that he was still at Grand Pré, and dared not move, as he was confident that the country between that place and Vouziers was occupied by the Prussians. The officer who brought the message, traversing the very ground along which the general must have marched, proved that he was badly informed, and was deficient in enterprise. However, on the arrival of the message, General Dumont, who commanded the division of which the Bordas brigade was a part, set out to Grand Pré to disengage his lieutenant.

Meanwhile General Douay had received a letter from the Marshal, telling him to hold his position; that he would support him; that he had despatched the 1st corps to Terron, the 5th to Buzancy, whilst the 12th would remain in second line at Le Chêne. There was a rumour that the Germans were in strength (100,000) at Grand Pré, and during the day that followed the men eagerly longed for their appearance. But when midday arrived, then one, then two o'clock, and there was not the sign of a single helmet, the intelligent French soldiers began to recognise that their generals had been again mistaken. It seemed to them in the highest degree ridiculous that, marching as they were, to give the hand to Bazaine, they should remain halted on the mere rumour, unconfirmed by a single fact, that the Prussians were close in front of them.

M'Mahon had never favoured the plan of marching upon Verdun to help Bazaine. According to his views, Paris, about to be seriously threatened, was the point upon which the army should fall back. His views were completely shared by the Emperor. Fully believing that the attempt to reach Verdun would be fatal to the army and to the country, M'Mahon resolved then, during the 27th, to renounce the forward movement and to retreat on the capital. That night the army fell back accordingly, and reached the town of Le Chêne. Thence M'Mahon despatched one telegram to Bazaine, informing him that the arrival of the Crown Prince at Chalons had forced him to fall back on the strong places in the north; another to Palikao, telling him of the retreat and of his reasons for it.

The telegram reached Paris that night. To the Empress and the Count of Palikao it was alike unwelcome. But little, they felt, was wanting to cause an insurrection in Paris which must be fatal to the dynasty. The return of the Emperor at the head of a defeated and discouraged army would suffice to produce an outbreak which would be irresistible. At all costs, then, it must be prevented. This selfish and shallow reasoning decided the minister of war to despatch positive instructions to M'Mahon to march on Montmédy. To him it was nothing that such a march, possible, if directed with energy on the 25th, had become on the 27th an act of pure madness. It was to send the army to destruction. The death of the Emperor during a general immolation would probably be accepted by the Parisian mob as an obliteration of all past grievances and the dynasty would be saved.

Both the Emperor and M'Mahon recognised the meaning of the order. But they prepared immediately to obey it. That same night, a night of storm and tempest, the army began to retrace its steps. The men were thoroughly discouraged. The orders and counter-orders, the hesitations, the apparent ignorance of their leaders, had shaken all their faith. On the 28th a skirmish between the rearguard of the 7th corps and the sight of the burning village of Falaise showed them that their march to Le Chêne had given the Germans the time they required to forestall them everywhere. What was equally discouraging was the certainty that their general-in-chief was absolutely ignorant of the whereabouts of the main army of the enemy.

The first intention of the Marshal had been to despatch the 7th corps by way of Buzancy to Stenay, where it could have crossed the Meuse. But hearing, by rumour only, that the Prussians had already reached Stenay, he directed that corps to march so as to be able the following day to cross the Meuse at Mouzon. At the same time the 5th corps, which had had a skirmish with the enemy at Buzancy, was directed to retreat on Nourat, the 12th on Mouzon, the 1st to move to Raucourt. The 7th corps during its march was watched by the German skirmishers the Uhlans, who appeared and disappeared without exchanging a shot.

That evening General Douay, perceiving his men exhausted by fatigue and want of food, had authorised their halting for the night at a place a few miles short of the camping ground ordered by the Marshal. The latter galloped down the following morning to demand the reason. It was then arranged between them that whilst the 1st division and the convoy of provisions should continue the march to Mouzon, the other two divisions should proceed by Raucourt and Autrecourt to cross the Meuse at Villers. The Marshal hoped to reach with all his troops the right bank of the river that night.

The march was a sad one. Firing, heavy firing, was heard on the right. It was evident that the Germans were attacking in force the 5th corps between Buzancy and Beauclair. At any moment the 7th corps might find itself in contact with the enemy, and at the moment the divisions of the 7th corps were scattered. General Douay sent orders that they should march direct on Raucourt. His orders to cross the Meuse that night were precise, and he adopted the only means by which they could be carried out.

Under many difficulties the 7th corps was approaching Raucourt when, at a turn of the road, it encountered the terrified remains of the brigade of the 1st division which had been escorting the convoy of provisions, and which, by an error of judgment, mistaking the route, had fallen in with the 5th corps just as it had been defeated by the Germans at Varniforet, near Beaumont. The troops entered Raucourt helter-skelter, their generals as ignorant as they were regarding all the circumstances of the attack and the position of the Germans. They now hesitated as to the direction they should take on quitting Raucourt, whether they should still, under the altered circumstances, march on Autrecourt and cross the Meuse at Villers. It was five o'clock, and the men had marched since the early morning. No food was to be had at Raucourt, for the Marshal and the 1st corps had passed through it during the day and had not left behind even a loaf of bread. It was decided, then, despite the fatigue and hunger of the men, who had eaten nothing for two days, to push on by the defile of Haraucourt to Remilly, a distance of rather less than five miles. They were but just in time. As the rearguard of the corps marched out of Raucourt the Germans entered it, and two of their batteries, posted on a height to the left, played upon the retreating Frenchmen. Such was the discouragement of the troops, that if the Germans had pushed on and had vigorously attacked them in the narrow and still narrowing defile of Haraucourt, they would have been destroyed almost to a man. But, fortunately for the French, the Germans contented themselves with a continuous fire from their guns, sufficiently terrifying under the circumstances, for the road was encumbered by that portion of the baggage which had preceded the army corps.

At length a turn of the road took the retreating force out of the line of fire. Autrecourt was reached. Thence the defile opened out, and the wearied and famished soldiers reached the heights of Remilly. Below them was the Meuse, that Meuse so longed for, so despaired of. Beyond could be discerned, in the faint glimmer of the twilight, the fortified walls of Sedan. Early the following morning the French army took a position on the heights of La Moncelle, Duigny, and Givonne, on the right bank of the rivulet of that name, a tributary of the Meuse, flowing to the east of Bazeilles; their line continued to the east by Illy and Floing until it rested on the Meuse near the peninsula of Iges. There we must leave them whilst we follow the Crown Prince of Saxony and the 3d army in their march from Metz, on the morrow of the victory of Gravelotte, and describe how he manœuvred so that M'Mahon should take the direction he desired.

. On the 19th, the day after that battle, the two armies directed to operate against M'Mahon had begun their movements. The 4th corps marched direct to the Meuse, whilst the 3d army, with which were the King and the headquarter-staff, crossed that river, and pressed on to Bar-le-Duc. A brigade of Hartmann's Bavarian corps was left before Toul, to replace a division of the 4th corps which had fruitlessly assailed that fortress, and which now took its place with the 4th corps. At Ligny, on the Meuse, two and a half miles below Bar-le-Duc, the Crown Prince had, on the 20th, a long interview with Moltke, Blumenthal, and afterwards also with the King. Information had reached him that M'Mahon had quitted Chalons with his army, and the question to be considered was, whether he would march to Paris, or take a flanking position, whence he could assail the German armies as they should march in that direction. It was decided that under any circumstances the Crown Prince should continue his march on Chalons. Whilst he was marching in that direction, information reached him that M'Mahon had been moving towards Rheims, but suddenly quitting that line, had turned in a northerly direction towards Rethel. It was clear, then, that he had no intention of making for Paris, but was probably bent on marching, by a circuitous route, to relieve Bazaine. To baffle the French Marshal in this attempt, it was decided to give to the expeditionary force a wheeling movement to its right, so as to move in a northerly direction. On the 26th of August, then, the 4th army took the road to the north, whilst the 3d marched to Clermont (en Argonne). To support these, and to prevent any possible dash of the French towards Metz, the 3d and 9th corps were detached from the investing army to Etain. On the 27th a detachment of the Saxon cavalry, commanded by Count Lippe, surprised the 12th regiment of Chasseurs near Buzancy; beat them after a hard fight; slew many of them; and caused a considerable panic in the French army. The Germans only fell back when two French corps moved to the support of their comrades. The day following, the King, who was at Varennes, despatched orders to the Crown Prince of Saxony to take with his army a defensive position on the left bank of the Meuse. He was however empowered, in case he should not find overwhelming numbers in front of him, to occupy the road between Vouzier and Stenay, advancing thence to Beaumont. The following day, the 29th, the Crown Prince despatched the 3d corps to occupy this road. At Nouart, his advanced guard came suddenly upon the rear-guard of the French, and a fight ensued which lasted till evening, and ended in the defeat of the latter. On the body of a French staff-officer, there was found a plan of the operations which the French were intending to execute. After studying this, the German commander decided that the right wing of the 4th army should push on at once to Stenay, supported by the 1st Bavarian corps, which formed the right wing of the 3d army; that that army, with three corps and the Würtemberg division, should move on Le Chêne, whilst the 6th corps should serve as a reserve behind the left wing. It was hoped to catch the French army ranged between Stenay and Le Chêne.

On the 30th of August, the advancing German columns surprised the 5th corps (de Failly's) in camp before Beaumont, threw it into the greatest confusion, drove it from its position, and went on to attack the 7th and 12th corps. These the Germans, after a bloody fight, forced back on the road to Carignan, thus compelling the Marshal to retreat on Sedan. On receiving this information, the King directed that whilst, on the 31st, the 4th army should compel the French left wing to fall back in an easterly direction, the 3d army should attack the French, if they should be still on the left bank of the Meuse, and, operating against their right wing, should hem them in in the narrow space between that river and the Belgian frontier. But M'Mahon had no thought of taking a position which would probably have compelled him to violate the soil of a neutral country. He marched that night into Sedan, and ranged his troops so as to meet the German attack the following morning. Expecting the attack to come from the east, he placed there his strongest force, his right wing was at Bazeilles, resting on the Meuse, the left was at Illy. The ground in front of his main defence was naturally strong, the entire front being covered by the Givonne rivulet, and the slopes to that rivulet, on the French side of it.

The possibility that the French marshal would accept battle at Sedan, had been considered at the German headquarters on the night of the 31st, and arrangements had been made to meet his wishes. The army of the Crown Prince of Saxony (the fourth army) occupied the right of the German forces, the Bavarian corps formed the centre, and the Prussians the left wing. The advanced troops of the army were ranged in the following order. On the right stood the 12th corps, then the 4th Prussian corps, the Prussian guards, and finally the 4th cavalry division, their backs to Remilly. From this point they were linked to the 1st and 2d Bavarian corps, opposite Bazeilles; they, in turn, to the 11th and 5th corps; and they, at Dom-le-Mesnil, to the Würtembergers. The 6th Prussian corps was placed in reserve between Attigny and Le Chêne.

One word, and one only, as to the nature of the ground on which the impending battle was to be fought. Sedan lies in the most beautiful part of the valley of the Meuse, amid terraced heights, covered with trees, and, within close distance, the villages of Donchéry, Iges, Villette, Glaire, Daigny, Bazeilles, and others. Along the Meuse, on the left bank, ran the main road from Donchéry through Frenois, crossing the river at the suburb Torcy, and there traversing Sedan. The character of the locality may best be described as a ground covered with fruit gardens and vineyards, narrow streets shut in by stone walls, the roads overhung by forests, the egress from which was in many places steep and abrupt. Such was the ground. One word now as to the troops.

The German army before Sedan counted, all told, 240,000 men; the French 130,000. But the disparity in numbers was the least of the differences between the two armies. The one was flushed with victory, the other dis-spirited by defeat. The one had absolute confidence in their generals and their officers, the other had the most supreme contempt for theirs. The one had marched from Metz on a settled plan, to be modified according to circumstances, the drift of which was apparent to the meanest soldier; the other had been marched hither and thither, now towards Montmédy, now towards Paris, then again back towards Montmédy, losing much time; the men eager for a pitched battle, then suddenly surprised through the carelessness of their commanders, and compelled at last to take refuge in a town from which there was no issue. There was hardly an officer of rank who knew aught about the country in which he found himself. The men were longing to fight to the death, but they, one and all, distrusted their leaders. It did not tend, moreover, to the encouragement of the army to see the now phantom Emperor, without authority to command even a corporal's guard, dragged about the country, more as a pageant than a sovereign. He, poor man, was much to be pitied. He keenly felt his position, and longed for the day when he might, in a great battle, meet the glorious death which France might accept as an atonement for his misfortunes.

The battle began at daybreak on the morning of the 1st of September. Under cover of a brisk artillery fire, the Bavarians advanced, and opened, at six o'clock, a very heavy musketry fire on Bazeilles. The masonry buildings of this village were all armed and occupied, and they were defended very valiantly. The defenders drove back the enemy as they advanced and kept them at bay for two hours. Then the Saxons came up to the aid of the Bavarians, and forced the first position. Still the defence continued, and the clocks were striking ten when the Bavarians succeeded in entering the place. Even then a house-to-house defence prolonged the battle, and it was not until every house but one[1] had been either stormed or burnt, that the Germans could call the village, or the ruins which remained of it, their own. Meanwhile, on the other points of their defensive position; at Floing, St Menges, Fleigneux, Illy, and, on the extreme left, at Iges, where a sharp bend of the Meuse forms a peninsula of the ground round which it slowly rolls; the French had been making a gallant struggle. In their ranks, even in advance of them, attended finally by a single *aide-de-camp*, all the others having been killed, was the Emperor, cool, calm, and full of sorrow, earnestly longing for the shell or the bullet which should give a soldier's finish to his career. M'Mahon, too, was there, doing all that a general could do to encourage his men. The enemy were, however, gradually but surely making way. To hedge the French within the narrowest compass, the 5th and 11th corps of the third army had crossed the Meuse to the left of Sedan, and were marching now to roll up the French left. But before their attack had been felt, an event had occurred full of significance for the French army.

Early in the day, whilst yet the Bavarians were fighting to get possession of Bazeilles, Marshal M'Mahon was so severely wounded that he had to be carried from the field into Sedan. He made over the command of the army to General Ducrot. That general had even before recognised the impossibility of maintaining the

---

[1] The house is called 'A la dernière Cartouche,' and is the subject of De Neuville's splendid painting.

position before Sedan against the superior numbers of the German army, and had seen that the one chance of saving his army was to fall back on Mezières. He at once, then, on assuming command, issued orders to that effect. But it was already too late. The march by the defile of St Albert had been indeed possible at any time during the night or in the very early morning. But it was now no longer so. The German troops swarmed in the plains of Donchéry, and the route by Carignan could only be gained by passing over the bodies of a more numerous and still living foe. Still Ducrot had given the order, and the staff officers did their utmost to cause it to be obeyed. The crowded streets of Sedan were being vacated, when suddenly the orders were countermanded. General Wimpffen had arrived from Paris the previous day to replace the incapable De Failly in command of the 5th corps, carrying in his pocket an order from the minister of war to assume the command-in-chief in the event of any accident to M'Mahon. The Emperor had no voice in the matter, for, whilst the regency of the Empress existed, he no longer represented the government. The two generals met, and after a somewhat lively discussion, Ducrot was forced to acknowledge the authority of the Minister. Wimpffen then assumed command. His first act was to countermand the order to retreat on Mezières, and to direct the troops to reassume the positions they had occupied when M'Mahon had been wounded. This order was carried out as far as was possible.

Meanwhile the Germans were pressing more and more those positions. About midday the Guards, having made their way step by step, each one bravely contested, gave their hand to the left wing of the 3d army. Then Illy and Floing, which had been defended with extraordinary tenacity, as the keys of the advanced French position, were stormed. The conquest of those heights completed the investment of Sedan. There was now no possible egress for the French. Their soldiers retreated into the town and the suburbs, whilst 500 German guns hurled their missiles, their round shot and their shells, against the walls and the crowded masses behind them.

Vainly then did Wimpffen direct an assembly in mass of his men to break through the serried columns of the enemy. In the disordered state of the French army the thing was impossible. The Emperor, who had courted death in vain, recognised the truth, and, desirous to spare the sacrifice of life produced by the continued cannonade, ordered, on his own responsibility, the hoisting of a white flag on the highest point of the defences, as a signal of surrender. But the firing still continued, and Wimpffen, still bent on breaking through, would not hear of surrender. Then Napoleon, his heart bleeding at the continued slaughter, despatched his chief *aide-de-camp*, General Reille, with a letter to the King of Prussia, in which he wrote that 'not having found death at the head of his troops, he surrendered his sword to his Majesty.' King William replied that he accepted the sword, and begged him to send some fully authorised officer to arrange regarding the capitulation. That same evening, about a quarter to eight o'clock, Wimpffen, who had been converted to the opinion that further resistance was impossible, after a conference with the Emperor, rode out to concert with Moltke and Bismarck the conditions they were willing to accept. He found them at the chateau of Bellevue, near Donchéry. The interview was very painful for the French general. He had but to hear the decision of the Prussian leaders, and to accept it. The decision was a very simple one. It had but one clause;

The French Army surrenders. 295

that the French officers and soldiers should surrender as prisoners of war, with arms and baggage. Vainly for three hours did Wimpffen exert all his eloquence to obtain better terms. The only concession he could obtain was that the officers who should sign an agreement, on their honour, not to serve against Germany during the war, should be allowed to return to their homes.

The following day these conditions were more formally accepted. The Emperor delivered his sword to the King of Prussia, and was sent to Wilhelmshöhe as a prisoner. 88,000 men (including one marshal, thirty-nine generals, and 3230 other officers) with 10,000 horses, 4000 cannon, seventy mitrailleuses, and an enormous quantity of stores fell into the hands of the victors. One of the great armies of France had suddenly been wiped out of existence.

Whose was the fault? Impartial history will not hesitate to charge the entire responsibility to those short-sighted politicians who, to save a dynasty, refused to admit within the defences of Paris an army which, well commanded, would have prevented the ultimate capitulation, but preferred to send it to certain destruction. It is surely fair to denounce such a policy as 'infamous. It is pleasant to record that it brought no advantage to its authors.

CHAPTER XV.

THE LAST PHASES OF THE WAR.

IT seemed as though there were nothing left for France to do but to bow down before her enemy and surrender. She had lost two great armies, the one closely blockaded in Metz; the other surrendered at Sedan. More than that, the defeat at Sedan caused in Paris—the Paris which had insisted on the war—a revolution. The dynasty which had not wanted the war, which had entered upon it almost under the compulsion of the Parisian mob, was expelled because that war—their war—had been uusuccessful. The Parisians vented their own shortcomings on the Bonapartes. How was Paris to defend herself against the enemy flushed with victory? Judging from past history, it might be inferred that if the French possessed a nature similar to that of the Prussians, she could and would do nothing. In 1806 the great Napoleon had conquered Prussia, East Prussia excepted, in a month. After the battle of Jena and Auerstädt, fought eight days after the declaration of war, Prussia had lain prone for the French to trample upon, shamefully yielding her fortresses, in many cases to inferior forces and without striking a blow. In twenty-two days after those battles it was all over with Prussia. And now France had received blows more severe and more deadly than those of Jena and Auerstädt: she had the consciousness that her military system was rotten to the core; that her superior officers were mostly men who had gained their positions, not by services in the field nor by merit, but through the favour of the court; that a new system had to be inaugurated whilst the victorious enemy was thundering at the gates of her capital. These facts were recognised by France, by Germany, by Europe. By all,·but the first, further resistance was deemed impracticable. No one else took into consideration the difference of race between the conquerors and the conquered of Sedan. Even the leaders of the German armies reasoned as though the consequences of Jena must form a precedent. As Prussia, after one great defeat—for Jena and Auerstädt were but two parts of one battle, fought the same day and at the same hours—had fallen into a panic and shamefully yielded, so must France, after misfortunes still more deadly, follow her example and allow her enemy, without striking a blow, to take all that he required.

But it is to the eternal glory of the French people that they did not follow the example of Prussia in 1806. Throughout the beautiful country so famed for the intellectual position achieved in the world by the children of its soil, there was not one cry for surrender. There was not even a panic. But one sound was heard, high above all others: 'Let us enlist; let us take to arms; the country must be defended.' Jules Favre, one of the Republican ministers who had led the assault upon, and who had succeeded the ministers of, the Empire, expressed only the universal feeling of France, when, in an interview with Bismarck after Sedan, he exclaimed, after listening to the demands for surrender of districts and fortresses by that statesman : 'Not one inch of our territories, not one stone of our fortresses will we surrender.' Under the actual circumstances France came very near making good those brave words.[1] Had Bazaine been other than Bazaine; had a genius and a patriot commanded the army in Metz, the issue of the war would, thanks to the universal patriotism of the French nation, been far different from that which I am about to record. Certainly, under those circumstances, there would have been no 'Refounding of the German Empire.'

The capture of Sedan and of the army which fought there closed the first phase of the war. Up to that time the action of the Germans had been really a defensive action, for although they had fought on French soil, such action was the consequence of the early disorganisation of the French armies. They had assumed 'an offensive defensive attitude.' But now this was all changed. The offensive was no longer defensive. The enemy must be smitten hip and thigh. The sieges of Strasburg and Belfort must be pushed: a siege-train must be sent for; orders must be given to make quick work with the fortress of Toul, to open the line which led from Nancy to Paris.

But the movement on Paris did not wait for the accomplishment of these designs. On the 31st of August and the 1st of September, the day before the battle of Sedan, Bazaine had made a serious attempt to break out from Metz by assailing the German troops posted on the right bank of the Moselle. This attempt, called by the French the battle of St Barbe, by the Germans of Noisseville, was of a very determined character. The French, marching from the fortress early on the morning of the 31st, took possession of Colombey, and developed their masses in front of it. For some reason they did not at once hurry

---

[1] Of more than one battle it might be said, as a distinguished German officer wrote of the Battle of Wörth : 'We were within an ace of losing the battle; but the French did not know it.' *Vide* Major Henderson's lecture in the Royal United Service Institution Journal for August 1892.

Bazaine fails to break out from Metz.

to the attack. Before them stood the troops commanded by General Manteuffel, 36,000 infantry, 4800 cavalry, and 138 guns, watched from the other bank by the army of Prince Frederic Charles, ready to send reinforcements to any point where they might be required. It was not till four o'clock that Bazaine, who had brought out all his available troops, attacked the fewer but very strongly posted troops of the enemy, and by half-past six had succeeded in wresting from them the village of Noisseville and the large brewery to the south of it. Thence he pushed forward, taking Montoy, Coincy, other hamlets, and, at nine o'clock, Servigny. But there their successes terminated. Their many efforts to force their way into Poix and Failly were repulsed. At ten o'clock the Germans retook Servigny, but, pressing on against Noisseville again and again, they were always driven back with loss. Meanwhile, considerable reinforcements had joined Manteuffel from the left bank by St Barbe and Marloy-Charly, whilst a brigade standing idle at Courcelles was pushed against Ogy. Aided by these troops, which increased his army to 69,000 infantry and 290 guns, Manteuffel, early the following morning, covering his movements by a strong and continued artillery fire, renewed his attack on Noisseville, and by nine o'clock had recovered it and all the places he had lost the previous evening. The French then, baffled and discouraged, re-entered Metz. I cannot resist the impression that they were not led with the vigour necessary to insure success. It would surely have been better to sacrifice every man than to have returned to a position which deprived France of her chief army.

Meanwhile other German troops were pressing forward on the road to Paris. On the 5th of September the King of Prussia entered Rheims. On the 8th Laon surrendered;

and, on the 15th, the advanced troops of the 3d and 4th armies halted within three hours of the capital of France, making a half-circle round its defences.

The revolution had brought to the head of affairs in Paris a certain General Trochu. It required, it must be admitted, a man of strong character and supreme genius to dominate at such an epoch the fickle population of that city, and Trochu, though possessing only second-rate abilities, was essentially a charlatan. He could talk big, could profess a confidence which he did not feel, and promise success which, by such a man as he was, was not to be attained. The resources which, within the defences, he could oppose to the German armies were not very formidable. He had not, alas, the army of 130,000 men which had been sent to certain destruction at Sedan. But he had the 13th corps under General Vinoy, and the 14th under General Renault, and 18,000 marines, excellent soldiers, a total of 88,000 regular troops. He had also in the camps of Vincennes and St Maur 100,000 Garde-Mobiles, only very imperfectly disciplined; 10,000 volunteers from the provinces, resolute men, prepared to give their lives for their country; the National Guard, composed of sixty old and a hundred and ninety-four new battalions which, with other miscellaneous volunteers of Paris, numbered perhaps 200,000 men, not, however, thoroughly to be depended upon. Altogether the defenders numbered about 400,000, but of these only the 88,000 regular troops and the 10,000 volunteers from the provinces could be reckoned as trustworthy soldiers. At a later period the trustworthy defenders were augmented by about 122,000 additional men.

Amongst those who escaped from Sedan, had come to Paris was General Ducrot. The German authorities assert that he had been released after the battle of that

Plan of Defence.

name on giving his word of honour that he would remain at Pont-à-Mousson, and take no further part in the war. This charge Ducrot always indignantly denied, and certainly it has never been proved. To him Trochu committed the command of the second army, and it was at the head of that army that he was the first to come in contact with the German assailers of Paris. The first army of defence, commanded by General Thomas, consisted of the National Guard; Ducrot's of the regular troops; whilst a third army, composed of seven volunteer divisions, was given to General Vinoy. The object of General Trochu was that the second army should break through the lines of the investing army, whilst the first army should occupy the defensive works of the city and the forts, and the third should divert the enemy's attention by breaking out at other points. At a later period the unmarried men of the National Guard were formed into separate battalions and employed as soldiers of the line.

Space will not permit me to recount in detail all the minute events of the siege which followed. It must suffice to record that, on the 15th of September, Ducrot made a vigorous attempt to prevent the complete investment of the city by attacking the Germans on the south front on the left bank of the Seine. The engagement took place at Sceaux, between Petit-Bicètre and Chatillon. The 2d Bavarian corps had crossed the Seine at Villeneuve-St-Georges, when, between Sceaux, Villejuif, and Montrouge, it came upon three divisions of Ducrot's army. Supported by the 5th Prussian army corps, which, under the command of the Crown Prince of Prussia, was marching on Versailles, the Bavarians drove the French from the heights of Plessis-Piquet, and forced them to take shelter behind the southern forts. Some intrenchments which the French had thrown up at Moulin-le-Tour, seven guns, and about 300 prisoners fell into the hands of the victors. After this the 3d German army had no difficulty in establishing itself in a position embracing the southern and south-eastern front of the city, from Sèvres to the Marne; the 4th army faced the north-east and northern front, the cavalry the west front, so far as the windings of the Seine would permit it. On the 5th of October the Crown Prince took up his headquarters at Versailles, those of the King being at Ferrières, the seat of the Paris Rothschilds. Here took place, on the 19th October, the famous interview between the French foreign minister, Jules Favre, and Bismarck, in which the former made his declaration that France would surrender neither one inch of her territories nor one stone of her fortresses. The interview remained without result.

Meanwhile, the fortress of Toul had surrendered to the Germans on the 24th of September. Strasburg, after a siege of six weeks, surrendered to vastly superior numbers, after it had seen its lunettes taken, and a practicable breach effected, on the eve of the completion of the preparations to storm it, on the 27th September. German troops were thus made available for other enterprises.

The investment of Paris was completed by the end of September. The German position remained, however, essentially defensive. The chiefs of the army had to await the arrival of the siege-train before they could begin their active operations. On the 30th of September, General Vinoy made the second sortie from the south-front, but after a fight of six hours' duration he was forced back. Then, for a time, the French contented themselves with a continuous artillery fire from the forts. That from the fort on Mont-Valérien, armed with marine-guns of heavy calibre, greatly incommoded

Bazaine surrenders. 303

the left wing of the 3d army. The forts on the southern side, Issy, Vauvres, Montrouge, Bicêtre and Ivry; Fort Charenton on the south front; the forts on the east front, and the redoubts connecting them all, kept up a fire which prevented a close approach of the enemy. On the 13th of October took place the third sortie, again from the southern face, only to be repulsed: on the 22d, a fourth, from Mont-Valérien, under General Vinoy, with the same result. By this time the German troops, freed by the conquest of Toul and Strasburg, had come into line. Others were to be expected, for the Germans were besieging Neu-Breisach and Verdun; were blockading Pfaizburg and Bitsche, and were marching to besiege Belfort.

On the 21st, the day of their fourth sortie under Vinoy, the cannonade from Mont-Valérien set fire to St Cloud, which was destroyed. Just a week later, a fifth sortie was made on the northern assailants. They succeeded in driving the Prussians from Le Bourget, and occupying it. But two days later, the 30th, the Prussian guards recovered it, after a fight which lasted several hours, and which cost many men to the attackers and the attacked.

It is impossible to leave this month of October without recording an event which was fatal to the hopes which many Frenchmen still entertained of ultimate success. On the 27th of October Marshal Bazaine surrendered Metz and his whole army, consisting of three marshals of France, 6,000 generals and officers, and 173,000 fighting men, to the German besiegers. The plea he assigned was the failure of provisions for so large a force. It is doubtful, however, whether such a plea can be accepted as justification for an act which dealt so deadly a blow to France; more than doubtful whether Bazaine had done all that a general could do for the preservation of his army and the destruction of that of the enemy; certain that political considerations — for Bazaine was a strong supporter of the Bonaparte dynasty and hated the faction which ruled in Paris — greatly swayed the mind of the general. Subsequently to the great sortie of Noisseville (31st August), he had made but two feeble attempts, on the 27th of September and the 7th of October, to break out. Since the 24th of September he had entered, through a certain Regnier, into secret negotiations with the German commander, which had for their object the conclusion of peace, combined with the free departure from Metz of his army to restore the imperial authority. With the same object he had, on the 25th of September, despatched General Bourbaki to England on a mission to the Empress, and on the 12th of October his chief of the staff, General Boyer, to the German headquarters at Versailles. But all his plans were baffled. The opinion expressed by some of his generals, that the army would not lend itself to such a course was the main cause of the failure of the negotiations. Disappointed in his hopes, then, Bazaine, on the 27th of October, surrendered.[1] This act made the Germans masters of one of the strongest fortresses in Europe, with 800 heavy guns, 102 mitrailleuses, and

---

[1] After the conclusion of the war, Bazaine was brought to a court-martial (October 6, 1871). After a patient trial which lasted two months, he was declared, the 6th December, guilty of treason, and sentenced to death and to degradation of rank. The then President of the Republic, Marshal M'Mahon, commuted the death-sentence into one of imprisonment for twenty years. Confined in the fort of the island St Marguerite, near Cannes, Bazaine escaped, and lived in Spain till his death. There can be no question that Bazaine, as a general, was quite unequal to the task imposed upon him.

300,000 Chassepôts, and placed at the disposal of the King the entire blockading army of Prince Frederic Charles for employment in the north and south of France, whilst he himself should push the siege of Paris with vigour.

Amongst the members of the government which had tumultuously wrested the administration from the Empress-Regent was a very eloquent advocate, named Gambetta. A man of great energy, determination, insight, and will-power, Gambetta had recognised in the early days of the siege the necessity of organising and utilising, outside of Paris, the energies which the disasters of France had roused in her sons. Before the complete investment of Paris, some of the members of the administration had been sent to Tours, to organise there the national movement, but it was felt, by none more strongly than by Gambetta, that they required an energetic head, and he resolved himself to assume the direction, from Tours, of the national resources. No other means of quitting Paris being available, he embarked on a balloon on the 7th of October, reached Tours, assumed there the ministry of war, and became practically dictator of France. Thence he issued a proclamation to the people of France, urging them to continue their resistance to the bitter end, and directed that all men, capable of bearing arms, should lend their hands to the work, and should join the troops of the line at Tours. In this way he formed an army of the north, and an army of the Loire, and, later, an army of the east. In all respects he displayed a fertility of resource which astonished the world. He obtained arms, uniforms, munitions, and other necessaries from foreign countries, especially from England. He bestowed the greatest pains in selecting as generals of the new levies men who should be real soldiers. Faidherbe, Aurelles de Paladines, Chanzy, were his creations. Under his inspiring influence the war in the provinces assumed a very serious complexion. France had responded nobly to the call he had made upon her people. Early reverses gave vigour to the new levies, and they fought with energy against the Bavarians under Von der Than at Arthenay and Orleans, and against the division Wittich at Château-dun and Chartres. But he was fighting against increasing odds. Soon, every day brought reinforcements to the Germans. The surrender of Metz enabled them to concentrate their resources to nip in the bud a movement which, if made whilst the Germans had still been detained before that fortress might have compelled the raising of the siege of Paris. When Metz surrendered, the King, not quite sensible of the danger to be apprehended from the rising of the departments, directed Manteuffel to assume command of the 1st army, and proceed with it in the direction of Orleans, whilst Prince Frederic Charles should march southwards with a portion of the 2d, sending the other portion to Versailles to strengthen the forces besieging Paris. The Bavarians, under Von der Than, was likewise ordered to operate on the Loire.

Meanwhile, Gambetta had raised the Loire army to a strength of 150,000 men. The command of it he had given to General Aurelle de Paladines. His object was to recover Orleans and to open the road to Paris. In the beginning of November Aurelle pressed along the right bank of the Loire, in the hope of retaking that city. Von der Than had taken a strong position at Coulmiers, barring the way. There, on the 9th, Aurelle attacked him, and, getting the better of a very fierce fight, forced him on the 10th to retreat on Toury, twenty-seven miles to the south-east of Chartres, to join there the division Wittich and the cavalry division of the Crown Prince of

Saxony. The same day the Germans evacuated Orleans, leaving open the road to Paris. The consternation of the German leaders at Versailles was considerable, and, in great haste, they despatched from before Paris two divisions to keep at bay the army of Aurelle until Prince Frederic Charles should arrive with the main portion of the 2d army. Aurelle, when he heard of this disposition of the enemy's troops, had already begun his march to Paris. But, learning the position of the two German divisions above referred to, strengthened by the 5th army corps under General Voigts-Rhetz, he turned aside to attack them at Beaune-la-Rolande. Defeated there, he fell back on Orleans, and took a position in front of the woods near that city. Attacked there on the 3d December, he was compelled to fall back within the city. The following day the heads of the two German armies of the north and the west, pushed their way into the suburbs. The French then, in virtue of a convention made with the German commander, the Grand Duke of Mecklenburg-Schwerin, evacuated the city, which the Germans entered by agreement after midnight. The French fell back towards Tours, followed by the enemy's cavalry. The Germans held Orleans till the end of the war, making it the headquarters of operations in that part of France.

Gambetta, upon the result of the movements of Aurelle, removed that officer from the command, and, dividing the Loire army into two parts, confided the direction of one to General Bourbaki, but recently returned from his mission to the Empress Eugénie in England, the other to General Chanzy. Bourbaki took a position at Bourges, and awaited there the army of Prince Frederic Charles, which he was aware was marching in his direction. Chanzy, meanwhile, had occupied Beaugency. Against him marched the army commanded by the Grand Duke of Mecklenburg. It seemed that the final success of the war depended upon the result of the two attacks which would follow these movements. But the German chiefs at Versailles resolved to leave Bourbaki for the moment and concentrate all their energies against Chanzy. They sent orders to that effect to Frederic Charles. Leaving a portion of his troops to watch Bourbaki, the Red Prince marched with the 9th and 10th corps to support the Grand Duke. Meanwhile Chanzy had obtained an advantage over the advanced corps of the west army at Meung (December 7), but on the following day was beaten at Beaugency by the Grand Duke, and fell back on the forest of Marchenoir. He retook, however, the offensive on the 10th, but after a fierce artillery combat was forced again to fall back. He then marched on Blois, followed by a corps of the enemy, which, on the 13th, occupied that city. Chanzy then marched on Vendôme. At that place Gambetta joined him and held a council of war, with the result that Vendôme was evacuated, and the army fell back on Le Mans. The Grand Duke followed, beat the rearguard of the French at La Morée, and occupied Vendôme on the 16th. He then pressed on, in two divisions, against Tours and Le Mans. The first surrendered after a feeble opposition (December 21), but, in obedience to instructions, the Germans did not enter the town until a month later (January 19), but contented themselves with destroying the railway to Le Mans and cantoning in the neighbourhood. Chanzy attempted once again to resume the offensive near Vendôme (December 31), but was repulsed with loss.

Meanwhile, in the north, General Faidherbe had been appointed by Gambetta to succeed General Farre in command of the army which had been defeated by the

Prussians at Amiens the 20th of November. Faidherbe took a very favourable position on the Hallue, with about 54,000 men, mostly raw levies, when he was attacked, the 23rd of December, by Manteuffel with two divisions, and forced to fall back behind Arras. Manteuffel followed on the 26th to Bapaume, and despatched thence a considerable portion of his army to invest Peronne. Faidherbe took advantage of this diversion to attack the Germans at Bapaume (January 2). Repulsed that day, he renewed his assault the day following, and after a very severe fight, in which the Germans suffered at least as much as their assailants, fell back towards the close of the day on Arras and Douai. Peronne fell on the 10th. Faidherbe then attempted to make his way southward, but he was caught on the 17th by Von Goeben at Beauvois, thrown back on St Quentin, and there, on the 19th, completely defeated.

It would require too much space to describe how the other partisan leaders of the new levies were, one after another, driven into inaction. It must suffice to record that General von Kamecke, who had belonged to the army before Metz, forced the surrender of Diedenhofen on November 24th; of Montmédy, December 14th; of La Fére, November 27th. General von Senden, who replaced him early in December, took Rocroy by a *coup-de-main*, January 15th, Mezières having previously surrendered, January 2d. Colonel von Krensky captured Longwy the 25th of January. Previously, Verdun had capitulated, November 8th, and Pfalzburg, December 12th. These captures meant the taking of many prisoners, many guns, and many stores. Belfort, besieged from November 3rd, still held out, and did so until the end of the war. So, likewise, did Bitsche.

So far the operations of the armies raised at the call

of Gambetta had failed. The too early surrender of Metz had foiled plans which, had Bazaine been able to hold on a fortnight longer, might have compelled the raising of the siege of Paris. Nor was Bourbaki more successful. Commissioned by Gambetta to march with the 15th, 18th, 20th and 24th army-corps, in all nearly 150,000 men, to effect a junction with the force which Garibaldi had raised to assist France, and to march them to the relief of Belford; to recover Alsace and to break the communications of the German army before Paris and the Rhine; Bourbaki was compelled, by a demonstration made against his flank by General Werder (January 9) to suspend his forward march. This delay gave Werder time to reach the intrenched and partly-armed (with siege guns) position, covering twenty-one miles, from Frahier by way of Echanne and Luze, to the German headquarters at Héricourt; thence southwards to Montbéliard and Delle, commanding the road by which Bourbaki must advance. In this position Werder repulsed the fierce attacks made upon him by the French the 15th, 16th and 17th of January. The position of Bourbaki had now become serious. Before him was Werder in a position he could not force. Marching to attack his left flank was Manteuffel, with a newly-organised army of old soldiers. He resolved then to retreat on Besançon. But Manteuffel, marching with great haste, rendered this task very difficult. He accomplished it, however, only to find himself still more embarrassed. The march over the rough paths of Côte d'Or and the Jura with scanty supplies, hemmed in by the foe, hindered by ice and snow, had completely demoralised his raw levies. A march of ten days rendered the condition of his army most deplorable. But worse was in store for him. Whilst at Besançon, urgently occupied with the cares of his army, he had received, the

Paris is left to its Own Resources. 311

evening of the 27th of January, a letter from Gambetta, informing him that he and the other generals Gambetta had nominated were publicly spoken of as traitors. In despair alike at the position of his army and at this odious calumny, Bourbaki made over the command of his army to General Clinchant, and attempted to commit suicide. The attempt failed, but Bourbaki was carried with the army into Switzerland, whither Clinchant marched, and where, surrendering to the neutral powers whose territories it had invaded, it was disarmed.

The attempts made by Gambetta and his generals to raise the siege of Paris having thus been foiled, there remained, then, to the government of that city, pressed hard by the besieging Germans, but the attempt to secure the best terms possible of surrender. The many sorties made by her defenders had been repulsed; the hope by which the spirits of her defenders had been so long buoyed up were vanishing fast: famine was approaching with giant strides; the strong places outside the circle of her defences were falling one after another; the fire of the enemy was, by the nearer approach of their troops, becoming more concentrated and more severe. Peace must be had. On January 28th, then, there was concluded at Versailles an armistice for three weeks. Then a national assembly was summoned to Bordeaux to consider how peace might be restored. In that assembly M. Thiers received full administrative powers, including the power of nominating his own ministers. He himself, with Jules Favre, undertook the negotiations with Bismarck. To ensure the success of those negotiations the armistice was twice prolonged. This was done at the instance of Thiers, for the conditions insisted upon by Bismarck were hard, and the French statesman struggled with all his energies to induce him to abate his demands. Especially did he strive to save Metz, or, at least, to receive Luxemburg in compensation.

But his endeavours were fruitless. The utmost that Bismarck would do was not to insist upon securing the still unconquered Belfort. Despairing of moving him further, Thiers and Favre gave way on the 24th of February, and signed the preliminaries of peace. They were (1) the transfer to Germany of the north-east portion of Lorraine, with Metz and Diedenhofen, and of Alsace, Belfort excepted: (2) the payment to Germany by France of one milliard[1] of francs in 1871, and four milliards in the three years following; (3) the Germans to begin to evacuate French territory immediately after the ratification of the treaty; Paris and its forts on the left bank of the Seine and certain departments at once; the forts on the right bank after the ratification and the payment of the first half milliard. After the payment of two milliards the German occupation of the departments Marne, Ardennes, Upper Marne, Meuse, the Vosges, and Meurthe, and the fortress of Belfort[2] should cease. Interest at five per cent. to be charged on the milliards remaining unpaid from the date of ratification; (4) the German troops remaining in France to make no requisitions on the departments in which they were located, but to be fed at the cost of France; (5) the inhabitants of the sequestered provinces to be allowed a certain fixed time in which to make their choice between the two countries; (6) all prisoners to be at once restored; (7) a treaty embodying all these terms to be settled at Brussels. It was further arranged that

---

[1] A milliard is one thousand millions.

[2] The Germans had failed to capture Belfort, but, on the conclusion of the armistice, the French government had ordered the garrison to capitulate with all the honours of war.

the German army should not occupy Paris, but that the Emperor—for such he had become—should content himself with marching through a portion of the city.

On the 28th of February Thiers laid these conditions before the assembly at Bordeaux. On the 1st of March they were accepted by 546 votes against 107. On the same day the Emperor and his staff, with a portion of the German army, entered Paris, the remainder following the next day, and the whole evacuating the city on the 3rd.

The peace congress met at Brussels the 28th of March, but its proceedings were almost immediately suspended by the revolution which then broke out in Paris. When the French troops had put down the revolt, their leaders displayed some hesitation as to adhering to the conditions of the preliminary treaty. Finally, however, the negotiations were resumed, May 6, at Frankfort, the negotiators being Bismarck and Jules Favre. The definitive treaty was signed on the 10th, the chief alteration in the terms being the shortening of the period for the payment of the idemnity.

Thus ended a war which, although it gratified the pent-up wishes of German enthusiasts, most assuredly, by the manner of its ending, especially in the matter of the hard conditions insisted upon by the victors, laid the foundations of enmity and future warfare between the two most important countries of the continent.

CHAPTER XVI.

THE CROWNING OF THE EDIFICE.

THE successes of the German armies in 1870 had removed every obstacle to the carrying into effect that union of Germany which had been the dream of enthusiasts for years, and had seemed for a few months possible on the morrow of the revolution of 1848. Then Austria had stopped the way. Nor when the Prussians had triumphed over Southern Germany in 1866, had Bismarck felt himself strong enough to push the matter to its logical issue. He made, it is true, an agreement with the German States outside of Austria for a common defence; but the arrangement went no further. There were symptoms, indeed, during the years between 1866 and 1870 that Bavaria and Würtemberg would gladly hail an opportunity to break the bonds which fettered them. But the skilful use made by Bismarck alike of the action, and of the invented action, of the Emperor Napoleon in the matter of the Hohenzollern candidature to the throne of Spain, in the first place; and the success of Germany in the war, in the second, not only diminished the prejudices of Bavaria and Würtemberg, but disposed the entire German nation to seize the opportunity of the successes of 1870 to complete the union in the manner the most likely to satisfy the aspirations of the German sovereign who had contributed so largely to render possible those successes. The fact indeed that the

The German Empire is refounded. 315

victories gained had been the direct result of German unity of action under the guidance of Prussia forced itself on the minds of every thinking man in Germany ; and it was determined by a large majority to complete without delay the work begun in 1866. Baden led the way. The King of Bavaria was persuaded to follow. Conferences opened at Versailles at the end of October, and soon announced a favourable result. On the 15th of November the heads of the new imperial constitution were agreed to by Baden and Hesse ; on the 23rd by the King of Bavaria; on the 25th (at Berlin) by Würtemberg. Various small concessions, demanded by several States to save their dignity were granted ; but the principal articles—those especially which demanded one diplomatic representation, one assembly for all the States of the union, and one supreme command of the army—were insisted upon by Prussia. The combined States proposed to assume the title of the German Empire. Its chief was to be the King of Prussia, with the title of German Emperor.

When the question came to be considered in the assemblies of the several States there was not found quite the same unanimity. The parliaments of Hesse, Baden, and Würtemberg indeed accepted the new constitution without opposition. In the lower House of Bavaria, nearly one-third of the members voted against it.[1] But before this debate had taken place (January 11), the matter had been actually concluded. On the 1st of January, 1871, the King of Bavaria, writing on behalf of all the sovereigns and ruling princes of Germany, informed the King of Prussia that he had been unanimously chosen to be the first ruler of the German Empire with the title of German Emperor. On the 19th of the same month the acceptance of the dignity by the King of Prussia was proclaimed

[1] The numbers were 48 against 102.

with imposing ceremony at Versailles. On that date the German Empire was refounded.

More than twenty-two years have elapsed since that memorable ceremony. Many of the actors in it have disappeared. The Emperor himself, his noble-hearted son, whose deeds as Crown Prince of Prussia have been recorded in these pages; the Red Prince; Von Roon, the organiser of victory; Moltke, the great strategist; and many others, have been called to their last account. There still remains amongst his countrymen one—the man without whose dogged resolution, absolute want of scruple, fertility of resource, fiery energy, and strength of will, the task had been impossible. It was, emphatically, Bismarck's work. To bring it to a successful conclusion, he had defied alike the parliaments and the people; had led his master and his country over abysses, in the traversing of which, one false step would have been fatal. Aided a great deal, it must be admitted, by the wretched diplomacy of Austria, by the deterioration of the powers of the French Emperor, and by his sublime audacity, he had compelled to his will all the moral difficulties of the undertaking. Von Roon and Moltke had done the rest. No longer, however, is Prince Bismarck allowed to put forth his hand to sustain the work which he created. For him it had been better to die, like Von Roon, like Moltke, keeping to the end the confidence of his sovereign, than to feel himself impelled, dismissed from office, to pour out his grievances to every passing listener, to speak in terms not far removed from treason of the sovereign who had declined to be his pupil. Was it for this, he seems to mutter, that I forced on the war which gave Prussia Schleswig and Holstein in 1864; that I compelled unwilling Austria to declare war in 1866; that, by the freest circulation of exaggerated state

ments,[1] I roused a bitter feeling in Germany against
France, and excited the statesmen, and, above all, the
mob, of Paris in 1870?—for this, that, the work accomplished, an empire given to the Hohenzollerns, I might
be cast aside like a squeezed-out orange? Well might
these be his thoughts, for it was he who made possible
the task of German unity, though in a manner which
will commend itself only to those who argue that the
end justifies the means.

Whether the new empire will last or will crumble away
is a question which, happily, I am not called to answer.
But I may say that its chances of vigorous life would
have been greater if the German negotiators of the
treaty had not insisted upon the too great spoliation of
their enemy. By that insistance they sowed the seeds
of future wars; they planted a discord which will, for
years to come, foment the natural jealousy of neighbours.
During the twenty-two years which have elapsed, they
have failed to conciliate the people torn unwillingly from
their long connection with that France of which it was
their pride and their glory to form a part. All these
circumstances constitute difficulties which a little less
greed would have avoided, and which may yet re-open
the question as to whether the Refounded German
Empire will emulate, in the length of its existence,
the Empire founded by Charlemagne.

[1] *Vide* Fyffe's 'History of Modern Europe,' vol. iii. pp. 419-20.

THE END.

INDEX

---o---

A.

ALBERT, The Archduke, *vide* The War of 1866, pages 175-82; visits Paris to concert military co-operation, 206.

Aurelle de Paladines appointed to command the army of the Loire. 306; *vide* The Franco-German War, 306, and onwards.

Austria, Empire of, founded in 1804, 3; is fully occupied for eighteen months after the revolution of 1848 by her internal affairs, 9; for the moment seems a wreck, 10; recovers herself. 20; and places Prussia in a position of inferiority, 20-34, *vide* Schwarzenberg; is baffled by Prussia in her attempt to enter the Zollverein, 38-40; war of. with France and Italy, 53-6; offers of assistance to, from the Prince Regent of Prussia, 54-6; rejects them, and also plans for reorganising the Bund, 56-7; bends under the pressure of Bismarck, 77; attempts to conciliate Prussia, 79-80; is baffled by Bismarck, 80; is hoodwinked by Bismarck on the Schleswig-Holstein question, 82-4; becomes the catspaw of Bismarck, and wages war on Denmark, 84-5; obtains by war, conjointly with Prussia, the cession of Holstein, Schleswig, and Lauenberg, 90; is over-reached by Prussia, is forced to complain, and then is deceived into signing the treaty of Gastein. 92-5; Bismarck forces war upon, 99-102; terms on which, had first obtained Venetia, 103; La Marmora proposes to buy Venetia from, 97, 104; the Emperor of, refuses to bargain away any part of his dominions, 104; the Emperor of, offers Venetia to Italy as the price of her neutrality, but is refused. 105; refuses proportion made by Napoleon III. to the three powers, 106; furious at Bismarck's intrigues, appeals to the Diet, which supports her, 106-7; popularity of, in Germany, on the eve of the war of 1866, 110; stupidity of the administration of, note to, 110, *vide* War of 1866, 119-188; effect in the capital of the battle of Königgrätz, 188; critical position of, 190; accepts the armistice of Nikolsburg and the peace of Prague, 190-1; reconciles herself with Hungary. 204; responds favourably to the overtures of Napoleon, 205; understanding of, with Italy, 207; policy of, on the outbreak of the Franco-German War, *q.v.* 228-9.

B.

BADEN, The first shock of the French Revolution of 1848 felt at, 8; the courts of justice of, sentence Oscar Becker to twenty years imprisonment, 68.

Bavaria, Effect of the Revolution of 1848 in, 8; War of 1866 in. *vide* War of 1866, pages 182-187.

Bazaine, Marshal, *vide* Franco-German War, 224-304; surrounding Metz, 303-4 and *note*.

Bazeilles, position of, 291; storming of, 292.

Becker, Oscar, attempt of, to assassinate King William of Prussia, 68-9.

Benedek, Ludwig von, previous career and character of, 117; campaign of, in Bohemia. *vide* War of 1866, 132-73.

Benedetti, Count, is sent to Nikolsburg to negotiate with Bismarck, 190; several proposals made by, and to, Bismarck, 197-201; *vide* the Hohenzollern incident, 210-21.

Berlin, Revolutionary feeling aroused in, by the events, in Paris, of 1848, 11-20.

Beust, Count, effects the reconciliation of Austria and Hungary, 204; arranges an alliance between Italy and Austria, 207; policy of, on the outbreak of the war of 1870, 228-9.

Beyer, General. *vide* the War of 1866, 119-74, and 184-87.

Biarritz, Meeting between Napoleon III. and Bismarck at, 97-8.

Bismarck, Otto Edward Leopold, Count von, is appointed Chief of the Prussian ministry, 70; previous career of, 70; character of, 73; threatens the House, and invokes the employment of 'blood and iron,' 74; dissolves the parliament, 75; struggles daringly with the new one, and prorogues it, 75-7; gives the foreign policy of Prussia an aggressive character, 77; bullies Austria, and conciliates Russia, 77-9; persuades his master to reject the plan of Austria, 80; resolves to use the Schleswig-Holstein question as a lever against Austria, 82; makes a catspaw of

Index.

Austria, 82-4; his first move in the game, 84; causes the King, with Austria as his ally, to declare war against Denmark, 85; resolves to obtain the conquered provinces for Prussia, 92; the way he sets about it, 93; the card up his sleeve, 94; forces Austria to demand that he show his hand, 94-5; outwits Austria, and persuades her to accept the treaty of Gastein, 95; proceeds to Biarritz to gain Napoleon III., 97; gains him, 98-9; arranges to sign an offensive and defensive treaty with Italy, 99; picks a quarrel with Austria about the duchies, 100; plays the part of the wolf with the Austrian lamb, 101; accuses Austria of forcing on a war, 101; evasive answer of, to Count Karolyi, 101; makes a bid for the support of the rest of Germany, 102; signs an offensive and defensive treaty with Italy, 102; plays with the French Emperor, 105-6, and *note*; breaks with Austria by ordering Prussian troops to enter Holstein, 106; begins the war of 1866, 107; *vide* War of 1866, 119-88; how, had planned the war, and what he hoped to win by it, 192-3; how he played with Napoleon, 195-203; refuses Napoleon Luxemburg, and breaks with him, 203-4; plans of, 203-4; means whereby, strengthened his position, 207-8; how he 'managed' his master, 209, and following pages; *vide* The Hohenzollern incident, 210-21; France declares war against Germany, 223; *vide* Franco-German War, The, 222 to the end; the present position of, 316-7.

Bittenfeld, Herwarth von, previous career of, 116-17; *vide* War of 1866, 132-173.

Blome, Count, Austrian Minister, is completely bamboozled by Bismarck at Gastein, 95.

Bohemia, War of 1866 in, *vide* War of 1866, 132-73.

Bonin, von General, *vide* War of 1866, 146-50.

Bourbaki, General, is sent by Bazaine to the Empress Eugenie, 304, and *note*; takes a position at Bourges, 307; great difficulties experienced by, 310; attempts suicide, 310; the army of, disarmed, 311.

Brandenberg, Count, is appointed Chief Minister in Prussia, 19; is sent to negotiate with the Czar, fails, and dies, 32.

Bruck, Charles Louis von, attempts to guide the commercial policy of Austria in a right direction, 38; fails before the opposition of Prussia, 39-40.

Bund, The, *vide* Germanic Federation.

C.

Canrobert, Marshal, *vide* Franco-German War, 226 and onwards.

Chanzy, General actions of, with the Germans, in 1870, 307-9.

Charlemagne founds the Holy Roman Empire, 1.

Clam-Gallas, Count, *vide* War of 1866, 135-173.

Clinchant, General, succeeds Bourbaki in command of his army, which is disarmed in Switzerland. 311.

Colombey, Battle of, *vide* Franco-German War, The, 257-8.

Confederation of the Rhine, The, devised by Napoleon in 1806, 4; is accepted by the German princes, 4; composition of, 4, *note*; advantages and disadvantages of, to France and Germany, 5; weighty French opinion against it, 6; death of, 6; succeeded by the Germanic Federation, 6.

Coulmiers, Germans defeated at, 306.

Crimean War, The, Negotiations which preceded, 44-6; Prussia assumes a policy of isolation with respect to, 47; conclusion of, 48.

Custoza, Battle of, *vide* The War of 1866, pages 175-82.

Czar Nicholas, The, assists Austria in her struggles with Hungary, 20; favours Austria against Prussia, 32; causes the Crimean War, 44-7.

D.

Danish War, The, begins, 87; the attack on Danewerke, 87; Prince Frederic Charles succeeds only by the aid of the Austrians under Gablenz, 88; Düppel besieged by Prince Frederic Charles, 88; taken, 89; Gablenz beats the Danes at Oeversee, and takes Schleswig, 88; reflections on the conduct of France and England regarding, 89-91; conclusion of, 91.

Denmark, question of Schleswig-Holstein cause breach between, and Germany, 14; which is settled, 15-34; the death of King Frederic of, brings it again into prominence, 81; strength of the feeling in, 81-2; King Christian of, appeals to the faith of treaties, 82; refuses the demands of Prussia and Austria, and is forced to wage war, 85; is forced, by war, to cede Holstein, Schleswig, and Lauenberg to Prussia and Austria, 91.

Dreyse, John Nicholas, invents the needle-gun, 41-3.

Drouyn de Lhuys resigns office because of the foreign policy of his master, 199.

Ducrot, General, receives command of the army of Sedan on the field of battle from M'Mahon, who desires, too late, to march on Mezières, 293; when he has to transfer the command to Wimpffen, 293; commands an army corps in Paris, 300; charged by the Germans with having broken his parole, indignantly denies the charge, 301.

E.

England, reflections on the conduct of, regarding the Schleswig-Holstein War, 90-1.

F.

Faidherbe, General, experiences of, in the War of 1870, 308-9.

Failly, De, General, *vide* Franco-German War, The, 226, and onwards.
Falkenstein, General Vogel von, *vide* War of 1866, 119-174, and 184-187.
Fleischacher, General, *vide* War of 1866, 147.
France, *vide* Napoleon III.
Francis II., is elected Emperor of Germany, 2; varied fortune of in the wars of the Revolution, 2; breaks up the Holy Roman Empire, and becomes Francis I., Emperor of Austria, 3; declares war against France, 3; is beaten, and signs the peace of Pressburg, 3.
Francis-Joseph, Emperor, becomes Emperor of Austria, 20; *vide* Empire of Austria.
Franco-German War, The. France declares war against Germany, 222; state of the French army, 222-3; the French Generals—Bazaine, 224; M'Mahon, 225; Canrobert, 226; De Failly, 226; Frossard, 226; the French artillery, 226; condition of the Prussian and German armies, 226-7; vain hope of Napoleon III. to detach the minor states from Prussia, 227; France fails to obtain allies, except under the condition of a striking success at the outset, 228-30; preparations made by Moltke, 230; concentration of the French armies, 231; the Emperor's plan is found, for reasons assigned, to be unworkable, 232; the Prince Imperial undergoes 'the baptism of fire' before Saarbrücken, 233; Moltke's system of gaining intelligence keeps the French in a state of alarm, 233; a report reaches the French head-quarters of a defeat at Weissenburg, 234; desultory orders issued in consequence, 234-5; not communicated to the several corps or divisions, 234-5; movements of M'Mahon, 235; Douay defeated at Weissenburg, 235; the 3d German army bivouacks on French ground, 236; M'Mahon orders up De Failly, who does not come, 236; takes post at Wörth, 236; is attacked and defeated there by the Crown Prince, 237-8; position and march of the 2d German army corps under Prince Frederic Charles, 239; he marches to concentrate at Alsenz-Grunstadt, 239; comes in touch with the 1st army on his right, 240; Steinmetz concentrates the 1st army at Tholey, 241; pushes on to find the Spicheren heights occupied, 241; movements of General von Kamecke, 241.

The Battle of Spicheren.

Description of the Spicheren plateau, 241; position at, of Frossard's corps, 242; is promised support by Bazaine, 243; resources of Frossard, 243; force of General Kamecke, 244; attacks, and is repulsed by the French, 244; renews the attack, 245; finds he can make no impression, 245; Frossard fails to take advantage of the position, 246, and *note*; timely movement of General Laveaucoupet, is baffled by arrival of reinforcements, 246; Kamecke greatly dares, 247; progress on the Prussian left, 247; and at Stiring-Wendel, 247; Von Goeben arrives, and takes command, 247; the Prussians make progress, 248; fight for the Gifert wood, 249; the French fall back, 249; possibilities at Stiring-Wendel, 250; vigorous defence of the Spicheren knoll by the French, 250; gallantry of General Laveaucoupet, 251, and *note*; at length the Prussians prevail, 251; why Frossard was not reinforced, 251; conduct of Bazaine, 252; of General Montaudon, 253; of Castagny, 253; of Metman, 253; to whom the loss of the battle of Spicheren was due, 254.

The Battle of Colombey.

Napoleon III. appeals to the people of Paris, 255; the Parisians reply by compelling his ministry to resign, and giving full powers to the Count of Palikao, 256; position of three French army corps on right bank of the Moselle, 257; they are attacked at Colombey by General von Goltz, 257; and are forced to lose a day, 258; slowness of Bazaine's movements, 258; resolution of the Germans to hold on to their prey, 261-2.

The Battle of Vionville.

The French occupy Vionville in force, 261; Alvensleben resolves to cut them off from Verdun, 261; hesitations of Bazaine, 262; battle of Vionville, 262-4; forces Bazaine to rest where he was, and cuts him off from Verdun, 264; the King of Prussia resolves to push his advantage to the utmost, 264-5.

The Battle of Gravelotte.

Force at the disposal of the King of Prussia, 265; plan of battle of the, 265; at mid-day the Germans attack the left of the French centre, but make but little progress, 267; they mistake the French centre for the extreme right, 268; the Saxons meanwhile take Sainte-Marie-aux-Chênes, 267; up to five o'clock the assailants have effected but little against the centre; they fail almost equally against the French left; they make, that is to say, no impression, 269; at four, Steinmetz renews his attack on the French left, 269-70; but recoils before the French defence, 270; they make no impression on the real French left, 271; Steinmetz attacks the right of the French left, and the left of the French centre, but finds it impregnable, 271-2; the extreme French right, 272; the Germans prepare for an attack, 272-3; the French position there, 273; the first attack practically repulsed, 274; possibilities before Canrobert, 275; are practically neglected, 275; Canrobert contracts his defence against the new attack, 276; his defences are forced, and the French retire into Metz, 277; causes of the loss of the battle, 277-8; numbers and losses on both sides, 278, and *note*; blockade of Metz, 279.

Sedan.

M'Mahon had it in his power to march on Paris, 280; the Empress and the Count of Palikao determine that for dynastic reasons he shall not do so, 280-1; marches and countermarches of M'Mahon, 281; the

X

troops lose confidence, 282-3; rumours regarding the German movements, 283; counter marches to Le Chêne, and telegraphs the reasons to Bazaine and to Paris, 284; is ordered by the Regency to march on Montmédy, 284; the Emperor understands that he is to be sacrificed, 284; M'Mahon obeys, 284; difficulties and terrors of the march, 285-9; finally takes post before Sedan, 289; movement of the German columns to cut off M'Mahon, 289-90; the nature of the ground before, 290-1; numbers of the two armies, 291; the battle of, begins, 291; the Bavarians attack Bazeilles, and, after a desperate resistance, storm it, 292; the Germans make their way, 292; M'Mahon is wounded and makes over command to Ducrot, 292; who desires to retreat on Mezières, when he has to make over command to Wimpffen, 293; the Germans press home their advantages, 293-4; Napoleon on his own responsibility hoists the white flag, his heart bleeding, 294; Wimpffen, convinced at last that no alternative remains, interviews Moltke and Bismarck, 294; the conditions of the surrender accepted, 295; whose was the fault? 295.

The last Phases of the War.

The Parisians vent their fury on the dynasty, 269; but resolve to continue the war à l'outrance, 297; Sedan closes the first phase of the war, 298; Bazaine feebly attempts to break out from Metz, 298; but is foiled, 299; the Germans press on towards Paris, 299-300; number of troops available in Paris, 300; commanders of the several corps, Ducrot, Thomas, Vinoy, 301; Ducrot is repulsed in a sortie, 301; the Germans post themselves at Versailles, 302; more German troops arrive, 302; Vinoy makes a sortie out, is repulsed, 302; a third sortie shares the same fate, 303; and a fourth, 303; Bazaine surrenders Metz, 304-5, and *note;* Gambetta leaves Paris in a balloon, 305-6; displays great fertility of resources, 306; consequences of the fall of Metz, 306-7; strength and composition of the armies raised by Gambetta, 306; easy advantages of, 307; neutralised by the reinforcements available to the Germans by the capture of Metz and other places, 307-8; Germans defeated at Coulmiers, but attack Aurelle again, defeat him, and occupy Orleans, 307; Gambetta removes Aurelle, and gives one army to Bourbaki, the other to Chanzy, 307-8; Chanzy eventually beaten, 308; Faidherbe experiences the same fate; 308-9; Bourbaki, after experiencing many difficulties, attempts suicide, 310-11; the army of, now commanded by Clinchant, is disarmed in Switzerland, 311; Paris left to her own resources, 311; Thiers is authorised to conclude peace, 311; associated with Jules Favre signs preliminaries, 312; Conclusion of the War, 312-13; Result of, to Germany, 314-7.

Frankfort, effect of the Revolution of 1848 in, 8; the thinkers of Germany flock to, in 1848,

15; the ante-parliament is constituted at, 16; the National Constitutional Assembly is formed at, 16; *vide* National Constitutional Assembly, Peace of, Terms of the, 311-3.

Frederic, Crown Prince of Prussia, appointed to command the 2d Army in 1866, previous career and character of, 116; *vide* War of 1866, 119-173; gains the combat of Weissenburg and the battle of Wörth, 234; *vide* Franco-German War, The, 226, and onwards.

Frederic Charles, Prince, commands the Prussians in the Danish War, 87-8; carries Danewerke, only through the assistance of General Gablenz, 88; besieges Düppel, 88; and takes it, 89; previous career of, 115; *vide* War of 1866, 119-173; *vide* also Franco-German War, The, 226 and onwards.

Frederic William IV., King, *vide*, Prussia.

Frossard, General, *vide* Franco-German War, The, 242 onwards.

Fyffe's Modern Europe, regarding the Zollverein, 37-8; regarding Prussia's action before and during the Crimean War, 47, *note;* 106, *note;* regarding the Franco-Prussian War, *notes* to 218-221, and last page.

G.

GABEL, *vide* War of 1866, 134.

Gablenz, General, by his flank attack enables Prince Frederic Charles to take Missunde (the left of the Danewerke), 87-8; takes Schleswig, and defeats the Danes at Oeversee, 88; order by method of administration in Holstein, 100; *vide* War of 1866, 119-73.

Gambetta leaves Paris to organise defence in the provinces, 305; *vide* Franco-German War, 306 to end.

Gastein, treaty of, Bismarck forces the, on Austria, 92-5; clauses of the, 95-6, the plain English of the, 96.

Germanic Federation, The, (The Bund) planned by five German Powers in 1814, 6; is promulgated in 1815, 7; unsatisfactory nature of, 7; displays only a genius for Austrian predominance, 8; is shaken to the dust by the revolution of 1848, 8; The Diet of, ceases to meet for three years, 9; is then galvanised into life by Felix Schwarzenberg, 9; King William of Prussia attempts the reform of, 69; plan of the Emperor of Austria to reform the Bund rejected, 80; the decisions of, with regard to Schleswig-Holstein, set aside by Austria and Prussia, 84-5; appealed to by Austria, the Diet decides, by nine votes to six, in her favour, 106.

Germany, by the fall of Napoleon, had exchanged one tyranny for another, 15; intellect of, represented at Frankfort in 1848, 15; feeling throughout, on the eve of the war of 1866, 109-11; *vide* War of 1866, 119-190; reasons why, after 1866, war had become almost a necessity for, 208-9; state of the armies of, in 1870, 226; *vide* Franco-German War, The, 226 to end.

Gitschin, *vide* War of 1866, 134; description of, 141, and further.

Goeben, General, *vide* The War of 1866, pages 122-174, and 184-187. *Vide* also Franco-German War, pages 247 onwards.
Goltz, General von, well-inspired conduct of, at Colombey, 257, *vide* Franco-German War, The; 257 and onwards.
Gramont, Duke of, *vide* Hohenzollern Incident, The, 210-221.

H.

HABSBURG, The House of, gives Emperors to the Holy Roman Empire, 2; representative of that empire in the revoluntary period, 2.
Hanover refuses permission to the ruler of Prussia to traverse her country for the purpose of connecting Minden with Jadebusen, 57; *vide* War of 1866, 119-130.
Henderson's, Major, The Battle of Spicheren quoted, 223, 4-6; 241, 6-9; 254.
Hesse-Cassel, affairs of, in 1848, 30-32; rivalry of Austria and Prussia in, 29-33.
Hohenzollern Incident, The, General Prim pitches upon Prince Leopold of Hohenzollern as a candidate for the throne of Spain, 210-1; they reach the ears of the French Emperor, but the matter is explained, 211; revives in 1870, 211; turmoil in Paris, fanned by the Duke of Gramont, 212; Napoleon does not wish for war, 212; his war minister, Lebœuf, 213; determination of Moltke, Bismarck and von Roon, to force on a war, 214-5; the Duke of Gramont aids them, 215; Benedetti and the King of Prussia smooth away all difficulties, 215-6; Gramont still for war, 216-7; his despatch gives the Berlin triad their opportunity, 217; they spread abroad, especially in Paris, false news, 218-9; which excite the Parisians to a point beyond control, 219-20; the peace party are forced to give way, 220; and the Emperor is forced to declare war, 220-1.
Hozier's The Seven Weeks' War, 141, 4, 6, 9, 153, 183.
Hühnerwasser, *vide* War of 1866.
Hungary, rising and submission of, in 1848-9, 9-20; a factor against Austria in the War of 1866, 109-190; reconciliation of, with Austria, 204; opposes active alliance with France against Prussia, 206.

I.

ITALY, anxiety of, to obtain the cession of Rome and Venetia, 97; signs an offensive and defensive treaty with Prussia, 102; *vide* La Marmora, 103-7; *vide*, also, The War of 1866, 176-82; obtains the cession of Venetia, 190; understanding of, with Austria, 207; policy of, on the outbreak of the Franco-German War, 229-30.
Italy, Northern, revolts from the Austrian yoke, 9, 20; succumbs, 20; assists England and France in the Crimean War, 48; reconstitutes Italy in alliance with France in 1859, 56.

J.

JOHN, The Freiherr Franz von, chief of the staff to the Archduke Albert in Italy, *vide* The War of 1866, 175-82.

K.

KAMECKE, General von, attack of, on Rotherberg, *vide* Franco-German War, The, 241 and onwards.
Karolyi, Count, strange interview of, with Bismarck, 101.
Königgrätz, The battle of, *vide* War of 1866, pages 154-174, consequences of, 188.

L.

LA MARMORA, General de, asks Austria to cede Venetia for money, 97, 103-4; but is refused, 104; refuses in his turn to accept Venetia as the price of Italy's neutrality, 105; signs an offensive and defensive treaty with Prussia against Austria, 102; *vide* The War of 1866, 176-182.
Langensalza, campaign and battle of, 119-130; *note* to 147, *vide* War of 1866.
Laveaucoupet, General, action of, at Spicheren, *vide* Franco-German War, 246-50, and *note*.
Lebœuf, Marshal, sketch of, *vide* Hohenzollern Incident, The, 210-21.
Lowenfeld, General von, *vide* War of 1866, 150.
Leopold, Archduke, *vide* War of 1866, 150-2.
Luxemburg, Story of the attempt of Napoleon III. to obtain Luxemburg, 201-3, 205.
Liebenau, *vide* War of 1866, 137.

M.

M'MAHON, Marshal, *vide* Franco-German War, The, 225-235; movement of, after his defeat at Wörth; march to and battle at Sedan, *vide* Franco-German War, The, 280-95, is severely wounded, and makes over command to Ducrot, 292.
Malet's Overthrow of the Germanic Confederation by Prussia in 1866, *notes* to 101, 104, 107, 110, 121, 127, 187, and *preface*.
Mannheim, liberal meetings at, prior to the revolution of 1848, 8.
Manteuffel, Count, confidential whispers to the King of Prussia, 33; is appointed minister, and negotiates the surrender of Olmütz, 33; reactionary policy of, 35-6; administers the foreign affairs of Prussia in a manner humiliating to the country, 36-7, 43-4; is dismissed by the Regent, 53.
Manteuffel, General, son of preceding, maintains strict discipline in Schleswig, 100; *vide* War of 1866, 119-174, and 184-187; *vide* also Franco-German War, The, 306 to end.
Marbot, General, contemporaneous opinion of, regarding the Federation of the Rhine, 6.
Martin's Life of the Prince Consort, regarding Prussia's action on the eve of the Crimean War, 47

Mecklenburg-Schwerin, The Grand Duke of, operations of, against the French in 1870, 307-10.
Mensdorf - Pouilly, Count, succeeds Count Rechberg as Foreign Minister at Vienna; character of, 104.
Metz, Battles before, and surrender of, *vide* Franco-German War, The, pages, 255-79; and 304-5.
Mexican Expedition, injurious effect of the, to Napoleon III., 195-211.
Moltke, von, previous career of, 112-4; character of, 114-5; the real director of the movements of the Prussian army in 1866, 114; *vide* War of 1866, 119-188; *vide* Hohenzollern Incident, The, 210-221; *vide* further Franco-German War, 230 to end.
Montmédy, M'Mahon's march on, 280-291, and its consequences, 291-5.
Münchengrätz, *vide* War of 1866, 135 and further.

N.

Nachod, *vide* War of 1866, 150.
Napoleon Bonaparte turns the tide against Germany, 2; grants the peace of Lunéville, 2; regrets his moderation, 3; becomes Emperor of the French, 3; defeats Austria in 1805 and forces on her the peace of Pressburg, 3; devises the plan of the ' Confederation of the Rhine,' 44.
Napoleon III. wages the Crimean war in alliance with England, 46-8; wages the war of 1849, in alliance with Sardinia, 33-6; has an abortive interview with the Prince-Regent of Prussia in June 1860, 64; reflections on the conduct of, with respect to the Schleswig-Holstein War, 89-90; is completely humbugged by Bismarck at Biarritz, 97-9; proposition made by, to Austria, Prussia, and Italy, 105; is the plaything of Bismarck, 106; disappointment of, at the early termination of the Austro-Prussian war, 189; hopes still entertained by, 192-3; professions of, before the war, 194; begins to feel that he has been duped, 195-6; again plays the game of Bismarck, 197-203; until Bismarck breaks with him, 203; is baffled by Bismarck in his attempt to gain Luxemburg, 201-3; is forced by the United States to eat the leek, 202; courts Austria, 205-6; alliances made by, only shadowy, 206-7; still tries to assert the prestige of France, 209; is prematurely old, 209; results to, of the plébiscite, 210; *vide* Hohenzollern Incident, The, 210-21; declares war against Prussia, 222; *vide* Franco-German War, page 222; hopes of, 227-31; joins the army, 231; plans of, 231; pronounced impossible, 232; affair of, at Saarbrücken, 232-3; conduct of, on hearing of the past disasters, 234; and of Wörth, 238; transfers the command to Bazaine and joins M'Mahon, 256; lost communication of, to Bazaine, 256; powerlessness of, in the presence of the orders of the Empress-Regent, 280-1; understands that he is to be sacrificed, and the reason, 284; courts death at the battle of Sedan, 292; is sent prisoner to Wilhelmshöhe, 295.

National Assembly, The, of Frankfort, constituted in 1848, 16-17; appoints Archduke John of Austria to be regent of the Empire; dilatory proceedings of, and their causes, 17, elects Frederic William IV. to be German Emperor, 18; consternation of, at his refusal, 23-4; succumbs and dissolves itself, 25; reflections on the mistakes of, 26.
Needle-gun, The, origin of, 40-41; is accepted, after many trials, by Prussia, 42-3.
Nickolsburg, Armistice of, 189-91.

O.

Olliver, Emile, *vide* Hohenzollern Incident, 210-221; is forced to resign, 256,
Olmütz, The edict of, explains the policy of Austria in 1849, 21-2; the treaty, called the surrender of, forced on Prussia, 33.
Orleans, fighting at and near, in 1870, 306-7.

P.

Palikao, Montauban, Count of, is appointed Minister-President in France, 256; combines with the Empress-Regent to prevent M'Mahon's march on Paris, 280-1; orders M'Mahon to march on Montmédy, 284.
Paris combines with Bismarck to cause the war of 1870, 219; expels the Napoleonic dynasty, 300; siege of, *vide* Franco-German War, The, 300 and onwards,
Podol, *vide* War of 1866, 139.
Prague, Treaty of, 191.
Prausnitz, the two villages of, *vide* War of 1866, 148.
Prussia, King Frederic William IV. of, character of, 10; conduct of, in Berlin in 1848, 11-13; private opinion of, 14; position of, 14; hails the chance of intervening in the affairs of Schleswig-Holstein, 15; is elected by the National Assembly of Frankfort to be German Emperor, 18; position of Frederic William in Prussia, 18-20; is dazed by the recovery of Austria, 20; hesitations caused in the mind of, by the policy of Austria, 20-23; refuses the proffered crown of Germany, 23; dismisses the Prussian parliament, 24; hopes to obtain supreme power in Germany by other means, 27-8; shuffling character of, 29; has his cause pleaded before the Czar, who gives it against him, 32; succumbs to Austria, 33; appoints Manteuffel minister, 33; succumbs all round, 34; baffles the attempt of Austria to enter the Zollverein, 38-40; internal policy of, reactionary, 43; external policy of, humiliating, 43-4; proposition of, on the eve of the Crimean War, properly rejected, 45; slavish devotion of, to the Czar, 46-7; hatred of, of Napoleon III., 47; institutes a foreign policy of isolation, 47; is refused participation in the initiatory stages of the discussions for peace, 48; is seized with a cerebral disorder, and hands over affairs to his brother, 49. For the remaining history of Prussia, *see* King William.

Prussian Parliament, The, receives unfavourably the army reforms of Von Roon, 62 ; the Regent acts in spite of them, 63 ; receives with no great favour the speech from the throne, 66-7 ; again opposes the military budget, 70 ; is dissolved by Bismarck, 74-5 ; re-assembles in a resolute mood, 75 ; and opposing Government, is prorogued, 77 ; refuses supplies for an attack on the duchies, 84 ; the new supports the policy of the old, 86-7 ; still opposes the King in 1866, and is dismissed after a session of eight days, 111.
Prussian Army, The, efforts of the King and Von Roon to reorganise, 62, 63, 74, 76, 111 ; members of, on the eve of the war of 1866, 111, *vide* War of 1866, 119-73 ; state of, in 1870, 226, *vide* Franco-Prussian War, 226 and onwards.

R.

RAMMING, General von, *vide* War of 1866, 150-2.
Rechberg, Count, Foreign Minister of Austria, is duped by Bismarck, 83.
Reichenberg, *vide* War of 1866, 136.
Revolution of 1848, The, shakes every State in Germany. 8 ;
Roman Empire, The Holy, Duration of, 1 ; succession to, devolves on Francis II., 2 ; ceases to exist, 4.
Roon, Theodore Emil, Count von, is appointed Minister of War, 58 ; previous career of, 59-60 ; the third of the illustrious triad, 61 ; plans of, for forming an efficient army, 62 ; are badly received by the Prussian Parliament, 62-3 ; persists in them, 63 ; again, 74 ; but again, 76 ; brings the Prussian army into a state of perfection, 111 ; *vide* Hohenzollern Incident, The, 210-221.
Rotherberg. The description of, and fight for, *vide* Franco-German War, The, 241 and onwards.

S.

SAARBRÜCKEN, combat at, 233 ; the ridge of, *vide* Franco-German War, The, 241 and onwards.
Schleswig-Holstein, position of the duchies of, in 1848, 14 ; Prussia supports, against Denmark, and then signs an armistice, 15-34 ; re-opening of the question, 81 ; action of Bismarck and Austria with respect to, 82-5 ; war declared, 85 ; concluded by the cession of, with Lauenberg, to Austria and Prussia, 91 ; becomes the lever by which Bismarck endeavours to oust Austria from Germany, 91-107.
Schwarzenberg, Prince Felix, 9 ; share of, in the re-habitation of Austria, 20 ; tries to prevent the ascendency of Prussia, 21 ; daring measures adopted by, to this end, 22 ; supports his policy with a tried army, 28 ; finds the pear ripe, 29 ; obtains the assent of Czar, 32 ; and strikes the blow which for twelve years placed Prussia in a position of inferiority, 33-4 ; death of, 37.
Sedan, the march to, and the battle before, *vide* Franco-German War, 279 and onwards.

Steinmetz, General von, *vide* War of 1866, page 150 and onwards ; at Spicheren, *vide* 241-254 ; at Gravelotte, 64-78.

T.

THIERS, M., is authorised to conclude peace, 311 ; concludes it, 312-13.
Trautenau, *vide* War of 1866, 146.
Trochu, General, takes the lead in the defence of Paris, 301.
Turnau, 136.

V.

VENETIA, mode in which Austria first obtained possession of, 104 ; Austria refuses to cede, for money, 104 ; *vide* La Marmora, 103-7 ; ceded to Italy, 190.
Victor Emanuel, King of Italy, *vide* the War of 1866, 175-82.

W.

WAR of 1866, The, long and persistent efforts of Bismarck to bring about, 82-108 ; general feeling in Germany on the eve of, 107-10 ; condition of the hostile forces, 111; the Prussian Government notifies to its generals that the war has begun, 119 ; position of the Prussian armies, 119-20 ; of the Austrian armies, 120 ; of the Bund armies, 121 ; Prussia makes a dash at Hanover, 121 ; condition of Hanover, 121, and *notes* ; Prussia carries all before her, 122 ; the Hanoverian army is brought into a condition in which it can move, 122 ; distribution of the Hanoverian army, 124 ; possibilities before it, 123 ; the Prussians are gathering round it, and have one corps in front of it, 124 ; the Hanoverians push on, 124 ; are deluded by Prussian trickery to halt between Langensalza and Eisenach, and to remain there the next day, 125 ; position of the Prussian forces, 125 ; the King of Hanover feels that he has been entrapped, 125 ; receives no assistance but only advice from Prince Charles of Bavaria, 126, and *note* ; the Hanoverian army takes post at Langensalza, 126 ; is attacked there by the Prussians, 127 ; whom it defeats with loss, 128 ; question arises whether to push on into Thuringia, 128 ; the King prefers to negotiate, 129 ; and Hanover surrenders to Prussia, 129 ; enormous advantages to Prussia, 129-30 ; Prussian troops enter and occupy electoral Hesse ; 130-1 ; the armies of Bavaria and the Bund, 133 ; the story turns to Bohemia, 134.

The Campaign in Bohemia.

Prince Frederic Charles moves towards Gitschin, 134 ; Von Bittenfeld makes for Gabel, 134 ; Benedek moves from Olmütz, 135 ; plans of Benedek, 135 ; how Moltke regards them, 135 ; Clam-Gallas is posted at Münchengrätz, 135 ; Frederic Charles occupies Reichenberg, 136 ; drives the Austrian skirmishers from Liebenau, 137 ; fights the combat of Podol, 138 ; gallantry of the

Austrians, 138; Von Bittenfeld drives the Austrian skirmishers from Hühnerwasser, 140; Clam-Gallas abandons Münchengrätz and falls back on Gitschin, 140-1; Rearguard combat, 141: fights there a severe combat, when he is ordered by Benedek to fall back on the main army, 142-4; plans of the Crown Prince for entering Bohemia from Silesia, 145; Benedek badly served by his intelligence department, 145; Von Bonin's corps marches on Trautenau, 146; is beaten by Gablenz, 147; the Prince of Würtemberg resolves to avenge him, 147; mistake made by Fleischacher with respect to the two villages called 'Prausnitz,' 148-49; consequent defeat of Gablenz, 148-49; the Prussian Guards occupy Koniginhof, 149; Benedek directs Ramming to smite the Prussian force as it issues from Nachod, 150; severe combat of Nachod and victory of the Prussians, 150-52; who force the Austrians to retire on Josephstadt, 152; opposite principles on which the rival armies acted, 153; Benedek concentrates his army, 156; position taken by, near Königgrätz, 156; strength and weakness of position, 158; Benedek removes his chief of the staff on the morning of the battle and replaces him by a new man, 159; movements of the Prussian army from July 1, 159; Prince Frederic Charles resolves to attack, 160-1; makes no impression, 162-4; the Prussian leaders begin to doubt the result, 164-5, 168-9; movements of the Crown-Prince, 165; the Prussian Guards reach Choteborek and get a view of the position, 166; the first division drive the Austrians from Recitz, 167; they prepare to attack Chlum and Rosberitz, 167-8; a haphazard movement on the Austrian right-rear induces Benedek to denude Chlum, 170; this movement, followed by the attack of the Prussian Guards, decides the battle, 171; general advance of the Prussians 172-3; the Austrians retreat on Hohenmauth, 173; the defeat a decisive one, 174.

The War in Italy.

Forces at the disposal of the King of Italy, 176; the Italians cross the Mincio, 176; inferior strength of the Austrian army, 179; brilliant movement of the same, 180; takes the Italian army in detail and by surprise, 180; and defeats it, capturing Custoza, 182; the Austrians always superior at the decisive points, 182.

The War in Bavaria.

The Bund and Bavarian armies and their commanders, 182-83; insulting refusal of Prince Charles of Bavaria to assist Hanover, 183, and *note*; the Prussians form the army of the Main, 53,000 strong, under Vogel von Falkenstein, Manteuffel, Goeben, and Beyer, 184; Beyer fights a cavalry combat at Dermbach, 185; Goeben catches the Bavarian army at Kissingen, 185; Falkenstein dashes on Aschaffenburg, and smites the enemy at Fronhefen and Laufach, 185; Manteuffel replaces Falkenstein and outmanœuvres the enemy on the Main, 186; gallantry of Von Hardegg, 186; imbecility of Prince Charles of Bavaria, 187; is followed close when news of an armistice arrives, 187; reflections on Prince Charles of Bavaria.

The end of the War.

Position of the armies of the two nations after Königgrätz, 188; action of the French Emperor, 189; critical position of Austria, 191; Austria accepts the conditions of the Armistice of Nikolsburg, 190-91; followed by the peace of Prague, 191-92.
Weissenburg, Combat of, 234-6.
William, King of Prussia, becomes Stellvertreter of his brother in 1857, 49; previous career of, 49-51; character of, 51-3; is nominated Regent and appoints new ministers, 53; action of, with reference to the Franco-Italian War, 53-6; proposals of, to Austria, rejected, 54-7; also to Hanover, 57; recognises the absolute necessity of organising an efficient army, 57; plans of, for that purpose, 57; selects Count von Roon to carry them out, 58; supports Von Roon in his contest with the Prussian Parliament, 63; interviews Napoleon III., and baffles him, 63-5; his policy, the peaceful re-assertion of Prussia's influence, 65; becomes King by the death of his brother, 66; manly speech of, to Parliament, 66; opposition of Parliament, 67; mistrust of, in Prussia, 68; attempt to assassinate, 68; urges reform of the Bund, 69; refuses to submit to the votes on the military budget of the Lower House, 70; appoints Count von Bismarck to be his chief minister, 70; supports his ministers in their struggle with Parliament, 74-7; is willing to accept the plan of the reform proposed by Austria, but is persuaded by Bismarck to refuse it, 80; supports Bismarck in his overriding of the Parliament, 86-7; obtains by war, conjointly with Austria, the cession of Holstein, Schleswig, and Lauenberg, 91; allies of, in the war of 1866, 107-8; unpopularity of the war in the dominions of, 108, and *note* to 109; *vide* War of 1866, 119-188; advantages gained by, for Prussia, by the War of 1866, 192-93; is personally a stranger to the lower intrigues of Bismarck, 209; *vide* the Hohenzollern Incident, 210-221.
Wörth, Battle of, 235-8.

Z.

ZASTROW, General von, *vide* Franco-German War, The, 248.
Zollverein, The, effects of the institution of, between 1828 and 1836, 37; extension of, 38; efforts made by Austria to enter, 386; baffled by Prussia, 39-40.

COLSTON AND COMPANY, PRINTERS, EDINBURGH.

www.ingramcontent.com/pod-product-compliance
Lightning Source LLC
Chambersburg PA
CBHW031433230426
43668CB00007B/515